Read Write Inc.

Literacy and Language
Handbook

2

Janey Pursglove and **Charlotte Raby**
Series developed by **Ruth Miskin**

OXFORD
UNIVERSITY PRESS

OXFORD
UNIVERSITY PRESS

Great Clarendon Street, Oxford, OX2 6DP,
United Kingdom

Oxford University Press is a department of the University of Oxford.
It furthers the University's objective of excellence in research, scholarship, and education by publishing worldwide. Oxford is a registered trade mark of Oxford University Press in the UK and in certain other countries.

First Edition published in 2013

British Library Cataloguing in Publication Data
Data available

ISBN: 978-0-19-833071-4

3 5 7 9 10 8 6 4

Paper used in the production of this book is a natural, recyclable product made from wood grown in sustainable forests. The manufacturing process conforms to the environmental regulations of the country of origin.

Printed in Great Britain by Ashford Colour Press

Acknowledgements

Cover: Tony Ross

Illustrations by: Galia Bernstein; Leo Broadley; Anthony Browne; Margaret Chamberlain; Ross Collins; Peter Cottrill; Lizzie Finlay; Julie Fortenberry; Alexandra Huard; Garry Parsons; Korky Paul; Andrés Martínez Ricci; Tony Ross; Lily Trotter

Design by Q2A

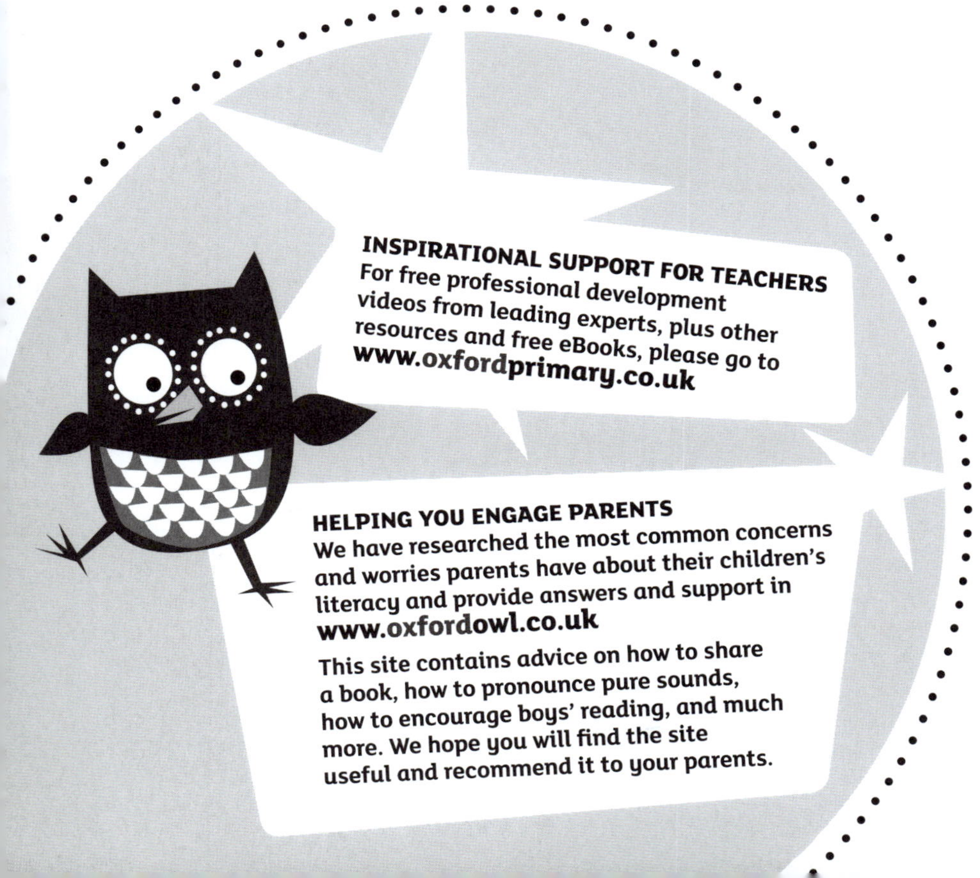

Contents

Introduction

What is Literacy and Language?

Literacy and Language is a complete literacy programme for children in Years 2–6 (Primary 3–7). It is designed to stimulate and challenge children's thinking and create enthusiastic, lifelong readers and writers.

It provides explicit guidance for developing children's reading comprehension and writing composition with support for teaching grammar, vocabulary development, critical thinking and spoken language. It gives you all the support you need to teach outstanding, consistent literacy lessons every day, and to deliver the new National Curriculum confidently.

The core purpose of the programme is to ensure that children, as the National Curriculum aims state:

- read easily, fluently and with good understanding
- develop the habit of reading widely and often for both pleasure and information
- acquire a wide vocabulary
- use grammar correctly
- appreciate our rich and varied literary heritage
- write clearly, accurately and coherently, adapting their language and style in and for a range of contexts, purposes and audiences
- use discussion in order to learn; they should be able to elaborate and explain clearly their understanding and ideas
- are competent in the arts of speaking and listening, making formal presentations, demonstrating to others and participating in debate

Literacy and Language resources for each year:

Anthologies of complete stories, plays, poems and non-fiction texts	a **Pupils' Book** containing writing, grammar, comprehension and vocabulary activities related to the Anthology texts	a **Homework Book** providing further practice and consolidation of grammar points and writing tasks	**Software** with a wide variety of teacher-led activities and teacher support, for use on an interactive whiteboard	a **Handbook** giving clear day-by-day lesson plans for each Unit

Resources

Anthologies

Literacy and Language is based on Anthologies of carefully chosen complete stories, plays, poems and non-fiction texts by leading children's authors including Michael Morpurgo, Jeremy Strong, Roger McGough, Geraldine McCaughrean, Jamila Gavin, Roy Apps and Susan Price.

The range of stories, plays, poems and non-fiction texts in *Literacy and Language* provide an opportunity for children to study texts which are absorbing, challenging and deep enough to dive into, while being accessible to all children.

The children's increasing familiarity with a wide range of stories, plays, poems and non-fiction texts will generate a desire for more reading for pleasure. Wider reading lists are provided for every Unit.

Unit 6

Chocolate Planet
Jon Blake

The Planet Wob was a boring place. Nothing smelled tasty and nothing tasted of anything. Turnip fields stretched as far as the eye could see.

Gala was fed up with eating turnips. Every night she looked up at the Planet Um, hanging in the streaky sky. Everyone said there were chocolate mines on Um.

One evening, Gala was lying in a turnip field with her friend, Frag. The Planet Um was glowing a silky, milky brown.

Gala's mouth watered.

"Let's go there," she said.

"It could be dangerous," said Frag.

"It could be delicious," replied Gala.

"There could be scary things," said Frag.

"Nothing scares me," replied Gala.

As usual, Gala got her way. The two friends borrowed a spaceship from Rent a Rocket. They packed sky baskets, lunar bags and cosmic jars. Gala planned to harvest every last speck of chocolate.

It was a long journey to Um. Frag began to feel peckish. "Did you pack any food?" he asked Gala.

Gala produced two lovely round turnips.

"You shouldn't have bothered," moaned Frag.

14 15

All the texts in the Anthologies are complete and are just the right length for children to read during the lesson and to develop reading stamina.

Unit 4

Beauty and the Beast
Gill Howell

Once upon a time, there was a merchant who had three daughters. He loved all three but kept a special place in his heart for Beauty, the youngest daughter. Beauty was always sweet-natured and cheerful, unlike the other daughters, who were often grumpy and jealous.

A day came when the merchant had to go away on important business. As he would be gone for some time, he said to his daughters, "What gifts would you like me to bring you?"

The eldest asked for jewels. The second asked for fine clothes.

Beauty said, "Dear father, there is nothing I need. Just your safe return." Her father insisted, so she replied at last, "Then bring me the loveliest rose you can find."

The merchant's business went well and finally he began his long journey home. In his bag were the gifts for his daughters…apart from Beauty's rose.

'I will find one on my journey,' he thought. Instantly, a great storm broke out across the sky.

Through the lashing rain, the merchant saw a gleam of light. Hoping to find shelter, he galloped towards it and discovered that it came from a **magnificent** castle surrounded by beautiful gardens.

14 15

All the fiction and non-fiction texts include rarer vocabulary, which the children explore through Word power activities prior to reading the text.

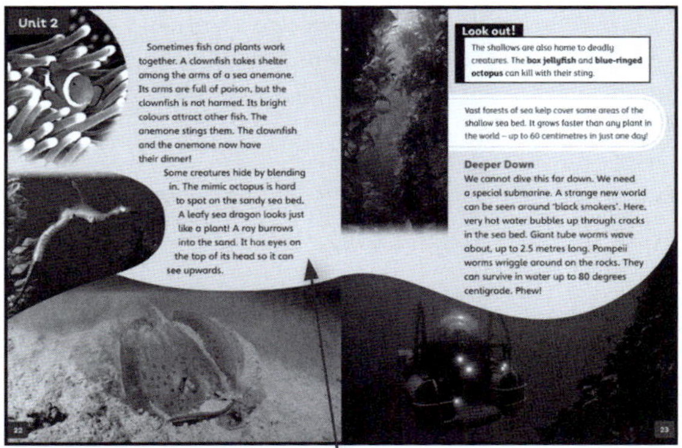
Unit 2

Sometimes fish and plants work together. A clownfish takes shelter among the arms of a sea anemone. Its arms are full of poison, but the clownfish is not harmed. Its bright colours attract other fish. The anemone stings them. The clownfish and the anemone now have their dinner!

Some creatures hide by blending in. The mimic octopus is hard to spot on the sandy sea bed. A leafy sea dragon looks just like a plant! A ray burrows into the sand. It has eyes on the top of its head so it can see upwards.

Look out!
The shallows are also home to deadly creatures. The **box jellyfish** and **blue-ringed octopus** can kill with their sting.

Vast forests of sea kelp cover some areas of the shallow sea bed. It grows faster than any plant in the world – up to 60 centimetres in just one day!

Deeper Down
We cannot dive this far down. We need a special submarine. A strange new world can be seen around 'black smokers'. Here, very hot water bubbles up through cracks in the sea bed. Giant tube worms wave about, up to 2.5 metres long. Pompeii worms wriggle around on the rocks. They can survive in water up to 80 degrees centigrade. Phew!

22 23

Each non-fiction text is a model of a particular form with a clear purpose, aimed at a specific audience. The high-interest, often humorous non-fiction texts provide further stimulus for reading widely and often.

Pupils' Book

Lively activities in the Pupils' Book develop children's writing, grammar, comprehension and vocabulary skills. The activities are linked to the Anthology texts and help children consolidate and apply what they are learning.

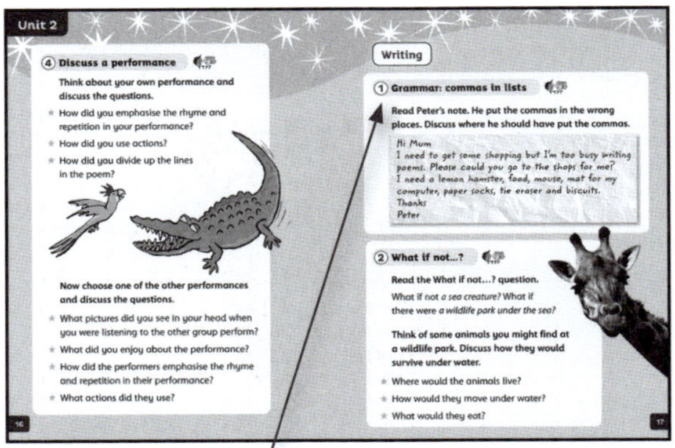

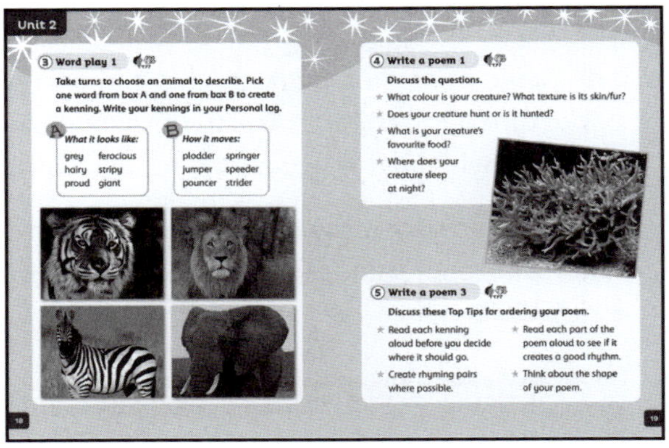

Grammar is taught in context and through writing to make it meaningful for children.

Partner work is embedded in the programme – many of the activities are rooted in discussion, which helps to develop children's spoken English.

There are **activities** to enhance children's **spoken vocabulary** and ultimately their vocabulary for writing.

Homework Book

The Homework Book contains weekly activities which allow children to practise and embed the grammar, writing and other language and literacy skills they have learnt in the lessons.

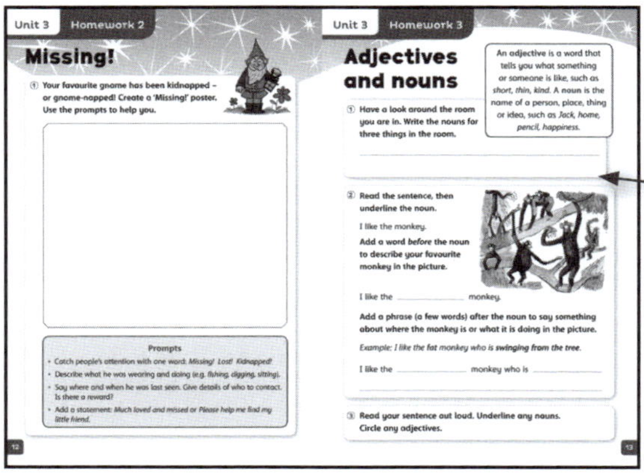

The activities are accessible and engaging, with age-appropriate glossaries and information boxes to ensure children can work independently at home.

Software

The Software is integral to the programme and is used for whole class teaching.
It contains a range of resources to support your teaching.

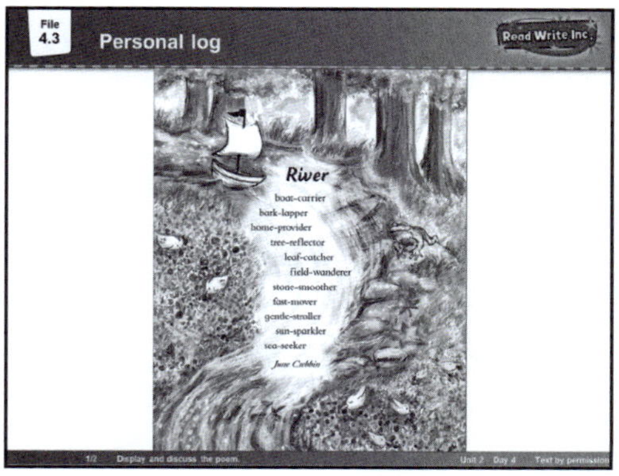

There are fully illustrated texts, including stories, plays, poems and non-fiction texts from the Anthologies, to display and explore as a class.

Audio and video clips are used to introduce drama activities or stimulate discussion.

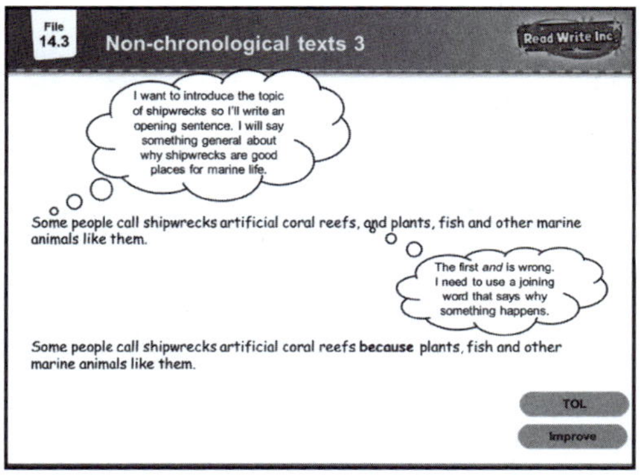

There are **modelled writing scripts** for the teacher to show how a text is built up, including how to 'Think out loud' to show children how to develop ideas.

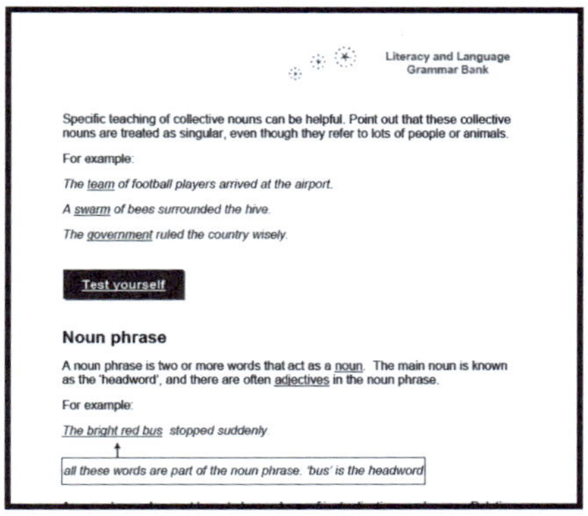

A **Grammar Bank** gives teachers clear explanations about every aspect of grammar in the new National Curriculum and practice tests for children (see p.9).

Files include:

- video, audio performances of the poems and plays, radio interviews, music and images
- drag and drop language activities
- writing plans which can be printed out for class use
- 'Think out loud' teacher scripts for modelled writing
- 'Power words' for classroom display
- ready-prepared 'Write a story' texts for modelled writing
- editable timetables.

The Software booklet provides more detailed information about the features of the Software.

All this support makes it possible for you to teach an outstanding literacy lesson every day.

Teaching Handbook

Teachers are given comprehensive, structured support from the detailed day-by-day lesson plans in the Teaching Handbook and timetables.

Overview timetables are provided in the Teaching Handbook and as editable files on the Software.

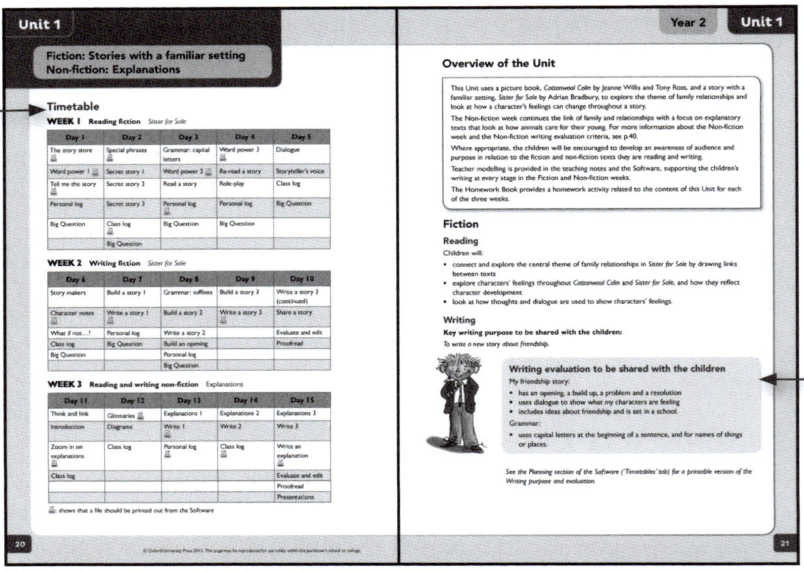

An overview of each Unit includes assessment criteria for reading and writing.

Lesson plans give detailed guidance for each activity.

Partner work ensures that every child is speaking every day, enriching their spoken English.

Activities are clearly matched to the new National Curriculum.

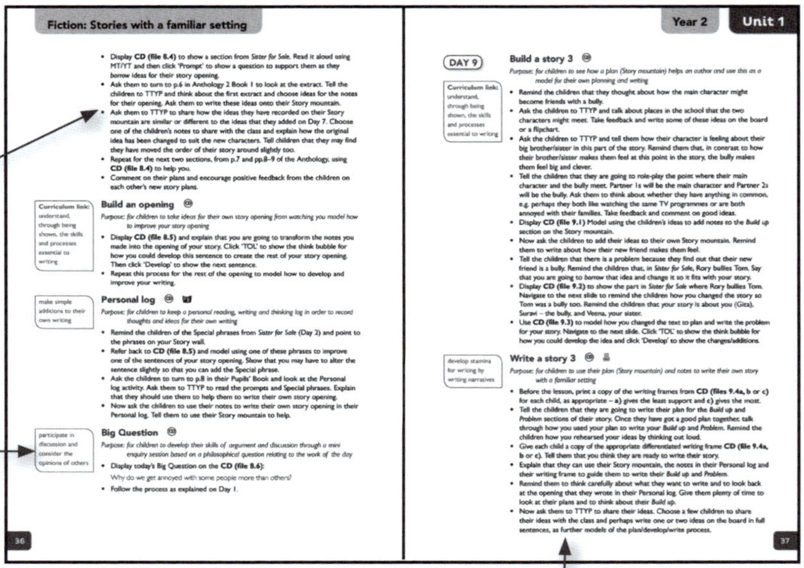

Children write every day, building up ideas, planning, developing longer pieces of writing, then evaluating, editing and proofreading their work.

What will children be taught?

Comprehension skills

At the heart of *Literacy and Language* is the enjoyment of and engagement with a variety of texts. Children are encouraged to take their own meaning from each text, becoming independent and critical thinkers. Comprehension activities are designed to help children to infer, summarise, question, clarify, predict and argue a point of view. The children also make connections between texts and their own experiences. The programme approach integrates reading, writing, thinking, and spoken language in all activities, to ensure the daily development of children's comprehension and wider literacy skills.

Grammar

Children are taught the importance of using grammar correctly, so they can communicate clearly and convey their meaning effectively. Comprehensive guidance is provided for teachers, supported by engaging Software, Pupils' Book and Homework Book activities.

Children meet examples of the grammar point they will study in the context of the story, playscript, poem or non-fiction text in the Anthology. The teacher then explains the grammar concept to the children, often using the Software and an activity in the Pupils' Book. Children are also taught the grammatical terms. When the teacher models the writing process the grammar concept is included so that children can see how to use it in their writing. When children do their main writing task they are reminded to include the grammar point as it is listed in the evaluation criteria. Children consolidate their knowledge of the grammar concept through activities in the Homework Book.

Grammar Bank

A Grammar Bank on the Software provides teachers with explanations about every aspect of grammar in the new National Curriculum. It contains a detailed, cross-referenced glossary of grammar terminology with clear examples and 'test yourself' exercises for teachers, with answers included. There are also grammar tests for children that provide practice in the type of questions they will meet in the English Grammar, Punctuation and Spelling Test.

The Grammar Bank allows teachers to consolidate their grammar skills and includes 'test yourself' sections.

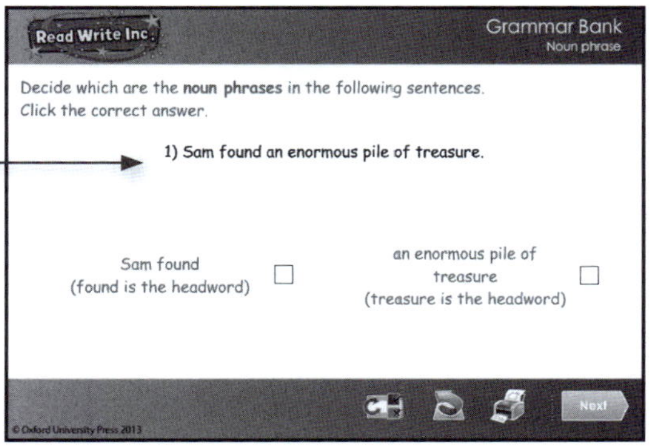

Three grammar, punctuation and vocabulary tests for each year provide meaningful practice for children for the English Grammar, Punctuation and Spelling Test.

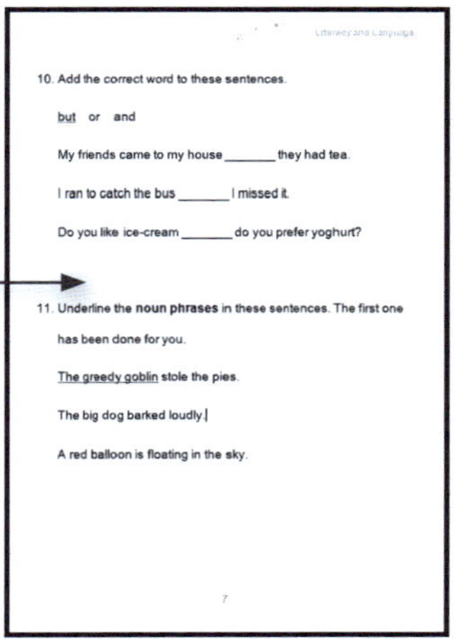

10. Add the correct word to these sentences.

but or and

My friends came to my house _______ they had tea.

I ran to catch the bus _______ I missed it.

Do you like ice-cream _______ do you prefer yoghurt?

11. Underline the **noun phrases** in these sentences. The first one has been done for you.

The greedy goblin stole the pies.

The big dog barked loudly.

A red balloon is floating in the sky.

7

Writing

Daily writing is at the heart of *Literacy and Language*. Alongside the main, extended writing activities, opportunities are taken every day to create shorter pieces of writing. This allows children to focus on very specific skills, build up their confidence and stamina for writing, and develop their understanding of audience and purpose.

As the new National Curriculum recommends, children are shown the process of writing. Using the resources for modelled writing and 'Thinking out loud', you can show what is involved in being a writer: making choices, alterations and additions while monitoring for sense and meaning. This de-mystifies the writing process for children while demonstrating the 'magic' of creating different effects with language. Writing in action shows children the power of language.

What they read, talk about and see through teacher modelling encourages children to experiment with language to express their thoughts and ideas accurately and independently. Most importantly, daily writing opportunities help children to develop a belief in themselves as writers.

Vocabulary development

The greater the children's vocabulary and the complexity of the language they hear and read, the richer their writing will be. The stories, plays, poems and non-fiction texts in the programme all include ambitious vocabulary. Before children read the texts, they are taught the meanings of more challenging words – both in the context of the story and in real life situations. The teacher and children use the vocabulary throughout the lesson, but also through the week, until the words become familiar. These new words and phrases are displayed and collected from one week to the next, keeping the favourite and most useful words displayed throughout the programme.

Spoken language

The new National Curriculum places huge emphasis upon spoken language. It states, 'The quality of and variety of language that pupils hear and speak are vital for developing their vocabulary, grammar and their understanding for reading and writing.'

Teaching children to articulate their thoughts and ideas out loud and to communicate what they know and understand is critical to the success of *Literacy and Language*. Children are taught to orally rehearse what they will write before putting pen to paper.

Teachers 'Think out loud' to show children what is involved in becoming an effective reader and writer. You can show children how you clarify and modify your understanding of what you read – how you infer and predict; build pictures in your mind; identify what's important; summarise key points; and importantly, persevere when things get tricky. In the same way, children are expected to 'Think out loud' with a partner to check their own understanding so their thinking is made clear to themselves as well as to you.

Literacy and Language uses carefully constructed partner work to make this possible. *Read Write Inc.* partner work is pacey, structured and meaningful – it keeps the children engaged throughout the lesson. Children answer every question with a partner, comment on each other's ideas, clarify each other's thinking, and build upon each other's thoughts and ideas. The teacher listens in carefully, selects children to give feedback and then selects others to build upon what they say. The teacher asks questions to take their thinking further and clears up any misconceptions.

Spelling

Read Write Inc. Spelling covers the National Curriculum spelling requirements and can be used alongside *Literacy and Language*.

How does the programme work?

Literacy and Language comprises six Units of work per year group. The Units are designed to be used over three weeks, but can also be used more flexibly, e.g. over a longer period if necessary as there is ample material and stimulus in the programme to extend tasks.

Whilst all literacy skills are developed throughout the programme, each week has a *particular* focus:

- Week 1 Reading fiction
- Week 2 Writing fiction
- Week 3 Reading and writing non-fiction

Children write every day in their Personal log (notebook, Daily log in Years 4, 5 and 6) so that writing becomes a habit. They record their thoughts, ideas, and reactions to the text, often as mind maps and story maps – some of which they will draw on for extended writing activities in Weeks 2 and 3.

Grammar activities are woven into the programme on the Software and in the Pupils' Book. In addition, the Homework Book provides an opportunity for children to consolidate and practise their grammar, writing and other literacy skills at home.

Thinking and discussion skills are practised through a daily 'Big Question' which is a philosophical question that children debate so that their spoken language is developed every day.

Week 1: Reading fiction

The story store

The main story (or poem or playscript) the children study in each Unit is introduced via a brief discussion of other texts containing similar themes, some of which will be familiar to most children. In Year 2, children are introduced to the theme through engaging picture books (see p.13) which are provided on the Software. This activity helps children to make connections between texts and their own experiences.

Secret story 1, 2 and 3

Literacy and Language uses a three layers of text approach to teaching reading and writing. Children are introduced to the text via Secret story 1, 2 and 3.

Secret story 1 introduces the children to the characters, setting, and plot through a series of clues, which the teacher explores by 'Thinking out loud' to make predictions about the story and build an idea of the 'bare bones' of the plot in the children's minds. This allows all children to access the basic story straight away. The ending is never revealed at this stage to ensure the children are motivated to want to read the full story.

Secret story 2 gives the children more information about the characters, setting and plot.

Being introduced to the text through Secret story 1 and Secret story 2 means that when the full story is revealed in Secret story 3, which is in the Anthology, the children can focus all their attention on the subtleties, nuances and their own interpretations of the text. The staged and guided access into the story means that children who need more support are undaunted by a challenging text and can immerse themselves in the world of the story as successfully as the children who need least support.

Week 2: Writing fiction

Build a story 1, 2 and 3

Having explored a text, children then see a new text being composed through the planning, oral rehearsing, drafting and editing stages. The teacher shows how a story is 'built up' via three layers of development (Build a story 1, 2 and 3). Using the pre-prepared resources, you are fully supported in the role of a writer as you model the composition of a text. This modelled writing deepens children's understanding of the writing process and enables them to compose confidently themselves.

Write a story 1, 2 and 3

With your support, the children then mirror the process you have modelled, drafting and revising so that they write ambitiously and accurately as they compose their own extended piece of writing.

The Software provides two versions of a story being written – Write a story 1 and Write a story 2. Through drama activities, teacher modelling and partner work, children build on these story frameworks, adding their own ideas, developing sentences and using them as models for planning their own plots, structures and characters. These prepare children to write the full story – Write a story 3.

Week 3: Reading and writing non-fiction

The fiction and non-fiction texts in each Unit are linked via one of the 'Big Questions' that children debated in the fiction weeks. Children explore examples of the non-fiction text type, focusing on audience, purpose, form and style. Then they use what they have learnt to plan and draft their own pieces of writing, with an audience in mind, through Write 1 and 2. A final piece is then written (Write 3), presented and evaluated through self and peer assessment.

Core activities

The core activities encourage children to engage fully with the text as they explore character, motivation, settings and themes.

Word power

Powerful, evocative vocabulary is explained and explored before children encounter it in the story, play, poem or non-fiction text. Teachers and children are also encouraged to use the 'Power words' outside the context of the story to ensure they become part of the children's own vocabulary store.

Think and link

Used at different points in the programme, this ensures that children question what they are reading and connect it to their wider reading, own experiences and current understanding of the world.

What if not...?

An opportunity for children to speculate on how a story would change if the writer altered any one aspect of character, plot or setting, developing their awareness of how one is affected by the other, e.g. in *Beauty and the Beast*, we ask 'What if not *a handsome prince?* What if the Beast had turned into *a frog* when Beauty kissed him?'

Build a sentence

Build a sentence is used to build a vivid, engaging description. The starting point is often a single word or a short phrase which is chosen because it is particularly powerful or unusual. The activity is used, with My turn/Your turn, to build up a sentence from a simple fragment to an ambitious, complex sentence that provides children with a model of good writing in microcosm. Teachers model making choices out loud, making changes and improvements, and repeating their sentence to themselves to ensure they can remember it. Sentences can be built up out loud, or written down.

Jump in

The purpose of Jump in is to help children remember vocabulary and phrases from the story. Jump in is used in *Literacy and Language* on subsequent readings of the fiction texts, to help children remember and assimilate the 'Power words' and 'Special phrases'. Once they get to know the story, ask them to join in the reading of the words in bold. Exaggerate particular words and phrases and use actions and facial expressions to help.

Class and Personal logs

Children write in a Personal log (notebook, Daily log in Years 4, 5 and 6) to:

- record responses to what they have read, thought and talked about
- experiment with vocabulary and text structures
- make notes, mind and story maps, diagrams and plans
- collect and paste related artefacts – tickets, photos, leaflets and drawings from home.

Big Question

A 'Big Question' is asked at the end of Days 1–8 and discussion should take about 10 minutes. These questions explore an idea linked to an aspect of the text covered that day, e.g. after reading *Beauty and the Beast*, the children debate: Should everyone be happy at the end of a story? The aim of the Big Question is to develop spoken language and argument skills. Children learn to justify ideas with reasons, negotiate, evaluate and build on the ideas of others, select the appropriate register for effective communication, as well as think in a deeper way about the more abstract issues that come from the text. Children are encouraged to express their opinions and enjoy a context in which there may be no right or wrong answers, just their own carefully considered opinions.

On Day 11 the non-fiction text is introduced through a brief re-examination of one of the Big Questions already discussed in the fiction weeks, helping children to make links between their own ideas and contextualising the new non-fiction text. For example, in Unit 5 children read *Chatterbox Ben*, a story about a boy who can't stop talking, and one of the Big Questions is: Can you say something without talking? This is briefly revisited on Day 11 when introducing different forms of communication.

Picture Books in Year 2

The same concepts and structures are used in *Literacy and Language* across Years 2–6. In Year 2, however, the Story store is enhanced by the use of high quality picture books as an introduction to the themes to be explored in the Anthology story, play or poem.

Authors and illustrators include Tony Ross, Anthony Browne, Jeanne Willis and Korky Paul.

Differentiation – guided assistance

It has been assumed that children in the *Literacy and Language* groups will all be fluent readers but not necessarily working at the same comprehension level. Differentiation is achieved by the amount of support pupils need in order to learn something new. The guidance in *Literacy and Language* ensures that children who need least support receive the necessary challenge and that others receive the necessary assistance to understand the texts they read and to write confidently.

The range of teaching and learning strategies embedded within the *Literacy and Language* resources allows *Literacy and Language* teachers to become skilful at ensuring that all children develop their ability to understand the texts they read, use the spoken word confidently and become accomplished writers.

Teachers support and challenge the children by:

- developing comprehension using the three layers of text approach for reading, allowing access to engaging and challenging texts for all children
- modelling your thought processes in planning for writing and editing using 'Think out loud' and the three layers of text approach for writing
- preparing children for writing using oral rehearsal
- providing differentiated writing frames where necessary
- asking and encouraging children to ask questions, with an emphasis on allowing thinking and talking time
- using partner and small group work developed to a high level to provide peer support and challenge
- encouraging use of the Personal logs to enrich and extend children's thinking, providing a 'safe' place for recording thoughts and ideas and to experiment with short pieces of writing
- using Challenge activities in Years 5 and 6 for class extension work.

Assessment and marking

Assessment is integral to the whole *Literacy and Language* programme. Partner discussion helps teachers assess what and how children are learning throughout the lesson.

The specific focus for both reading and writing is set out at the beginning of each Unit, along with the key purpose and evaluation criteria for children's main writing composition. Each set of partners is provided with a copy of the writing Evaluation criteria (see the Planning section of the Software, and navigate to the 'Timetables' tab for these) at the start of the writing process and this is used as a guide for editing and evaluating their own and their partner's work. The criteria are included in the Pupils' Book for selected Units, and as PowerPoints on the Software, to show that they are integral to the writing process. They also form the basis for the teacher's marking. Teachers are encouraged to mark the children's work thoroughly and give advice on their next steps based upon the Evaluation criteria.

Commenting on Personal logs

Teachers explain that the Personal log (Daily log for Years 4, 5 and 6) is an important part of being a writer – it is to a writer what a sketch book is to an artist. The children know that the logs will not be 'marked' in the same way as their exercise books. Teachers read the children's notes and ideas and respond with thoughtful notes and suggestions. These should be written in pencil, not pen; it will be like a dialogue on paper. Children should be aware that their privacy will be respected and that ideas from their Personal log will not be shared with others without their permission. Although the Personal log is for notes and ideas, it should be stressed that this book is special – it is not a rough book or jotter. Children can leave the front page empty so that, at the end of the year, they can make a contents page for the year's work.

Class logs

Class logs are used in Years 2 and 3 to demonstrate how to keep a Personal log, as well as to collect combined responses from the class. The teacher writes some of the most pertinent ideas in the log and sticks in photocopies of children's writing and pictures they collect. The Class log is displayed in a place where children can read it at other points of the school day. A blank page is left at the start to create a contents page.

How do you get started?

Book training

Ruth Miskin Training provides a one- or two-day in-school training course or a one-day central training course. A knowledgeable and experienced trainer ensures you can teach the new National Curriculum confidently, using *Literacy and Language*. Please note: *Literacy and Language* should be taught by qualified teachers.

Appoint the *Literacy and Language* leader. Choose a confident and organised teacher to meet the other teachers every week for 20 minutes to discuss one particular aspect of *Literacy and Language*, demonstrate lessons to teachers, observe other teachers, evaluate children's progress and teachers' marking.

Training can be booked at: www.ruthmiskintraining.com

How does the programme fit with Read Write Inc. Phonics?

As soon as children have completed *Read Write Inc. Phonics*, or are reading at NC Level 2a, they are ready to start *Literacy and Language*. Children who finish *Read Write Inc. Phonics* during Year 2 join a Year 2 *Literacy and Language* class. Children who finish in Year 3 join a Year 3 *Literacy and Language* class, and so on. We develop the same teaching strategies and principles used in *Read Write Inc. Phonics*:

Full participation: this is fundamental to *Literacy and Language*. Teachers use 'Think out loud' to show the children how to analyse, plan and organise their ideas. 'My turn/Your turn' is used to practise key activities and, crucially, partner work ensures that all children participate in the whole lesson.

Positive teaching: children learn at a much faster pace in an assertive and positive climate. They talk more readily in an atmosphere free from anger and tension. Praise for effective partner work is crucial.

Pace: each Unit has been planned to take three weeks. However, teachers might choose to add in extra time for some activities. You may also want to plan time for children to present and publish some of their final compositions.

Purpose: every part of the lesson has a very clear purpose. Please read the explanation behind the core activities on p.12. It is important to make the purpose of each activity transparent and easy to understand using child-friendly language.

Passion: this is a very supportive and detailed programme, which is why it works so well. However, it is the energy, enthusiasm and passion that teachers put into the lessons that bring the teaching and learning to life. Passionate teaching has impact.

Setting up Literacy and Language in your classroom

Timetable 70 minutes for *Literacy and Language* lessons. We also recommend that schools plan for an additional 20 minutes for Storytime every day. Suggested stories and poems to read to children are listed on www.ruthmiskintraining.com. In the Overview chart on pp.18–19, there are also suggestions for stories and books for wider reading which will link to the themes and genres explored in the Units.

Management signals

Use these signals to ensure teaching is effective and consistent throughout the school.

The 'stop' signal: when all children are engaged in partner work, you need to be able to get their attention quickly and easily without raising your voice. Hold your hand in the air and do not talk whilst it is raised. When children see the signal they should finish what they are saying and raise one hand in response. Do not start talking until everyone has returned the signal and you have lowered your hand.

'My turn/Your turn' signal (MT/YT): there are times when you will need children to copy what you do. *My turn:* touch your chest with your palm when it's your turn. *Your turn:* open your palm to children when it's their turn.

The 'Turn to your partner' signal (TTYP): before you ask a question, tap two fingers together to warn children they will need to turn to their partners to answer. Explain that the 'hands up' system for answering questions will not be used. Ask children to put one hand on their head if they need clarification or have a question to ask.

The 'Perfect partner position': partners should sit side-by-side and shoulder-to-shoulder. (If they face each other the noise level increases.) Number the partners 1 and 2. Children keep the same number for the duration of the whole Unit. See the Planning section of the Software and navigate to the 'Extras' tab for further guidance on choosing partners, and activities to ensure partners work effectively together.

Planning and preparation

All the planning is ready for you to use. However, a thorough understanding of the programme's multi-layered and integrated approach to teaching fiction, non-fiction and grammar is vital. The more prepared you are, the more successful your children will be.

First, gain a thorough overview of the whole Unit. Read the story and non-fiction texts in the Anthology, followed by the teachers' notes in the Handbook, and the activities in the Pupils' Book and Software. You will see how the individual layers unfold; how the reading activities feed into the writing and how the 'Big Questions' weave together the fiction and non-fiction texts. Each activity builds upon the next.

Study the timetable at the beginning of each Unit – it provides an overview of the activities for each day and shows when you need to print out any files from the Software such as evaluation sheets, modelled writing prompts, words for display, etc.

Prepare for your lessons using the teaching notes for the Unit. You could also use and adapt the flexible planning sheets on the Software.

Organising discussion

Setting ground rules for discussion

The ground rules for discussion should inform the whole school policy on teaching and learning so they become fundamental to every lesson in every curriculum area. Children should be taught, explicitly, the rules for working in a group or with a partner and take part in regular evaluations of what makes for effective discussion – see the Planning section of the Software, and navigate to the 'Extras' tab for the Effective discussion poster. Although the rules are similar for all ages, children's responses increase in complexity and sophistication year-by-year.

Display the Effective discussion poster in a prominent position. Praise the children for specific behaviour when partners co-operate successfully.

Short answers

Explain to the children that you will sometimes require a one- or two-word answer to questions – use a finger and thumb to show 'small'. This action tells partners to turn back to you quickly once they have said their answer to their partner.

One, two, three: if there is only one answer to the question, say '*One, two, three,*' and ask children to call out the answer together.

Popcorn: if there are lots of different one-word answers use Popcorn – children call out their answers in the pauses between other answers.

Wave: sweep your arm across the room in a wave. Children call out their answer as your arm sweeps over them.

Longer answers to explain why

Ask a question, then ask partners to TTYP (Turn to your partner). Listen in to different partnerships each time, sometimes building on their ideas. Do not get too involved with one partnership as it is important to observe how well all sets of partners work together – particularly in the early days. Do not give children too long to answer or let the discussion tail off. Importantly, make sure children carry on talking until you raise your hand to stop. It is very disruptive to discussion when children raise their hands/show thumbs or use any other signal to show that they have an answer ready. Select partnerships with helpful contributions to feed back to the group or do this on their behalf.

In-depth answers to consider different viewpoints, challenge claims politely, negotiate an agreement

As above but go backwards and forwards, asking other partnerships to build on the contributions of others.

Overview chart

Unit	Unit 1	Unit 2	Unit 3
Main grammar focus for the Unit	Capital letters Question marks Suffixes (-ful, -less)	Commas in lists Suffixes (-ing, -er, -est)	Sentences with different forms (exclamation and command) Adjectives, nouns and noun phrases
Fiction texts	*Cottonwool Colin* by Jeanne Willis and Tony Ross (A picture book) *Sister for Sale* by Adrian Bradbury (A story with a familiar setting)	*The Fish Who Could Wish* by John Bush and Korky Paul (A picture book) 'Tiger' by Usha Kishore 'River' by June Crebbin 'Don't Call Alligator Long-Mouth Till You Cross River' by John Agard (Poetry)	*Little Croc's Purse* by Lizzie Finlay (A picture book) *Oh Gnome!* by Lou Kuenzler (A playscript)
Fiction focus	Children explore the theme of family relationships and independence and look at how a character's feelings can change throughout a story. In the writing week, they create a new story about friendship which is set in a school.	Children read a variety of poems and explore poetic techniques. They listen to a recording of *Underwater Farmyard* by Carol Ann Duffy. In the writing week, they imagine a new sea creature and create a shape poem using kennings to represent it.	Children look at themes of honesty, friendship and persuasion. They explore how characters' thoughts and feelings are revealed by their actions, and identify important moments or characters. In the writing week, they create new play scenes.
Suggestions for wider reading	*Peter's Chair* – Ezra Jack Keats *Willy the Wimp* – Anthony Browne *Alfie and the Big Boys* – Shirley Hughes *The Works – Every kind of poem you will ever need at school* – Paul Cookson (see 'New School' – Kevin McCann, 'Younger Brother' – Trevor Millum, 'My Brother Bert' – Ted Hughes)	*Underwater Farmyard* – Carol Ann Duffy and Joel Stewart *Moon Zoo* – Carol Ann Duffy and Joel Stewart *The Rainbow Fish* – Marcus Pfister *Tiddler: The story-telling fish* – Julia Donaldson and Axel Scheffler *Meow Ruff: A Story in Concrete Poetry* – Joyce Sidman	*Aesop: The Complete Fables* – Aesop (see 'The Boy who Cried Wolf') *The Lying Carpet* – David Lucas *The Huge Bag of Worries* – Virginia Ironside *Angry Arthur* – Hiawyn Oram and Satoshi Kitamura *Something Else* – Kathryn Cave and Chris Riddell
Non-fiction texts	'Parents and their Young' (An explanation)	'Journey to the Deep' (A non-chronological text)	'The Super Car Boot Toy Sale!' 'Gnome, Sweet Gnome!' (Persuasive writing)
Non-fiction focus	Children explore how families in the animal world are different to families in the human world, beginning with information about how baby animals are cared for, then looking at the life cycles of frogs and sea turtles. At the end of the Unit, they write their own explanation of a frog's life cycle.	Children look at non-fiction texts about oceans, and learn how they are structured to help the reader find information. They will learn the difference between facts and opinions, and which is more useful in non-fiction texts. They write a short non-chronological text about shipwrecks.	Children examine persuasive texts in a variety of forms. They will identify how techniques such as layout and language can be persuasive, and will experiment with layout features like pictures, boxes, headings and shapes. They write and perform a voice-over for a film trailer.

	Unit 4	Unit 5	Unit 6
	Conjunctions (for co-ordination) Adverbs	Conjunctions (for subordination) Apostrophes for contractions	Verb tenses Tenses in texts
	Billy Monster's Daymare by Alan Durant and Ross Collins (A picture book) *Beauty and the Beast* by Gill Howell (A traditional tale)	*The Night Shimmy* by Gwen Strauss and Anthony Browne (A picture book) *Chatterbox Ben* by Adrian Bradbury (A story with a familiar setting)	*G.E.M.* by Jane Clarke and Garry Parsons (A picture book) *Chocolate Planet* by Jon Blake (A story set in a fantasy world)
	Children explore traditional (i.e. fairy) tales by looking at plot, settings, characters and the power of change. They will recognise Special phrases which are used in fairy tales, and identify the most important moments in a story. In the writing week, children will create a new fairy tale.	Children examine the themes of communication and relationships. They will explore what characters' speech and actions reveal about them. They will focus on personal writing, like diaries, and will write a diary entry about something that happened to a character they created.	Children look at the themes of envy and courage, and explore them within fantasy stories. They will think about key ideas in fantasy stories, and the importance of setting. They will use drama to explore character motivation, and they will write a fantasy story set in space.
	Little Beauty – Anthony Browne *The Big Ugly Monster and the Little Stone Rabbit* – Chris Wormell *The Works 4* – Pie Corbett and Gaby Morgan (see 'My Sister's a Monster' – Gillian Floyd) *Beauty and the Beast* – Michael Morpurgo and Loretta Schauer *Mixed Up Fairy Tales* – Hilary Robinson and Nick Sharratt	*Slightly Invisible* – Lauren Child (or any other Lola books that feature Soren Lorensen, Lola's invisible friend) *The Snowman* – Raymond Briggs *Not Now Bernard* – David McKee *The Tiger Who Came to Tea* – Judith Kerr	*Charlie and the Chocolate Factory* – Roald Dahl *Quick, Let's Get Out of Here* – Michael Rosen (see 'Chocolate Cake') *Aliens in Underpants Save the World* – Claire Freedman *We're Off to Look for Aliens* – Colin McNaughton *Dr Xargle's Book of Earthlets* – Jeanne Willis and Tony Ross *Man on the Moon* – Simon Bartram
	'How to Turn a Class Hamster into a Dinosaur' (An instruction text)	'Thrill City' – Email and Letter (Communication texts)	'Chocolate' (An information text)
	Children learn why different forms of instructions are useful for different purposes. They will recognise how adverbs of time and manner are used to make instructions clear and easy to follow. They write a clear set of instructions for how to make a thaumatrope.	Children look at formal and informal language by exploring different forms of communication for specific purposes and audiences. They will use formal and informal language to create an email, an invitation and a role-play.	Children develop awareness of information texts by exploring their key features and considering the importance of using different presentation methods. They will gather information about chocolate and present it in a chocolate exhibition.

Fiction: Stories with a familiar setting
Non-fiction: Explanations

Timetable

WEEK 1 Reading fiction *Sister for Sale*

Day 1	Day 2	Day 3	Day 4	Day 5
The story store 🖶	Special phrases 🖶	Grammar: capital letters	Word power 3 🖶	Dialogue
Word power 1 🖶	Secret story 1	Word power 2 🖶	Re-read a story	Storyteller's voice
Tell me the story 🖶	Secret story 2	Read a story	Role-play	Class log
Personal log	Secret story 3	Personal log 🖶	Personal log	Big Question
Big Question	Class log 🖶	Big Question	Big Question	
	Big Question			

WEEK 2 Writing fiction *Sister for Sale*

Day 6	Day 7	Day 8	Day 9	Day 10
Story makers	Build a story 1	Grammar: suffixes	Build a story 3	Write a story 3 (continued)
Character notes 🖶	Write a story 1 🖶	Build a story 2	Write a story 3 🖶	Share a story
What if not…?	Personal log	Write a story 2		Evaluate and edit
Class log	Big Question	Build an opening		Proofread
Big Question		Personal log		
		Big Question		

WEEK 3 Reading and writing non-fiction Explanations

Day 11	Day 12	Day 13	Day 14	Day 15
Think and link	Glossaries 🖶	Explanations 1	Explanations 2	Explanations 3
Introduction	Diagrams	Write 1 🖶	Write 2	Write 3
Zoom in on explanations 🖶	Class log	Personal log 🖶	Class log 🖶	Write an explanation 🖶
Class log				Evaluate and edit
				Proofread
				Presentations

🖶: shows that a file should be printed out from the Software

Overview of the Unit

This Unit uses a picture book, *Cottonwool Colin* by Jeanne Willis and Tony Ross, and a story with a familiar setting, *Sister for Sale* by Adrian Bradbury, to explore the theme of family relationships and look at how a character's feelings can change throughout a story.

The Non-fiction week continues the link of family and relationships with a focus on explanatory texts that look at how animals care for their young. For more information about the Non-fiction week and the Non-fiction writing evaluation criteria, see p.40.

Where appropriate, the children will be encouraged to develop an awareness of audience and purpose in relation to the fiction and non-fiction texts they are reading and writing.

Teacher modelling is provided in the teaching notes and the Software, supporting the children's writing at every stage in the Fiction and Non-fiction weeks.

The Homework Book provides a homework activity related to the content of this Unit for each of the three weeks.

Fiction

Reading

Children will:

- connect and explore the central theme of family relationships in *Sister for Sale* by drawing links between texts
- explore characters' feelings throughout *Cottonwool Colin* and *Sister for Sale*, and how they reflect character development
- look at how thoughts and dialogue are used to show characters' feelings.

Writing

Key writing purpose to be shared with the children:

To write a new story about friendship.

Writing evaluation to be shared with the children

My friendship story:

- has an opening, a build up, a problem and a resolution
- uses dialogue to show what my characters are feeling
- includes ideas about friendship and is set in a school.

Grammar:

- uses capital letters at the beginning of a sentence, and for names of things or places.

See the Planning section of the Software ('Timetables' tab) for a printable version of the Writing purpose and evaluation.

Resources

PB Pupils' Book, pp.4–12
A Anthology 2 Book 1, pp.2–17
CD CD on interactive whiteboard, Unit 1
GB Grammar Bank on CD
HB Homework Book, pp.4–6

READING FICTION

DAY 1

Curriculum link: participate in discussion about books, becoming familiar with a wide range of books

The story store

Purpose: for children to hear and enjoy a picture book story that introduces themes to be explored in the Anthology text

- Before the lesson, print out a copy of the TOL (Think out loud) points from **CD (file 1.2)**. In addition to this, make yourself a simple badge with a star to use as a Story star.
- Show the children your Story star. Explain that when they see this star it means that they are going to hear a wonderful story.
- Display **CD (file 1.1)** and show the front cover of *Cottonwool Colin* by Jeanne Willis.
- Ask the children to read the title and look at the picture, and then TTYP (Turn to your partner) to share what they think the story might be about. Collect feedback and show how much you value their ideas.
- Navigate through the pages by clicking on the foward arrow or the corners of the pages. Read the story aloud to the children with great enthusiasm and obvious pleasure. Use TTYP to explore a few aspects of the story as they arise, such as why they think Colin Smally is treated differently to his brothers and sisters, or how Colin might feel about being left out.
- Tell the children that they are going to help you to re-read the story.
- Navigate back to the beginning of the story. Use MT/YT (My turn/Your turn) to re-read the first page.
- As you re-read the story with the children, use the TOL points you printed from **CD (file 1.2)** and your own ideas and ask the children to TTYP to explore the connections between the words and the pictures. Focus on how the pictures give us extra information about the characters and what is happening. Draw children's attention to the way the font is used to emphasise certain words. Use the TOL points to explain how the font makes you read the words differently.

discussing their favourite words and phrases, new vocabulary

Word power 1

Purpose: for children to learn the meaning of specific vocabulary used in the story and increase their knowledge of synonyms

big *huge vast enormous* ***safe*** *secure sheltered protected*
scared *terrified petrified alarmed*

- Tell the children that there were some words in the story they heard that could be replaced with other words that mean the same thing.
- Display **CD (file 1.3)** to show the Power words and their definitions. Click 'Next' to show a sentence from the story and some synonyms.
- Drag and drop the synonyms into the sentence and use MT/YT to read the sentence aloud after each substitution.
- Ask the children to TTYP and choose which of the words they think is the most powerful/accurate. Ask them to Popcorn (see Introduction p.17) their answers. Drag the most popular choice into the gap.
- Navigate through the screens and repeat the process for the rest of the sentences.
- Print out the words from **CD (file 1.4)** to display on your Story wall.

Tell me the story

Purpose: for children to use language to explore feelings shown in illustrations

- Before the lesson, print out one copy of the feelings bubbles on **CD (file 1.5)** for each set of partners.
- Tell the children that you are going to explore some key moments from the story *Cottonwool Colin*. Explain that you want to think about how Colin and his brothers and sisters might be feeling at different points in the story.
- Display the first page of the story on **CD (file 1.1)** and look at the picture together. Ask the children to TTYP and discuss how they think the mice are feeling and take feedback.
- Now ask the children to look at the second page of the story and TTYP to discuss how they think Colin is feeling. Take feedback.
- Give each set of partners a copy of the feelings bubbles you printed from **CD (file 1.5)**. Tell the children that there are lots of words that could be used to describe how Colin and his brothers and sisters are feeling in the story.
- Navigate to p.9 ('She wrapped him up'.) Ask the children to TTYP to select which feelings bubbles they would use to describe how Colin is feeling, and which ones they would use to describe how Colin's brothers and sisters are feeling.
- Ask the children to write some of the feelings in their Personal log.
- Repeat the process for pp.21–22. ("Yes. If you must.")

Curriculum link: planning or saying out loud what they are going to write about

Personal log

Purpose: for children to keep a personal reading, writing and thinking log in order to record thoughts and ideas for their own writing

- Tell the children that, just like Colin, when you were a child you sometimes felt frustrated by not being allowed or able to do things.
- Ask the children to TTYP and discuss a time when they felt frustrated by not being *allowed* to do something. Take feedback and write some of their ideas onto the board, e.g. not being allowed to stay up late to watch a TV programme.
- Now ask the children to TTYP and discuss a time when they felt frustrated by not being *able* to do something that others could do. Take feedback and write some of their ideas onto the board, e.g. not being able to ride a bike without stabilisers when other children could.
- Remind the children that Colin got the chance to prove that he was able to do what his brothers and sisters could do. He had to be brave and keep on going, even when things did not go his way. In the end, Colin felt really proud of himself.
- Tell the children about a time when you were a child that you learned to do something that you found difficult at first, e.g. riding your bike without stabilisers. Tell them about the frustrations and setbacks and then explain how it felt when you did it for the first time, e.g.

  I felt frustrated when I was learning but proud when I…

  I felt annoyed when I couldn't do it but I felt excited when I finally could…
- Now ask the children to TTYP and discuss a time when they learned to do something difficult. Tell them to explain how they felt as they were learning to do it and then how they felt when they finally mastered it. Take feedback and model turning the children's ideas into sentences.
- Ask the children to write their sentences into their Personal log, reminding them to say their sentences to their partner before writing them down.

Curriculum link: participate in discussion and consider the opinions of others

Big Question

Purpose: for children to develop their skills of argument and discussion through a mini enquiry session based on a philosophical question relating to the work of the day

- Display today's Big Question on **CD (file 1.6)**:

  Can you help too much? *

- Ask the children to TTYP to talk about this question. Collect feedback and write some responses on the board.
- Click 'Prompts' to show some statements that may help to encourage discussion.

  ** This Big Question will be revisited on Day 11 – the first day of the Non-fiction week.*

DAY 2

recognising recurring literary language in stories

Special phrases

Purpose: for children to become familiar with some words and phrases that help to move a story on

It all started... *Then suddenly...* *From that moment on...* *Until...*

- Tell the children that *It all started...* is a Special phrase that is often used to tell you when something began. Say that writers often use phrases like this to move the story on. Tell the children that these phrases are often about time passing, e.g. *The next day...* or to signify a quick change in pace, e.g. *Then suddenly...*
- Ask the children to TTYP to think about any other phrases they have heard in stories. Give the children time to discuss and collect feedback.
- Tell them that *From that moment on...* and *Until...* are also examples of phrases that authors often use.
- Print the phrases from **CD (file 2.1)** and display on your Story wall for this Unit. Ask children to listen out for these phrases because you could use them at any time throughout the day.

making inferences, answering and asking questions, predicting

Secret story 1

Purpose: for children to be motivated to 'unlock the secrets' of a new story, and to make connections between the new story and the picture book story they have read

- Tell the children that it is time for a Secret story. Wear or point to your Story star. Explain that you have found some clues about a Secret story and you need their help to find out more. Convey your own eagerness and enthusiasm and draw them into your excitement.
- Display **CD (file 2.2)** to show the Secret story basket. TOL as you show your curiosity and interest about the contents of the basket.
- Click 'Secret'. One picture, word or phrase will emerge from the basket. Click 'TOL' to show a think bubble. Use this and your own ideas and TTYP to speculate about the significance of the contents.
- Navigate through the rest of the slides, revealing a different secret on each slide until the basket closes.
- Make sure you do not reveal the title, any surprises or the ending of the story at this stage!

Curriculum link: making inferences, answering and asking questions, predicting

Secret story 2 (CD)

Purpose: for children to hear more about the new story, to make links with their own experiences and make predictions. For the children to become more familiar with the story so far before they hear the full version

- Tell the children that there was one more item right at the bottom of the Secret story basket. Display **CD (file 2.3)**. Do not navigate past the first slide at this stage.
- Explain what a scroll is – you may also wish to prepare a real scroll from paper and ribbon. Say that you are really excited about what might be written on the scroll as it could tell us more about the Secret story.
- Navigate to the next slide to show the unrolled scroll and then click 'Audio' to hear the contents read out by a narrator.
- Navigate to the next slide and click 'Audio' to hear the first section again. Ask the children to TTYP to discuss the question the narrator poses and then take feedback. Repeat the process for the next two sections.
- On the penultimate slide, click 'Audio' to hear the narrator's final message.
- Finally, navigate to the last slide to show the scroll rolling up again.

checking the text makes sense as they read, making inferences, discussing sequence of events

Secret story 3 (A) (teacher only) (PB)

Purpose: for children to hear and enjoy the full version of the story for the first time

- Tell the children that they are now going to hear the whole story for the very first time. TOL about which parts you cannot wait to hear about.
- Ask the children to TTYP to share ideas about what they are looking forward to.
- Say that you need to switch your Storyteller voice on. Make it a special moment as if you are getting ready for a performance.
- Now turn to Anthology 2 Book 1 p.2 and read the full story to the children with great enjoyment, enthusiasm and expression to convey meaning.
- At the end of the story, ask the children to look at the Secret story 3 activity on p.4 in their Pupils' Book. Ask them to read and discuss the questions with their partner. Say that there are no right answers and encourage them to give their own ideas and opinions, as well as thinking about the events in the story. Take feedback from a few sets of partners.

making inferences on the basis of what is being said and done

Class log (CD) (PB)

Purpose: for children to share the process of keeping a class reading, writing and thinking log to record responses to texts and activities in a variety of forms

- Before the lesson, print a copy of the cover design for *Sister for Sale* from **CD (file 2.4)**.
- Tell the children that today they are going to begin the section of their Class log for this story. Show them the new title page with the heading *Sister for Sale* on it and paste the cover that you printed from **CD (file 2.4)** onto it.
- Remind the children of the character in *Sister for Sale* and ask them to TTYP to talk about their first thoughts about each character. Take feedback.
- Create a mind map for each character in the Class log. Using the children's ideas model adding some points for Molly under the headings: *What is she like? How does she feel about Tom? How does she help Tom?*
- Give each set of partners three sticky notes. Ask the children to turn to the Class log activity on p.5 in their Pupils' Book. Explain that they need to TTYP to discuss the questions about Tom and write their ideas onto the sticky notes.
- Ask some of the children to add their sticky notes to the mind map for Tom in the Class log. Share their ideas by reading out some of the sticky notes.

- Give each set of partners another three sticky notes. Using the Class log activity on p.5 of the Pupils' Book, ask the children to complete the same process for Rory.
- Tell the children that the story is set at school and ask them to TTYP and talk about places in their school where the story could be set.
- Explain that they can bring things in to be pasted into the Class log, e.g. pictures of their birthdays or of sisters and brothers, stories about families or school. Make sure you bring in anything that could be relevant as well.

Curriculum link: participate in discussion and consider the opinions of others

Big Question (CD)

Purpose: for children to develop their skills of argument and discussion through a mini enquiry session based on a philosophical question relating to the work of the day

- Display today's Big Question on **CD (file 2.5)**:

  Is it easy to be a good friend?

- Follow the process as explained on Day 1.

DAY 3

Year 2 Grammar learning how to use punctuation correctly, including capital letters

Grammar: capital letters (CD) (PB) (HB)

Purpose: for children to revise and consolidate their understanding of when capital letters should be used

- Read the statement below aloud to the children and ask them to complete it. Say that you would like them to give a choral response.

  We always know when a new sentence begins because it will have a ______________.

- Check that all the children gave the correct answer. Clarify if necessary and repeat if a few children were unsure of the answer. Write the completed sentence on the board or flipchart under the heading *Capital letters*.
- Now ask them to TTYP to discuss where else capital letters are used. Tell them to Popcorn their answers, e.g. names of people and places, days of the week, months of the year. Record correct examples on the board or flipchart and correct any misconceptions.
- Throughout the day, make sure you use terminology that you want the children to become familiar with where appropriate, e.g. *'I'm just writing today's date – "Wednesday" is a* proper noun *isn't it? That means it needs a capital letter.'*
- Teach the children the punctuation action for a capital letter (see the Extras section of the Software).
- Display **CD (file 3.1)** to show a sentence linked to the story that they heard earlier. Use MT/YT to read it aloud. Now ask the children to TTYP to decide which words should have a capital letter.
- Explain you are going to read the sentence aloud slowly and they mime their punctuation action for *capital letter* whenever a word needs a capital letter.
- Click 'Sentence' to show a second sentence and repeat the activity.
- Tell the children to look at the Grammar: capital letters activity on p.6 of their Pupils' Book. Guide them through the instructions and then ask them to write the sentences in their Personal log with the capital letters in the right places.

Homework Book p.4 provides further practice on capital letters.

discussing their favourite words and phrases, new vocabulary

Word power 2 (CD)

Purpose: for children to learn the meaning of specific vocabulary used in the story and increase their knowledge of synonyms

almighty fuming loomed scarpered

- Tell the children that there were some words in the story they heard that are *powerful* because you might not hear them every day.
- Display **CD (file 3.2)** to show the Power words *almighty, fuming, loomed* and *scarpered,* and their definitions. Look at the words with the children and then use MT/YT as you read the sentences to them, putting special emphasis on the relevant words.
- Explain that the writer could have chosen different words that mean the same thing. Navigate to the next slide to show the first word and click 'Synonyms' to reveal its synonyms.
- Click 'Sentence' to show a sentence linked to the story containing the word. Use MT/YT to say the sentence, substituting *almighty* using the synonyms. Ask children to TTYP to decide which word they preferred.
- Navigate to the next slides and repeat the process for *fuming, loomed* and *scarpered.*
- These words and their definitions can be printed from **CD (file 3.3)** to display on your Story wall for this Unit. Let the children hear you using these words, e.g. *'I couldn't believe it when my friend ate my lunch when I wasn't looking – I was* fuming!*'*

Curriculum link: checking that the text makes sense to them as they read and correcting inaccurate reading

Read a story

Purpose: for children to gain a deeper understanding of the story when they see the text for the first time, and to demonstrate this understanding by reading with expression

- Ask the children to TTYP to recall the Special phrases (see Day 2).
- Let the children follow the text in Anthology 2 Book 1 pp.2–13 as you re-read the full version of the story aloud with great enthusiasm. Put special emphasis on the Power words (in bold), and ask the children to listen out for the Special phrases.
- Now tell the children that they are going to read the story without you. Ask children to take turns to read alternate sections with their partners. Tell them to make sure they use lots of expression in their reading. Explain that you will be listening in and hoping to hear some star storytellers.
- Give feedback to the whole class on the children's reading to model what skills and behaviour you expect.

making inferences on the basis of what is being said and done

Personal log

Purpose: for children to keep a personal reading, writing and thinking log in order to record thoughts and ideas for their own writing

- Before the lesson, print off the blank body outline and Word banks for each set of partners from printable **CD (file 3.5)**.
- Tell the children that, at the beginning of the story, Colin wished he could do all the things that his brothers and sisters were allowed to do. Remind them that you discussed how Colin must have felt. Say that Colin's mum was not being nasty, she was being over-protective and just wanted to keep him safe. You could say that Molly is a bit like Colin's mum – she just wants to keep Tom safe.
- Explain that, just like in real life, characters in stories can change how they feel at different times.
- Ask the children to TTYP and discuss how Molly makes Tom feel at different points in the story.
- Take feedback and make sure they understand that there is not a right answer – you are just asking for their opinion.
- Display **CD (file 3.4)** to show a blank body outline and explain that this represents the character of Tom in the story. Drag his name onto the body.
- Model dragging the word *annoyed* onto the body and explain that this is how Molly makes Tom feel. TOL (see next page) as you drag other words onto the body to show how Molly makes Tom feel at different points in the story.

At the beginning of the story Molly makes Tom feel annoyed and frustrated because she won't let him do anything for himself, but when she stands up to Rory she makes Tom feel proud and safe.

- Ask children to draw two columns in their Personal log, with the headings *Positive* and *Negative*. Ask them to write the words that you have dragged onto the body outline into the correct columns.
- Reset the activity and drag Molly's name onto the body outline. Model dragging two feelings onto the body to show how Tom makes Molly feel at different points in the story, e.g.

At the beginning of the story Molly feels protective of Tom, but when she realises that he is being bullied because of her, she feels sad.

- Give each set of partners a copy of the blank body outline and the Word bank from **CD (file 3.5)** Ask them to TTYP to complete the Role on the wall for Molly, to show how Tom makes her feel at different points in the story.

Curriculum link: participate in discussion and consider the opinions of others

Big Question (CD)

Purpose: for children to develop their skills of argument and discussion through a mini enquiry session based on a philosophical question relating to the work of the day

- Display today's Big Question on **CD (file 3.6)**:

Should we tell people how we really feel?

- Follow the process as explained on Day 1.

DAY 4

discussing their favourite words and phrases, new vocabulary

Word power 3 (CD)

Purpose: for children to develop their knowledge of and application of rarer vocabulary; for children to understand how writers use language for effect

anxious frustrated embarrassed terrified proud cool brave excited

- Remind the children that on Day 1 they discussed the story *Cottonwool Colin* and talked about what the characters might be feeling at different points in the story. Display the word cloud on **CD (file 4.1)**. Use MT/YT to read some of the words and TOL as you relate them to both *Cottonwool Colin* and *Sister for Sale*.
- Navigate to the next screen to show some negative feeling words. Use MT/YT to read the first word *anxious* and TOL to explain how someone might show that they are anxious: '*They might rub their hands together or pace up and down.*'
- Act *anxious* to show the children what you mean and repeat for the other words in the list.
- Now ask the children to take turns to choose one of the words and act it out for their partner. Can they work out which feeling their partner is showing them?
- Tell the children that you have some sentences describing characters acting out these emotions and you need their help to link the feelings to the descriptions. Navigate to the next screen to display the first two descriptions and read them using MT/YT. Ask the children to TTYP and decide which feeling is being displayed in the first sentence. Take feedback and drag the word to the box underneath the sentence. Repeat for the sentences on the remaining screens.
- These words and sentences, and the word cloud can be printed from **CD (file 4.2)** to display on your Story wall for this Unit. Let the children hear you using these words throughout the day and praise them if they use them.

Curriculum link: checking the text makes sense to them and correcting inaccurate reading

Re-read a story A

Purpose: for children to deepen their understanding of the story by increasing familiarity with the text

- Explain to the children that the characters in the story experience things from different points of view.
- Ask them to TTYP to recall a point in the story where Molly and Tom were feeling differently about the same event.
- Draw their attention to where Molly blows out Tom's candles and cuts his cake. Mime putting on a pair of glasses and tell them that you can see this through Molly's eyes; she thinks she is helping Tom. Mime putting on another pair of glasses and explain that you can now see this through Tom's eyes; he is frustrated that Molly has ruined his special moment.
- Explain that you want them to read *Sister for Sale* again really carefully. Tell them that Partner 1 can put on Molly's glasses and Partner 2 can put on Tom's glasses. Then they can TTYP to discuss how they feel at different points in the story.
- Ask the children to turn to p.2 in Anthology 2 Book 1 and to re-read the story with their partners, taking it in turns to read alternate sections and using expression and intonation to convey meaning and impact. Remind them to pause after each section to discuss how each character is feeling at this point in the story.
- For some groups, you may wish to read aloud to the children first as they follow the text in their copy of the Anthology. They can Jump in (see Introduction p.13) to say the Power words and Special phrases.

role-play to help pupils identify with and explore characters

Role-play PB

Purpose: for children to consider the reasons behind a character's actions

- Explain that an Agony Aunt is someone that you might contact if you have a problem that you need help resolving. Tell the children that they are Tom and that you are an Agony Aunt. Use the questions below to develop the children's understanding of Tom's motivations and feelings. After you ask each question, ask the children to TTYP to think how they might respond to the question in role as Tom.
- Questions could include the following: *Tom, can you tell me about the problems you are having with your big sister? Can you give me an example of when she treated you like a baby? How did you try to stop her? What other things does she try to do for you? How does it make you feel? Why do you think she tries to help you so much? What do you think you can do to sort the problem out?*
- When you have listened to all the information, say you will write a reply with some advice for Tom.
- Now ask the children to turn to the Role-play activity on p.6 of their Pupils' Book. Explain that Partner 1s should take on the role of the Agony Aunt and ask the questions, and Partner 2 should take on the role of Molly and answer the questions. Tell children to use the questions as guidance as they role-play an interview between the Agony Aunt and Molly. Move around, helping children as they conduct the interview.

writing for different purposes

Personal log CD

Purpose: for children to keep a personal reading, writing and thinking log in order to record thoughts and ideas for their own writing

- Ask the children to imagine they are Tom and writing to an Agony Aunt. Tell them to use the ideas they explored in the role-play to help them.

- Ask them to TTYP to share ideas and then write some sentences in their Personal log that would go in a short letter to the Agony Aunt. Remind them to say each sentence to their partner before writing it down.
- As the children write, move around the room looking for good examples to share with the class. Pick out points that you think are particularly effective.
- Ask the children to swap books with their partner and read each other's letters.
- Display **CD (file 4.3)** showing the Agony Aunt's reply to Tom. Read it aloud to the children and ask them to TTYP to discuss whether it was what they expected the Agony Aunt to advise. Take feedback.

Curriculum link: participate in discussion and consider the opinions of others

Big Question (CD)

Purpose: for children to develop their skills of argument and discussion through a mini enquiry session based on a philosophical question relating to the work of the day

- Display today's Big Question on the **CD (file 4.4)**:

  What happens if you keep a problem to yourself?

- Follow the process as explained on Day 1.

DAY 5

Dialogue (CD)

Purpose: for children to develop empathetic responses to characters and situations

- Tell the children that you are going to zoom in on the moment when Rory bullies Tom. Explain that you want to try to understand what the characters were thinking at that moment.
- Display **CD (file 5.1)** and read this section of the story aloud to the children. Point to the part where Rory taunts Tom. Read it to the children, making your voice sound sneering and cruel. Ask the children to take turns to practise changing their voices as they read Rory's dialogue.
- Click 'Highlights' to highlight the dialogue. Point to the speech, 'Little Baby Tom!' Explain to the children that, while Rory is saying these hurtful words, he is thinking all sorts of things. Ask the children to TTYP and discuss what Rory might be thinking. Ask them to Popcorn their answers. Draw a think bubble for Rory on the flipchart and use the children's ideas to fill it in.
- Click 'TOL' to display a think bubble for Rory. Ask the children to TTYP and discuss what this tells them about Rory, e.g. he wants other children to think he is funny. Take feedback and write children's ideas onto the flipchart.
- Ask the children to copy some of these ideas into their Personal log as they will be useful later when they are writing about the bully in their own story.
- Click 'TOL' again to hide Rory's think bubble and click 'TOL' again to see Molly's think bubble.
- Point out the empty think bubble for Tom. Ask the children to TTYP to discuss what Tom might be thinking and write a think bubble for Tom in their Personal log. Take feedback from a few sets of partners and select one idea to type into the think bubble on screen.

read accurately and fluently

Storyteller's voice (CD)

Purpose: for children to develop their awareness of dialogue and narrative and the need for storytellers to use different 'voices' to sustain the listeners' interest

- Display **CD (file 5.2)** to show a section of *Sister for Sale*. Click 'Dialogue' to highlight the dialogue in this section of the story.
- Explain that Tom's thoughts form another type of dialogue in this story. Click 'Thoughts' to highlight Tom's thoughts. Explain that this should not sound the same as the dialogue that is spoken aloud.

- Demonstrate how to read Tom's thoughts. Try out several different ways to read the sentence you are focusing on and TOL to explain what effect you were trying to create. Ask the children to TTYP and discuss which version of the sentences they liked best. Repeat this process for the other sentence in red.
- Explain that the other parts of the text belong to the storyteller and that they use a special storyteller's voice. Say that you are going to read all of the storyteller parts. Explain that you will use MT/YT to help the children to read the characters' dialogue and Tom's thoughts each time.
- Read your narrative/storyteller parts with expression to convey meaning.

Curriculum link: discussing and expressing views about stories

Class log

Purpose: for children to share the process of keeping a class reading, writing and thinking log to record responses to texts and activities in a variety of forms

- Give each set of partners two sticky notes. Tell them to TTYP to discuss which is the funniest part of the story and why. Ask them to write their answers on their sticky notes and come up to the front to stick them in the Class log.
- Pick out a few sticky notes to read aloud to the rest of the class and ask the children to explain their choices.

participate in discussion and consider the opinions of others

Big Question (CD)

Purpose: for children to develop their skills of argument and discussion through a mini enquiry session based on a philosophical question relating to the work of the day

- Display today's Big Question on the **CD (file 5.3)**:

  How does it feel to admit you made a mistake?

- Follow the process as explained on Day 1.

WRITING FICTION

DAY 6

Story makers

Purpose: for children to develop their understanding of how stories are created by writers and to learn that we can all become writers

- Show the children your Story star. Explain that it shows that this week we are going to find out more about how the stories we love are made. Tell them that if we can all find the secret to making great stories, we can all call ourselves Story makers.
- Ask the children to TTYP to share one or two ideas about what makes a good story. Collect feedback and write some of their ideas on the board. Copy some of them onto card and display them on your Story wall for this Unit.

Character notes (CD) A

Purpose: for children to understand the importance of characters in stories and to gather ideas to write a description of a character

- Before the lesson, print a copy of **CD (file 6.2)** for each set of partners.
- Tell the children that they are going to be writing a story similar to *Sister for Sale*. Tell them that they need to collect ideas about the characters before they start writing. Remind them of all the information they gathered about Tom and Molly in the reading week.

- Tell them that they are going to use their knowledge of the characters, Tom and Molly, to read the story as *writers*. Explain that they need to look out for effective words, sentences and phrases that the writer uses to describe how the characters feel and behave. They are going to use some of these ideas in their own stories.
- Display **CD (file 6.1)**. Say that you are going to read as a *writer*, looking for something that shows that Tom is really frustrated with his sister. Stop at '"Try again, Tom," Molly said' and click 'Highlight' to highlight the sentence. Click 'TOL' to show how you are going to use this section of the text to help you when you write about how frustrated your main character feels.
- Continue to read the story, repeating the process when you reach 'Before I could stop her...' and "Eat more cake!' I thought.'
- Give each set of partners a copy of **CD (file 6.2)**. Tell them to work with their partner to read *Sister for Sale* on pp.2–13 of Anthology 2 Book 1. Say that you want them to concentrate on the characters Tom and Molly and look for some ideas to *borrow* for their own story.
- Tell the children to copy the words, phrases or sentences they think would be useful onto their grids and write short notes to explain how they would use them in their story. Some ideas have already been included for them.
- Walk around, providing support and guidance and feed back to the class any examples that you think will be particularly useful.
- Tell the children to paste their grids into their Personal log.

Curriculum link: making inferences on the basis of what is being said and done

What if not...? (CD) PB

Purpose: for children to consider the effect that character and plot have on one another

- Remind the children of the part in the story *Cottonwool Colin* where Colin stands up for himself. Return to **CD (file 1.1)** and navigate to p.19 ("I got wet."). Read from here to the end of the story. Ask the children to spend a few minutes thinking about how the story *Sister for Sale* would change if Tom was more like Colin and stood up for himself.
- Ask the children to look at the first What if not...? question on p.7 of their Pupils' Book. Model how you TOL about the question What if not *an enemy?* What if Rory, the bully, were *Tom's friend?*

  Well, that would probably change the whole story. If Tom were friends with Rory then he might be following Rory and calling another child names. Molly might still come over to help the child but she would be very disappointed in her brother.

- Display **CD (file 6.3)** to show a section of *Sister for Sale* and read it aloud.
- Navigate to the next slide to show the same section of the story with What if not...? changes made. Click 'Highlights' to show the changes for comparison and then TOL using your own ideas to guide a discussion about the possible effects the changes would have on other characters and events in the story.

  Why might Tom become friends with Rory? How would Molly react to Tom being friends with a bully? What would Tom think when he saw Rory being cruel to another child?

- Collect feedback and write some of their ideas on the board.
- Make sure the children understand how the whole story would be affected if just one aspect was changed.
- Now ask the children to look back at p.7 in their Pupils' Book and TTYP to discuss the other What if not...? questions. Collect feedback and develop some of the answers.

Curriculum link: increase pupils' vocabulary, draw on and use new vocabulary

Class log

Purpose: for children to share the process of keeping a class reading, writing and thinking log to record responses to texts and activities in a variety of forms

- Remind the children of the work you did in the reading week about describing the characters and how they felt. Tell them that they are going to work together to write some sentences to describe the characters in the new story.
- Use the Not just activity (i.e. extending children's vocabulary by experimenting with more extreme synonyms) to model choosing better words to describe the characters.
- Say that you think the bully's behaviour was bad. *Not just bad… but terrible, Not just terrible… but horrendous.* Write the final version of the sentence in the Class log.
- Now ask the children to TTYP and do the same for Tom in the new version of the story. *When Tom saw Rory taunting Jack, he felt bad. Not just bad but…* Take feedback from the children to describe more accurately how Tom felt, e.g. *awful, dreadful.* Once you are happy with the sentence, write it in the Class log.
- Finally, repeat the process for Molly in the new version of the story. Ask the children to TTYP to describe how she felt when she saw Tom with the bully. *When Molly saw Tom with the bully, she felt sad. Not just sad but…* Take feedback from the children to describe more accurately how Molly felt, e.g. *dismal, downcast.* Once you are happy with the sentence, write it in the Class log.

participate in discussion and consider the opinions of others

Big Question (CD)

Purpose: for children to develop their skills of argument and discussion through a mini enquiry session based on a philosophical question relating to the work of the day

- Display today's Big Question on the **CD (file 6.4)**:

  Should we always stand up to bullies?

- Follow the process as explained on Day 1.

DAY 7

understand, through being shown, the skills and processes essential to writing

Build a story 1 (CD)

Purpose: for children to see a story grow through three stages of development and to see the first stage of a plan that will provide a model for their own planning

- Tell the children that, in order to write a story, an author has to make a plan. They gather together all their ideas and characters and work out what is going to happen when, and to who. Tell them that they are going to help you to build the plan for a new story about friendship, set in their school. (You are in role as the writer.)
- Display the Story mountain on **CD (file 7.1)**. Tell the children that there are going to be three characters in the story: the main character, their brother or sister and the main character's friend – the bully.
- Point out the four main headings for the different parts of the story.
- Remind the children of the ideas they came up with on Day 6 for how Tom became friends with Rory. Ask them to TTYP and decide why their main character might make friends with a bully, e.g. because they were trying to escape from their annoying sibling. Take feedback and TOL as you write some of their ideas into the Opening section.
- Repeat this process with the other boxes, focusing on the ideas below in each section:
  - Build up – explore the relationship between the main character and their new friend, the bully.
  - Problem – explore how the main character feels about their friend bullying others – should they stand by or take action?
  - Resolution – explore how the main character finds help (perhaps from their sibling).

Curriculum link: planning or saying out loud what they are going to write about

Write a story 1

Purpose: for children to develop the first stage of a plan for their story

- Before the lesson, print a copy of the Story mountain from **CD (file 7.2)** for each child or set of partners. (You may wish to print this on A3 paper to give the children more room to write.)
- Explain to the children that they are going to start working out their story plans. Give each child or set of partners a Story mountain from printable **CD (file 7.2)**.
- Ask the children to turn to the Write a story 1 activity on p.7 of their Pupils' Book. Tell them to TTYP to read through and discuss the Top Tips before they start planning their stories.
- Tell the children that they can now start to fill in their Story mountain. Walk around, supporting and guiding them as they work. The children can just add brief notes at this stage. They will add more notes later.
- Ask the children to TTYP to share their ideas. Choose one or two partners to share with the whole class.
- Use this opportunity to TOL about their ideas for characters and settings. This will give children the opportunity to check that their plans are clear.

writing down ideas and key words, including new vocabulary

Personal log

Purpose: for children to keep a personal reading, writing and thinking log in order to record thoughts and ideas for their own writing

- Tell the children that they are going to add more detail about the main characters.
- TOL as you use an example from *Sister for Sale* and adapt it to fit the new story.

  In the story, Tom felt cross and embarrassed because Molly was always trying to help him, even at school. I could use that.

  My main character, who I'm going to call Gita, could be hiding from her sister, Veena, at break time and bump into the bully, Suravi, in the toilets. Gita could tell Suravi that she was hiding from her bossy sister and that could be the beginning of their friendship. I'll add it to my Story mountain.

- Encourage the children to use the ideas they recorded in their Personal log when they were looking at the story as writers on Day 6 and add them to their Story mountain.
- Then model doing the same for the bully, showing how some of the ideas about Rory in *Sister for Sale* could be used in their story.
- Ask the children to add more detail about the bully in their story to their Story mountain.

participate in discussion and consider the opinions of others

Big Question

Purpose: for children to develop their skills of argument and discussion through a mini enquiry session based on a philosophical question relating to the work of the day

- Display today's Big Question on the **CD (file 7.3)**:

  Who or what makes you feel good about yourself?

- Follow the process as explained on Day 1.

DAY 8

Year 2 Grammar learning the grammar of word structure

Grammar: suffixes

Purpose: for children to develop their awareness of how suffixes can change the class and the meaning of a word

- Tell the children that that when we speak to each other we add *suffixes* to words all the time without even thinking about it.

- Display **CD (file 8.1)** to show a dictionary definition for the word *suffix* and read it aloud to the children.
- Remind the children of the characters Molly and Tom in the story *Sister for Sale*. Navigate to the next screen. Use MT/YT to read the incomplete sentence.
- Ask the children to TTYP and to use their knowledge of the story and characters to choose the most appropriate word to complete the sentence. Ask them to Popcorn their answers.
- Drag the chosen word into the gap. Use MT/YT to read the completed sentence.
- Say that *help* is the root word. Explain that by adding the suffixes *-ful* or *-less* to the root word we can create two different adjectives (describing words) which have different meanings.
- Navigate to the next screen to show a grid. Talk through the first row of the grid. Use MT/YT to say the sample sentence and exaggerate the word *help* in the sentence. Allow the examples to *show* the children how the grammar works rather than *telling* them with over-complicated explanations.
- Draw the children's attention to the next two rows. Use MT/YT to say the sample sentences, exaggerating the suffixes in the words *helpful* and *helpless*.
- Ask the children to TTYP to discuss whether they think the words *helpful* and *helpless* have the same meaning or different meanings. Take feedback and clarify if necessary, drawing out how *helpful* is positive and *helpless* is negative.
- Ask them to turn to p.8 in their Pupils' Book and look at the Grammar: suffixes activity. Tell them to take turns to read the words down each column. Explain that they should now make three new sentences. The first sentence should use a root word from the table, the second should use a word with the *-ful* suffix and the third should use a word with the *-less* suffix.
- Collect examples of their sentences and scribe some of them on the board or a flipchart, underlining the suffixes or writing them with a different colour pen.

Homework Book p.5 provides further practice on suffixes.

Curriculum link: understand, through being shown, the skills and processes essential to writing

Build a story 2 (CD)

Purpose: for children to see a story grow through three stages of development and to see the second stage of a plan that will provide a model for their own planning

- Tell the children that all good writers use ideas and words from other stories to help them to write their own stories. Explain that you are going to *borrow* parts of the story *Sister for Sale* to help you write your story, which you are going to call *My Friend the Bully*.
- Display **CD (file 8.2)** and explain that you want to use some of the ideas from *Sister for Sale* that show why Tom was so fed up with his sister. Say that you want to change the ideas so that they can be used in the opening of your story.
- Read the first extract chorally and ask the children to TTYP and think about how they might use the ideas in their story. Click 'TOL' to reveal the think bubble and the note that you will add to your Story mountain later.
- Repeat for the two further extracts. The last slide has two think bubbles.
- Display **CD (file 8.3)** to show yesterday's Story mountain with the new notes added to the story opening.

encapsulating what they want to say, sentence by sentence

Write a story 2 (CD) (A)

Purpose: for children to develop the second stage of a plan for their story

- Tell the children that they need to add details to the notes under the *Opening* heading on their Story mountain **CD (file 7.2)**.

- Display **CD (file 8.4)** to show a section from *Sister for Sale*. Read it aloud using MT/YT and then click 'Prompt' to show a question to support them as they *borrow* ideas for their story opening.
- Ask them to turn to p.6 in Anthology 2 Book 1 to look at the extract. Tell the children to TTYP and think about the first extract and choose ideas for the notes for their opening. Ask them to write these ideas onto their Story mountain.
- Ask them to TTYP to share how the ideas they have recorded on their Story mountain are similar or different to the ideas that they added on Day 7. Choose one of the children's notes to share with the class and explain how the original idea has been changed to suit the new characters. Tell children that they may find they have moved the order of their story around slightly too.
- Repeat for the next two sections, from p.7 and pp.8–9 of the Anthology, using **CD (file 8.4)** to help you.
- Comment on their plans and encourage positive feedback from the children on each other's new story plans.

Curriculum link: understand, through being shown, the skills and processes essential to writing

Build an opening (CD)

Purpose: for children to take ideas for their own story opening from watching you model how to improve your story opening

- Display **CD (file 8.5)** and explain that you are going to transform the notes you made into the opening of your story. Click 'TOL' to show the think bubble for how you could develop this sentence to create the rest of your story opening. Then click 'Develop' to show the next sentence.
- Repeat this process for the rest of the opening to model how to develop and improve your writing.

make simple additions to their own writing

Personal log (CD) (PB)

Purpose: for children to keep a personal reading, writing and thinking log in order to record thoughts and ideas for their own writing

- Remind the children of the Special phrases from *Sister for Sale* (Day 2) and point to the phrases on your Story wall.
- Refer back to **CD (file 8.5)** and model using one of these phrases to improve one of the sentences of your story opening. Show that you may have to alter the sentence slightly so that you can add the Special phrase.
- Ask the children to turn to p.8 in their Pupils' Book and look at the Personal log activity. Ask them to TTYP to read the prompts and Special phrases. Explain that they should use them to help them to write their own story opening.
- Now ask the children to use their notes to write their own story opening in their Personal log. Tell them to use their Story mountain to help.

participate in discussion and consider the opinions of others

Big Question (CD)

Purpose: for children to develop their skills of argument and discussion through a mini enquiry session based on a philosophical question relating to the work of the day

- Display today's Big Question on the **CD (file 8.6)**:

  Why do we get annoyed with some people more than others?

- Follow the process as explained on Day 1.

DAY 9

Curriculum link: understand, through being shown, the skills and processes essential to writing

Build a story 3

Purpose: for children to see how a plan (Story mountain) helps an author and use this as a model for their own planning and writing

- Remind the children that they thought about how the main character might become friends with a bully.
- Ask the children to TTYP and talk about places in the school that the two characters might meet. Take feedback and write some of these ideas on the board or a flipchart.
- Ask the children to TTYP and tell them how their character is feeling about their big brother/sister in this part of the story. Remind them that, in contrast to how their brother/sister makes them feel at this point in the story, the bully makes them feel big and clever.
- Tell the children that they are going to role-play the point where their main character and the bully meet. Partner 1s will be the main character and Partner 2s will be the bully. Ask them to think about whether they have anything in common, e.g. perhaps they both like watching the same TV programmes or are both annoyed with their families. Take feedback and comment on good ideas.
- Display **CD (file 9.1)** Model using the children's ideas to add notes to the *Build up* section on the Story mountain.
- Now ask the children to add their ideas to their own Story mountain. Remind them to write about how their new friend makes them feel.
- Tell the children that there is a problem because they find out that their new friend is a bully. Remind the children that, in *Sister for Sale,* Rory bullies Tom. Say that you are going to *borrow* that idea and change it so it fits with your story.
- Display **CD (file 9.2)** to show the part in *Sister for Sale* where Rory bullies Tom. Navigate to the next slide to remind the children how you changed the story so Tom was a bully too. Remind the children that your story is about you (Gita), Suravi – the bully, and Veena, your sister.
- Use **CD (file 9.3)** to model how you changed the text to plan and write the problem for your story. Navigate to the next slide. Click 'TOL' to show the think bubble for how you could develop the idea and click 'Develop' to show the changes/additions.

develop stamina for writing by writing narratives

Write a story 3

Purpose: for children to use their plan (Story mountain) and notes to write their own story with a familiar setting

- Before the lesson, print a copy of the writing frames from **CD (files 9.4a, b** or **c)** for each child, as appropriate – **a)** gives the least support and **c)** gives the most.
- Tell the children that they are going to write their plan for the *Build up* and *Problem* sections of their story. Once they have got a good plan together, talk through how you used your plan to write your *Build up* and *Problem*. Remind the children how you rehearsed your ideas by thinking out loud.
- Give each child a copy of the appropriate differentiated writing frame **CD (file 9.4a, b** or **c)**. Tell them that you think they are ready to write their story.
- Explain that they can use their Story mountain, the notes in their Personal log and their writing frame to guide them to write their *Build up* and *Problem*.
- Remind them to think carefully about what they want to write and to look back at the opening that they wrote in their Personal log. Give them plenty of time to look at their plans and to think about their *Build up*.
- Now ask them to TTYP to share their ideas. Choose a few children to share their ideas with the class and perhaps write one or two ideas on the board in full sentences, as further models of the plan/develop/write process.

- When they are ready, tell them to think about what they want to write and to say it aloud before they write it down to check it makes sense.
- As the children are writing, walk around encouraging and supporting. You may like to read out good examples for inspiration as they complete each section.

DAY 10

Curriculum link: develop stamina for writing by writing narratives

Write a story 3 (continued) (CD)

Purpose: for children to have time to complete their work, so they can see that you value the act of writing

- Ask the children to read though their story so far, referring to their Personal log for their *Opening* and their writing frames for their *Build up* and *Problem* and then TTYP to share what they have written.
- Explain that you now want them to work on the *Resolution* section (ending) of their stories.
- Display **CD (file 10.1)** to show your notes. Click 'TOL' and use it to help you explain your choices.
- Ask the children to write additional notes for their story's *Resolution* on their Story mountain.
- Once they have put a good plan together, navigate to the next slide on **CD (file 10.1)** to talk through how you used your plan to write your ending.
- Tell the children they are now ready to finish writing their story. Look at the last slide to show them your ending.
- Display **CD (file 10.2)** to show the children your completed story and read it aloud to them.
- Ask children to TTYP to discuss it.
- When the children have put together the ideas for their *Resolution,* ask them to use the *Opening* they wrote in their Personal log and the *Build up, Problem* and *Resolution* that they wrote onto their writing frames to write up their completed story onto paper.
- You should expect some children to write the story using very simple sentences, following your ideas closely as their guide. Others will go on to develop their stories further with a clear beginning, middle and end in a logical sequence and with some use of *storyteller* language. A few children should be able to develop the problem/resolution aspect of the story more fully, and write longer sentences with varied conjunctions and appropriate punctuation for effect.

Share a story (CD)

Purpose: for children to share their story with a new audience

- Tell the children that they are going to be storytellers and tell their stories to a new partner.
- Prepare them for this by getting them to rehearse their character voices for dialogue and rehearse a voice to read the characters' thoughts. Remind them that when you read *Sister for Sale* you used your Storyteller voice and emphasised certain words to create atmosphere. Ask them to practise reading their story aloud to their partner using their Storyteller voice.
- Ask all Partner 1s to find a new Partner 2 to listen to their story (for this activity only). Move around the room as they read their story, collecting good examples of storytelling to feed back to the children at the end of the session.
- At the end of the session, ask the children to TTYP and say what they enjoyed about their partner's story. Take feedback and comment on the observations.

Curriculum link: evaluating their writing with the teacher and other pupils; make simple additions, revisions and corrections

Evaluate and edit (CD)

Purpose: for children to evaluate their own and their partner's work against specific criteria and then discuss how they could improve their work

- Display **CD (file 10.3)** to show the evaluation prompts and read them together using MT/YT.
- As a model, select an example of work where the writing has met the criteria, and share this with the other children, explaining why it works well.
- Tell the children to take turns to read their partner's writing in pairs and discuss together how well each piece of writing has met the criteria.
- Ask children to discuss at least two changes they could make to improve their work.

proofreading to check for errors in spelling, grammar and punctuation

Proofread

Purpose: for children to proofread their work and make changes to improve the accuracy of their grammar, punctuation and spelling

- Now ask the children to proofread their work. If you have noticed that several children need to improve on a particular aspect of spelling, grammar or punctuation, use this as a focus for the Proofread activity. Write an example which includes common errors from the children's writing and use this as a model.
- The children should always be checking for standard use of punctuation and correct spelling of common exception words.
- The following points would be relevant as the particular focus for this Unit:
  - using capital letters correctly, ensuring they are used for names of people and places as well as at the beginning of a sentence
  - checking their spelling of words and phrases used to move time on, such as *suddenly*, *after* (they can find many of these in the Anthology text)
  - checking suffixes have been correctly added to the end of root words and these words have been used appropriately, e.g. *helpful, helpless, careful, careless*.

Further activity

- Publish: allow the children to type up their stories, making changes from the Evaluate and edit and Proofread activities, and make a class story booklet.

READING AND WRITING NON-FICTION

The Non-fiction week continues the theme of family and relationships with a focus on families in the animal world, beginning with information about how animals care for their young and then looking at explanations of life cycles.

See p.20 for the daily timetable for the Non-fiction week.

Non-fiction

Reading

Children will:

- think about why we read explanatory texts
- notice how explanatory texts are structured to make information clear, using key features such as *an introduction*, *technical language* and *questions*
- identify how adverbs of time are used to order information and how this helps the reader to follow the text
- understand why glossaries are useful and learn to organise information alphabetically.

Writing

Key writing purpose to be shared with the children:

To write an explanation of a frog's life cycle.

Writing evaluation to be shared with the children

My frog life cycle:

- gives information about the key stages in a frog's life
- uses technical language to give the reader information about frogs.

Grammar:

- includes conjunctions to link ideas in the same sentence
- includes adverbs of time to structure the text clearly.

See the Planning section of the Software ('Timetables' tab) for a printable version of the Writing purpose and evaluation.

DAY 11

Curriculum link: pupils should be guided to participate in discussion listening to, discussing and expressing views about a wide range of non-fiction

Think and link

Purpose: for children to develop an interest in explanations via one of the Big Questions they have explored

- Display the Big Question from Day 1 on **CD (file 1.6)**:
  Can you help too much?
- Ask the children to TTYP to recall some of the points they discussed when the question was introduced on Day 1 and take feedback.
- Remind the children that Tom's sister, Molly, tried to *mother* him. Ask them to TTYP and talk about what Molly did to mother Tom. Display **CD (file 11.1)** to show the image of a joey. Ask them to TTYP and decide what type of animal his mother is. Navigate to the next slide to reveal that his mother is a kangaroo.
- Navigate through the slides, repeating the process for each of the animals. As you show each slide, ask the children to TTYP and talk about what they think each parent would need to do to look after their offspring. When you reach the final slide, explain that baby cuckoos are often not looked after by their own mothers.

Introduction

Purpose: for children to understand why we read explanatory texts

- Tell the children that explanations are a type of information text that tell the reader how and why something happens. You are going to look at some questions which use *how* or *why*.
- Remind the children that when we ask a question in *spoken form*, we often raise our voices slightly at the end of the sentence we are saying.
- Teach or revise the punctuation mime for a question mark (see the Extras section of the Software) by raising your eyebrows and the pitch of your voice as you say '*How did you manage to do that?*' and draw a large question mark in the air. Exaggerate the rise in the pitch of your voice. (We may not always do this in natural speech, but it is a useful way to remind children when to use question marks.)
- Explain that when we *write* a question, we can say it like that in our heads to remind ourselves to add a question mark at the end.
- Write the sentence on the flipchart with the question mark in a different colour.
- Now ask the question '*Why is rain good for plants?*' Explain that you want them to TTYP to see if they can give an answer that explains what you need to know. Take feedback and listen out for conjunctions such as *because* and *so*. Explain that these are words we use when we want to link ideas together in the same sentence and we call them *conjunctions*.
- Explain that the text that they are going to read is all about how and why animals look after their young. Display **CD (file 11.2)** to show the first page of the Anthology text. Draw attention to the first *how* question. Ask the children to TTYP and talk about the different ways parents help their children. Do they think it is the same for the animal world?
- Before they read, ask the children to TTYP to think of some *how* and *why* questions that they would like to see explained in the text. Take feedback and write some questions onto the flipchart.
- Now ask the children to turn to pp.14–17 in Anthology 2 Book 1 and read the full text with their partner, taking it in turns to read alternate paragraphs. Afterwards take feedback to find out whether their questions were answered.

- Choose two sets of partners to give an example of a question that was answered in the text. Paraphrase their answers to form a short statement. Write it on the flipchart and tell them that a question is often answered with a statement. A statement is a sentence that doesn't need a question mark. It just needs a full stop.
- Read your statement out and drop your voice slightly at the end of the sentence and mime the action of punching in the air (see the Extras section of the Software).

Curriculum link: being introduced to non-fiction that is structured in different ways

Zoom in on explanations

Purpose: for children to become familiar with some of the key language features associated with explanations

- Before the lesson, print a copy of **CD (file 11.3)** on A3 paper and the list of conjunctions and adverbs of time from **CD (file 11.4)**.
- Display the words you printed from **CD (file 11.4)** on your Explanations wall and remind the children that they are adverbs of time and conjunctions.
- Display **CD (file 11.5)** and show the children the key features.
- Read each feature and explain that adverbs of time are words and phrases that show the order in which things happen. Remind them that conjunctions are words and phrases such as *and, but, or, so* that we use to link ideas in a sentence.
- Navigate to the next slide to show the first section of 'Parents and their Young'. Read the text together and tell the children that you are going to look at some of the key features in the text.
- Click 'Question' and 'Adverb of time' to highlight some of the key features. Explain that the adverb of time *First* shows the order of events.
- Now ask the children to turn to the Zoom in on explanations activity on p.9 in their Pupils' Book and TTYP to read the list of key features. Ask them to take it in turns to read each paragraph in 'Parents and their Young' on pp.14–15 of Anthology 2 Book 1 and see if they can find any key features.
- Take feedback from the children and highlight your A3 copy.

Homework Book p.6 provides further practice on explanations.

understand how different types of writing are structured

Class log

Purpose: for children to share the process of keeping a class reading, writing and thinking log to record responses to texts and activities in a variety of forms

- Now display the printed A3 copy of **CD (file 11.3)** on the board or flipchart. Ask the children to follow the text on pp.16–17 of Anthology 2 Book 1 as you read it to them and to look and listen out for any key features. Clarify if necessary.
- Now ask the children to TTYP to find examples of any key features listed on p.9 of their Pupils' Book.
- Collect examples and highlight them on your A3 copy. Paste the highlighted copy of the text into the Class log.

DAY 12

Glossaries

Purpose: for children to understand why non-fiction texts have glossaries and how they are organised

- Ask the children to find the words printed in bold in 'Parents and their Young' on pp.14–17 of Anthology 2 Book 1.
- Tell the children that the author has forgotten to write a glossary. Explain that a glossary orders the key words alphabetically and gives the meaning of the words.

- Display **CD (file 12.1)** to display the words that are shown in bold in the Anthology text. Click 'Definition' to show the definition for each word and share it with the children using MT/YT. Model using the word in a sentence, e.g. 'Reptiles *like to lie in the sun to warm up*.' Ask the children to TTYP and use the word in a sentence. Take feedback. Repeat the process for each of the words.
- Display **CD (file 12.2)** and tell the children that the words and their definitions need to be organised into alphabetical order. Explain that you do this by looking at the first letter of the word. Drag the words into alphabetical order using TTYP to ask the children to tell you where each word should go.
- Point to the words *protect* and *prey*. Explain that they have the same first and second letters, so the children will need to look at the third letter to see which word should appear first in the glossary. Ask the children to TTYP and decide which word should appear first.
- When all the definitions are in alphabetical order, print out the glossary and paste it into the Class log.

Diagrams (CD)

Purpose: for children to be able to understand how a diagram is used to organise information

- Display **CD (file 12.3)** to show the diagram showing the life cycle of a sea turtle. Use MT/YT to say each caption.
- Click 'Hide/Reveal' to hide the captions. Ask the children to TTYP and take turns explaining to their partner, in their own words, what is happening at each stage on the diagram.
- Move around as they do this, taking note of children who are confident and concise in their explanations. Use their examples as you feed back to the children.
- Click 'Hide/Reveal' to show the captions.

Curriculum link: explain the meaning of new words; writing down key words, including new vocabulary

Class log (CD)

Purpose: for children to share the process of keeping a class reading, writing and thinking log to record responses to texts and activities in a variety of forms

- Tell the children that they are going to write an explanation about the life cycle of a frog and so will need to use and understand some technical words about frogs.
- Display **CD (file 12.4)** to show the technical words and then use MT/YT to read the words together. Click 'Sentence' to show examples of the words used in context. Write the words into the Class log.
- Navigate to the next slide and click 'Definitions' to reveal definitions for each of the words. Click 'Definitions' to hide the definitions and tell the children that you want them to help you write a class definition of each word into the Class log.

DAY 13

discussing the sequence of events; learn about cause and effect in non-fiction

Explanations 1 (CD) (A)

Purpose: for children to sequence the text in an explanation with support

- Display **CD (file 13.1)** to show an explanation of the life cycle of a sea turtle. Say that the text is in the wrong order. Use MT/YT to read each sentence.
- Tell children to use the diagram of the turtle's life cycle on p.17 of Anthology 2 Book 1 to help work you to out the order of the text. Choose the sentence 'A sea turtle digs a hole on the beach and lays her eggs in the bottom of it.' and ask the children to TTYP and work out which picture on the diagram the text goes with. Ask the children where it should come in the paragraph and drag it into the correct position.
- Repeat this process for each sentence until the paragraph is correctly ordered. Read your final paragraph aloud using TOL to check it makes sense.

Curriculum link: discussing the sequence of events

Write 1

Purpose: for children to use a diagram to sequence the text in an explanation independently

- Before the start of the lesson, print a frog life cycle diagram for each child and print and cut out a set of sentences for each set of partners from **CD (file 13.3)**.
- Display **CD (file 13.2)**. Use MT/YT to read the captions for each part of the frog's life cycle. Explain that captions are short explanations which are not always full sentences and may only contain the most important details. Ask the children to TTYP to help you to decide where the captions should appear on the life cycle. Take feedback and drag the captions next to the correct pictures.
- Navigate to the next screen to show the diagram without captions and ask the children to TTYP and take it in turns to explain what is happening in each part of the life cycle.
- Navigate to the next screen to show some full sentences developed from the captions. Ask the children to TTYP and tell their partner how they would order the sentences to make a paragraph. Take feedback and agree where the explanation should start. Do not order the sentences at this point.
- Give each set of partners a print out of the life cycle diagram and a set of cut-out sentences from **CD (file 13.3)**. Ask them to work together, using the the frog life cycle to help them, to order the sentences so that they have an explanation of the frog's life cycle.
- When the children have finished, order the sentences together on **CD (file 13.2)** using feedback from the children.
- Give the children time to make any alterations and ask them to write the paragraph and paste the life cycle diagram into their Personal log.

writing for different purposes

Personal log

Purpose: for children to keep a personal reading, writing and thinking log to record thoughts and ideas for their own writing

- Before the lesson, print a copy of the frog photographs for each child from **CD (file 13.5)**.
- Tell the children that you have found some images of frogs that could go with their explanations. Display **CD (file 13.4)** and play the slideshow by navigating through the slides. After each picture ask the children to TTYP and discuss what they can see. Choose one picture and model writing a caption for it.
- Give each child a copy of the photographs from the slideshow **CD (file 13.5)**. Ask them to choose one of the photographs and write a caption for it on a new page in their Personal log. Tell the children to keep the pictures safe so they can add them to their explanations in their writing books later on.

DAY 14

understand, through being shown, the skills and processes essential to writing

Explanations 2

Purpose: for children to participate in improving an explanation

- Display **CD (file 14.1)** to show the paragraph about sea turtles that the children helped you to order on Day 13.
- Remind the children that conjunctions (e.g. *because, and*) can be used to link ideas and that adverbs of time (e.g. *first, next*) can be used to order ideas.
- Tell the children that you are going to improve the paragraph by using adverbs of time to order the sentences and conjunctions to add some additional information.

- Navigate to the next screen to show the first sentence and a list of adverbs of time. Improve the sentence by saying it aloud and choosing an adverb of time to add to the beginning and then drag it into the sentence. Share the sentence using MT/YT and TOL as you explain why you think it does/does not work.
- Navigate to the next screen and repeat the process.
- Navigate to the next screen to show the first sentence with an adverb of time added to the beginning. Tell the children that you are now going to use a conjunction to add some additional information.
- Orally improve the sentence by choosing a conjunction and some additional information and then dragging it into place. Share the sentence using MT/YT and TOL as you explain why you think it does/does not work.
- Navigate through the next two screens and repeat the process. The final screen shows how the completed explanation looks.

Curriculum link: making simple additions, revisions and corrections to their own writing

Write 2 PB

Purpose: for children to improve their explanations independently

- Ask the children to find the paragraph explaining the life cycle of a frog that they ordered and stuck into their Personal log on Day 13, and turn to the Write 2 activity on p.10 of their Pupils' Book.
- Tell the children that you would like them to improve their paragraph by using some of the words and phrases in their Pupils' Book. Say that they should break down this task by first adding in some adverbs of time from the first box and then selecting conjunctions and additional information from the second box.
- Explain that they will need to edit the paragraph by removing some words and adding in punctuation. Tell them to TTYP to discuss the changes before writing them into their Personal log.
- Move around, observing and supporting children. When the children are ready, feed back, using good examples.

writing for different purposes

Class log CD

Purpose: for children to share the process of keeping a class reading, writing and thinking log to record responses to texts and activities in a variety of forms

- Before the lesson, print a copy of the glossary text from **CD (file 14.2)** and cut up the six words and three definitions.
- Tell the children that they are going to help you create a glossary for their explanation of the frog's life cycle.
- Stick the words (not the definitions) on the board and ask the children to TTYP to decide how to order them alphabetically.
- Take feedback and clarify if necessary. Paste the words in the Class log in the correct order.
- Now show the children the definitions. Use MT/YT to read them one at a time and then ask the children to TTYP and decide which word they think each definition goes with. Paste the correct definitions next to the words in the Class log.
- Now ask the children to TTYP to think of a short definition for one of the remaining words. Choose two sets of partners to feed back and use their ideas to develop a clear definition. Write this in the Class log.
- Repeat the process for the remaining two words.
- Explain that they are going to add more detail to their explanations in the next lesson so some of these words might be useful then.

DAY 15

Curriculum link: understand, through being shown, the skills and processes essential to writing

Explanations 3

Purpose: for children to learn how to use notes to create sentences containing additional information

- Tell the children that you are going to work together to begin to expand and develop their explanation about the frog's life cycle.
- Display **CD (file 15.1)** to show some extra information about frogs, in note form. TOL as you model how to convert the first of the notes into a full sentence. Say it aloud before writing it in the text box.
- Ask the children to TTYP to decide how they could convert the second of the notes into a full sentence. When they are happy with their sentence, ask them to write it into their Personal log.

encapsulating what they want to say, sentence by sentence

Write 3

Purpose: for children to turn notes into sentences to create additional information independently

- Ask the children to turn to p.11 in their Pupils' Book and look at the Write 3 activity. Ask them to TTYP to read the notes about frogs.
- Tell the children that they are going to use the notes and create sentences to provide additional information. Tell them to write their sentences below their frog life cycle in their Personal log.

Write an explanation

Purpose: for children to write their own explanation

- Before the lesson, print a copy of the writing frame on **CD (file 15.3)** for each child.
- Tell the children that they are now ready to use their paragraph, sentences and the frog's life cycle to write an explanation text full of interesting information.
- Display **CD (file 15.2)** to show how you added more detail to and improved your explanation. Navigate through the slides and click 'Develop' to use the TOLs to model how you developed your explanation. Remember to suggest when you would use your picture and caption from the Personal log activity on Day 13.
- When you reach the final slide, read your completed explanation aloud. Remove it from display before you ask the children to write their own explanation. They can either write it straight into their writing books or use the writing frame on **CD (file 15.3)**.
- For more independent children, hide your completed explanation and ask them to write their paragraph using just the notes on their life cycle to support them.
- Monitor the children as they write.

evaluating their writing with the teacher and other pupils; make simple additions, revisions and corrections

Evaluate and edit

Purpose: for children to evaluate their own and their partner's work against specific criteria and then discuss how they could improve their work

- Ask the children to turn to p.12 in their Pupils' Book and look at the Evaluate and edit activity. Ask them to TTYP to read through the question prompts.
- As a model, select an example of work where the writing has met the criteria, and share this with the other children, explaining why it works well.
- Tell the children to take turns to read their partner's writing in pairs and discuss together how well each piece of writing has met the criteria.
- Ask children to discuss at least two changes they could make to improve their work.

Curriculum link: proofreading to check for errors in spelling, grammar and punctuation

Proofread

Purpose: for children to proofread their work and make changes to improve the accuracy of their grammar, punctuation and spelling

- Now ask children to proofread their work. If you have noticed that several children need to improve on a particular aspect of spelling, grammar or punctuation, use this as a focus for the Proofread activity. Write an example which includes common errors from the children's writing and use this as a model.
- Children should always be checking for standard use of punctuation and correct spelling of common exception words.
- The following points would be relevant as the particular focus for this Unit:
  - checking that punctuation has been used correctly, particularly question marks
  - checking their spelling of technical (subject specific) vocabulary, e.g. *tadpole, froglet, frogspawn*.

read aloud what they have written with appropriate intonation to make the meaning clear

Presentations (CD)

Children might need access to computers for this activity.

Purpose: for children to present their explanations clearly and effectively

- Display **CD (file 15.4)** and show the children a presentation of the frog's life cycle (images only).
- Navigate back to the second slide and TOL as you explain which sentence you would use for that slide. Type your sentence into the text box.
- Now ask the children to TTYP to talk about which parts of their explanation they would use with the next slide. Choose two sets of partners to feed back. Paraphrase as necessary before typing a sentence into the text box.
- Repeat the process for the rest of the slides.
- You may wish to plan an ICT session where children use the slides on **CD (file 15.4)** to create their own presentations with their partners. They could present their explanations to children from another class.

Fiction: Poetry
Non-fiction: Non-chronological texts

Timetable

WEEK 1 Reading fiction Poetry

Day 1	Day 2	Day 3	Day 4	Day 5
The poetry store	Poetic terms	Secret poem 2	Secret poem 3	Read a poem 3
Think and link 1	Secret poem 1	Word play	Read a poem 2	Performance
Role-play	Zoom in on settings	Word power	Repetition, rhythm and rhyme	Discuss a performance
Wishes and consequences	Class log	Think and link 2	Personal log	Class log
Personal log	Big Question	Read a poem 1	Big Question	Big Question
Big Question		Personal log		
		Big Question		

WEEK 2 Writing fiction Poetry

Day 6	Day 7	Day 8	Day 9	Day 10
Poetry makers	Build a poem 1	Build a poem 2	Build a poem 3	Write a poem 3 (continued)
Follow me	Write a poem 1	Write a poem 2	Write a poem 3	Evaluate and edit
Grammar: commas in lists	Word play 2	Layout	Personal log	Proofread
What if not...?	Personal log	Personal log		Performance
Word play 1	Big Question	Big Question		
Personal log				
Big Question				

WEEK 3 Reading and writing non-fiction Non-chronological texts

Day 11	Day 12	Day 13	Day 14	Day 15
Think and link	Zoom in on non-chronological texts	Grammar: suffixes 1 *-ing*	Grammar: suffixes 2 *-er* and *-est*	Write 3 (continued)
Introduction	Non-chronological texts 1	Questions	Non-chronological texts 3	Evaluate and edit
Non-chronological detectives	Write 1	Non-chronological texts 2	Write 3	Proofread
Class log	Class log	Write 2	Personal log	Publish
		Personal log		

: shows that a file should be printed out from the Software

Overview of the Unit

This Unit uses a variety of poems with unusual imagery to stimulate the children to write their own poems. The picture book *The Fish Who Could Wish* by John Bush and Korky Paul sets the scene for exploring the underwater world. The focus is on developing the children's enjoyment of poetry. They explore pattern, imagery, rhyme, alliteration, kennings and shape (concrete) poems using the poems 'Tiger' by Usha Kishore, 'River' by June Crebbin and 'Don't Call Alligator Long-Mouth Till You Cross River' by John Agard.

The Non-fiction week continues the theme of the underwater world with a non-chronological text about oceans. For more information about the Non-fiction week and the Non-fiction writing evaluation criteria, see p.68.

Where appropriate, the children will be encouraged to develop an awareness of audience and purpose in relation to the fiction and non-fiction texts they are reading and writing.

Teacher modelling is provided in the teaching notes and the Software, supporting the children's writing at every stage in the Fiction and Non-fiction weeks.

The Homework Book provides a homework activity related to the content of this Unit for each of the three weeks.

Fiction

Reading

Children will:

- explore poetic techniques, e.g. *rhyme, rhythm, repetition, alliteration*
- explore the form of shape (concrete) poems
- perform a poem, using emphasis to create meaning.

Writing

Key writing purpose to be shared with the children:

To write a poem describing a new sea creature.

Writing evaluation to be shared with the children

My poem:

- includes interesting information about my new sea creature, such as where it lives or what it eats
- uses at least one poetic technique, e.g. *rhyme, rhythm, repetition* and *alliteration*
- includes kennings arranged in an interesting shape.

Grammar:

- includes commas to tell the reader when to pause.

See the Planning section of the Software ('Timetables' tab) for a printable version of the Writing purpose and evaluation.

READING FICTION

Resources

PB Pupils' Book, pp.13–22
A Anthology 2 Book 1, pp.18–24
CD CD on interactive whiteboard, Unit 2
GB Grammar Bank on CD
HB Homework Book, pp.7–9

DAY 1

Curriculum link: participate in discussion about books, becoming familiar with a wide range of books

The poetry store

Purpose: for children to hear and enjoy a picture book poem that introduces themes to be explored in the Anthology texts

- Before the lesson, print out a copy of the TOL (Think out loud) points from **CD (file 1.2)**. In addition to this, make yourself a simple badge with a star to use as a Poetry star.
- Show the children your Poetry star. Explain that this means that they are going to hear a wonderful story that is written in the form of a poem.
- Display **CD (file 1.1)** to show the front cover of *The Fish Who Could Wish* by John Bush and Korky Paul. Ask the children to read the title and look at the picture and then TTYP (Turn to your partner) to share what they think the poem might be about. Collect feedback and show how much you value their ideas.
- Navigate through the pages by clicking on the foward arrow or the corners of the pages. Read aloud to the children with great enthusiasm and obvious pleasure, using expression to convey meaning and impact. Use TTYP to explore a few aspects of the poem as they arise, e.g. the unusual images, use of rhyme and the silliness of some of the fish's wishes.
- Tell the children that they are going to help you to re-read the poem.
- Navigate back to the beginning of the poem. Use MT/YT (My turn/Your turn) to re-read it. Stop at points to look closely at the illustrations of the other fish and discuss what they might be thinking about the wishing fish's antics.
- As you re-read the poem with the children, use the TOL points you printed from **CD (file 1.2)** and your own ideas and TTYP to explore the unusual things that appear as a result of the fish's wishes.

drawing on what they already know

Think and link 1

Purpose: for children to make connections between this story and other stories

- Ask the children to TTYP to recall some of the fish's wishes. Take feedback and write their ideas onto the board or a flipchart.
- Ask the children to TTYP to decide which wishes were just silly and which wishes might have upset the other fish, e.g. *the other fish would have been very cold when it started to snow under water.* Display **CD (file 1.1)** again and navigate through the pages, pointing out the illustrations which help them to make their decisions.
- Ask the children to TTYP to think about things characters want or wish for in other stories they might have read, e.g. *Cinderella, The Three Wishes, King Midas, Aladdin*. Ask: '*When the wish was granted did it make them happy?*' Take feedback and add some of your own ideas if necessary.

role-play to help pupils identify with and explore characters

Role-play

Purpose: for children to use accurate descriptions to make their own wishes

- Tell the children that a magical creature has given them a wish. Partner 1s are going to be the magical creature and Partner 2s need to ask the magical creature to grant their wish. Ask them to plan and practise a role-play of what might happen. Encourage Partner 2s to use accurate vocabulary to describe their wish, and Partner 1s to think carefully about what the consequences of the wish could be. Check they understand the meaning of the word *consequences*.

- Ask the children to perform their role-plays simultaneously as you walk around offering praise and encouragement. Then ask the children to swap roles and repeat the process. Ask two or three sets of partners to explain what the consequences of their wishes might be.
- Ask them to TTYP to decide if they need to change the way they ask for their wish to be granted to make sure they get exactly what they want. Take feedback.

Wishes and consequences PB

Purpose: for children to explore what might happen as a result of making wishes

- Tell the children that the fish's wishes made some odd things happen. Remind them of the consequences of some their wishes from the Role-play activity. Say that their wishes had to be very specific, so they got exactly what they wished for, e.g. if you wished you could fly you might never be able to land again.
- Ask them to turn to p.13 in their Pupils' Book and look at the Wishes and consequences activity. Ask them to TTYP to read through the first set of prompts under the heading *What will you wish for?* and to decide what they would use their one wish for. It does not have to be the same wish that they used in their role-play.
- Ask the children to TTYP and practise saying their wish using the opening: *I wish…* Record some of their wishes on the board or flipchart.
- Now ask them to TTYP and read through the second set of prompts under the heading *What will happen when you make your wish?* and to decide what might happen as a consequence of them making their wish.
- Take feedback and model orally forming your sentence, adding *but* to suggest ideas for what the consequences of the wish might be.
- Ask the children to TTYP and orally compose a full sentence explaining what their wish is and using *but* to add the consequences.
- Take feedback and repeat their sentences back to them, making sure you use *I wish* and *but* if they have not already added them. Model writing some of their sentences on the board or a flipchart.
- Ask the children to write their sentence into their Personal log. Remind them to begin with *I wish* and add *but* before they write down the consequences, and to say their sentence to their partner before writing it down.

Curriculum link: writing for different purposes; increase pupils' vocabulary

Personal log CD

Purpose: for children to keep a personal reading, writing and thinking log in order to record thoughts and ideas for their own writing

- Remind the children that there were lots of rhyming words in *The Fish Who Could Wish*. Write these examples on the board: *blue/true/do, ski/sea, delight/night, treat/eat, wish/fish, wise/ties*. Draw attention to the fact that some rhymes sound the same but have different spellings.
- You can use the Complex Speed Sounds chart to clarify or explain where the different spellings would be on the chart. The chart can be found on the CD by opening the 'Complex Speed Sounds chart' from the top of the resources list for Day 1.
- Ask the children to TTYP to think of one new rhyming word for the first set of rhymes, e.g. *blue/true/do* and *shoe*.
- Ask them to Popcorn (see Introduction p.17) their answers, and clarify if necessary.
- Tell them to write the original set of words in their Personal log, plus their new word and any other rhyming words they like.
- Repeat the process for each set of words.
- At the end of the activity, choose some rhyming pairs to add to your Poetry wall.

Curriculum link: participate in discussion and consider the opinions of others

Big Question

Purpose: for children to develop their skills of argument and discussion through a mini enquiry session based on a philosophical question relating to the work of the day

- Display today's Big Question on the **CD (file 1.3)**:

  Would it be a good thing if all wishes came true?
- Ask the children to TTYP to talk about this question. Collect feedback and write some responses on the board.
- Click 'Prompts' to show some statements that may help to encourage discussion.

DAY 2

Poetic terms

Purpose: for children to become familiar with some technical language particular to poetry: rhyme, repetition, adjective, stanza, line, alliteration, kenning

- Remind the children that *The Fish Who Could Wish* is a poem that tells a story. Ask them to look at the Poetry wall to remind themselves of some of the rhyming words they found. Tell them that some poems have rhymes in them but not all poems have to rhyme.
- Display **CD (file 2.1)** to show the poetic term *rhyme* and its definition. Read the term and its definition using MT/YT. Click on the term to reveal an example from the poem.
- Navigate through the next two slides and repeat the process for the other terms.
- The final slide shows the more complex poetic terms *alliteration* and *kenning*. The children will be introduced to these terms during the week. Read the terms and definitions with the children using MT/YT. (This is just to introduce the children to these new terms; they should not be expected to remember them at this stage.)
- Tell the children that during the week they will listen to and read lots of poems that will use these techniques and they will hear lots of examples.
- Write the poetic terms on card or print them out from printable **CD (file 2.2)** and display them on your Poetry wall for this Unit.

making inferences, answering and asking questions, predicting

Secret poem 1

Purpose: for children to listen to and make connections between a new poem and the picture book story

- Tell the children that it is time for a Secret poem. Wear or point to your Poetry star.
- Explain that you have found a Secret treasure chest that was hidden in a sunken shipwreck and that each day it will open to reveal a new poem. (Note that the Secret poem structure for poetry differs from the three layers of text approach used elsewhere in the programme. In this Unit children will be introduced to poetry and immersed in poetic imagery by listening to audio recordings of a variety of poems. They then re-read and re-tell the poems, building pictures in their minds and enjoying the sounds and rhythms of the words. The children draw on ideas from all of the poems in their own writing.) Display **CD (file 2.3)** to show the Secret treasure chest.
- Click the chest to start the animation and to play the audio of some lines being read from *Underwater Farmyard* by Carol Ann Duffy.
- Ask the children to listen to the poem a second time with their eyes closed and to make pictures in their mind as they hear the poem.
- Ask the children to TTYP to talk about some of the images that they saw. Take feedback and model linking the children's images to any similar images in *The Fish Who Could Wish*, e.g. '*You described seeing dark, deep waters, just like the deep waters in* The Fish Who Could Wish.'

- Ask the children to TTYP to talk about anything that they feel is similar in this poem to *The Fish Who Could Wish*. Take feedback.

Zoom in on settings

Each set of partners will need two strips of card or paper for this activity.

Purpose: for children to make links between the settings of the two poems they have heard

- Display **CD (file 2.3)** on the board and tell the children that they are going to listen to the poem again. Say that this time you want them to listen out for any words and phrases that they really like.
- Click the treasure chest to play the audio of the poem being read again.
- Ask them to TTYP to share the words and phrases they liked. Take feedback and encourage children to give reasons for their choices. You may need to model some examples for the children to help them with this activity, e.g.

  I really like the lines about the deep wet meadows which are blue and have sea-cows because they make me imagine a special place where the sea is like lush fields and I can see cows grazing contentedly.
- Tell the children that you are going to collect words that describe the underwater world to put on the Poetry wall.
- Listen to the poem once more, then ask the children to TTYP to identify words used to describe the underwater world. Take feedback and write some of the words onto the board or a flipchart.
- Give each set of partners two strips of card or paper and ask them to write down a word/phrase on each strip that has been used to describe the underwater world. Choose a few sets of partners to take it in turns to stick their words/phrases onto the Poetry wall and describe the images the words created in their minds.
- Remind the children that *The Fish Who Could Wish* had a similar setting to *Underwater Farmyard*. Ask the children to TTYP to describe the underwater world using some of the words they wrote down and the words on the Poetry wall.

Class log

Curriculum link: participate in discussion and consider the opinions of others

Purpose: for children to share the process of keeping a class reading, writing and thinking log to record responses to texts and activities in a variety of forms

- Tell the children that they are going to start a new section in the Class log for Poetry. Show the new title page with just the heading *Poetry* written at the top.
- Ask them to turn to p.14 in their Pupils' Book and look at the Class log activity. (These covers can also be displayed on the board from **CD (file 2.4)**.)
- Tell the children that they are going to be reading and exploring other poems and that some of them will also be about water and creatures that live in water. Explain that you would like them to look at the cover designs and TTYP to decide which design they would choose for the cover of a book containing a collection of poems about the underwater world, if they were the publishers, and why. Ask: *'How do they make you feel? Which one is most likely to make the reader pick up the book? Which is the clearest? What can you see in the images?'*
- Ask for feedback and vote for the best cover. Before the next lesson, print the best cover from **CD (file 2.4)** and paste it onto the title page in the Class log.
- Tell the children that they can offer things to be pasted into the Class log, e.g. pictures of strange sea creatures or the underwater world, or other poems that are linked to water. Make sure you bring in anything that could be relevant.

Curriculum link: participate in discussion and consider the opinions of others

Big Question (CD)

Purpose: for children to develop their skills of argument and discussion through a mini enquiry session based on a philosophical question relating to the work of the day

- Display today's Big Question on the **CD (file 2.5)**:

  Will there always be new things to find?*

- Follow the process as explained on Day 1.

  ** This Big Question will be revisited on Day 11 – the first day of the Non-fiction week.*

DAY 3

making inferences, answering and asking questions, predicting

Secret poem 2 (CD)

Purpose: for children to listen to a new poem and think about the imagery used in it

- Tell the children that it is time for another Secret poem. Wear or point to your Poetry star.
- Display **CD (file 3.1)** to show the Secret treasure chest. Click the chest to start the audio of the poem 'Tiger' by Usha Kishore. This poem will be read without its title.
- Tell the children that the poem is about an animal. Ask them to TTYP to decide which animal they think it is about. When you take feedback, encourage the children to use examples from the poem to back up their ideas.
- Navigate to the next slide to reveal that the poem is called 'Tiger'.
- Tell them they are going to listen to the poem a second time and that you want them to close their eyes and make images in their minds as they listen.
- After they have listened, ask them to TTYP to describe some of the images that they saw. Take feedback and link these images to what we imagine tigers to be like.

Word play (CD)

Purpose: for children to understand what kennings are and how they are created

- Tell the children that the poem they heard was made up of kennings. Say that a kenning is two words that give the reader an image of something without saying its name, e.g. a *tap* could be a *water-giver*. Tell them that in Old English, kennings were used to describe things (refer to any relevant topic work).
- Say that you are going to show them some kennings that were used in Old English.
- Display **CD (file 3.2)** to show an image of a whale and an image of a road. Click 'Kenning' to show the kenning *whale-road*. Ask the children to TTYP to say what they think a *whale-road* could be.
- Now click 'Image' to show what the kenning represents *(the sea)*. Navigate through the slides to repeat the process for a *wave-rider (boat)* and a *world-candle (sun)*.

discussing their favourite words and phrases, new vocabulary

Word power (CD)

Purpose: for children to learn the meaning of specific vocabulary used in the poem and increase their knowledge of synonyms

walker sprinter snarler

- Tell the children that you have chosen some kennings from the poem 'Tiger'. Say that the words in the kennings are powerful because they help you to create a clear picture in your mind of what the tiger is like. Say that they are going to help you to create some new kennings for the poem.
- Display **CD (file 3.3)** to show three kennings from the poem. Explain that the poet could have chosen different words that mean the same thing.

- Navigate to the next screen to show the beginning of the first kenning and a list of synonyms. Use drag and drop to substitute synonymous words into the gap. Use MT/YT to read it aloud after each substitution.
- Ask the children to TTYP to share which word they liked best.
- Navigate through the screens and repeat the process for the other kennings.
- These words and synonyms can be printed from **CD (file 3.4)** to display on your Poetry wall for this Unit. Let the children hear you using these words throughout the day and praise them if they use one.

Think and link 2 CD PB

Purpose: for children to explore how kennings can be used to describe characteristics

- Display **CD (file 1.1)** to remind the children of the story of *The Fish Who Could Wish*. Tell them they are going to create kennings to describe some of the things the fish wished for.
- Say that, like the author who used kennings to describe the tiger in the poem 'Tiger', they need to think about the characteristics of some of the things that the fish wished for.
- Navigate to pp.3–4 ('He wished for a castle.') of *The Fish Who Could Wish*. TOL to model creating some kennings for the castle, e.g. *'Who lives in a castle? It's usually kings and queens. How about a* royal-home. *This castle looks very tall and it's made of stone so it could be a* stone-tower *or a* tall-dwelling.'
- Next navigate to pp.5–6 ('He wished for a car.') to show the image of the car. TOL to model creating some kennings for the car, e.g. *'Cars move quickly so I could call it a* fast-rider *or a* speedy-mover. *Cars run on petrol, so I could say a* petrol-guzzler *or an* oil-drinker.'
- Now ask the children to turn to p.15 in their Pupils' Book and look at the Think and link 2 activity. Ask them to TTYP to read through the words in the Word bank and use them to create some kennings for the castle and the car that the fish wished for in the story. Take feedback and show how much you value their ideas. Write some of the children's kennings onto the board or a flipchart.

Curriculum link: checking that the text makes sense to them; making inferences

Read a poem 1 CD A

Purpose: for children to see the new poem for the first time and to read it with intonation and expression to show understanding

- Tell the children that there was another item in the Secret treasure chest. Display **CD (file 3.5)** to show a scroll.
- Navigate to the next slide to show the unrolled scroll with the poem 'Tiger' written on it. Read the poem, stopping after each kenning to TOL about the image the kenning creates in your mind.
- Ask the children to turn to p.18 in Anthology 2 Book 1 and take turns to read the poem to their partner, using lots of expression to make the reading exciting.
- Explain that you will be listening in and hoping to hear some star poetry readers.
- Give feedback to the whole class to model what skills and behaviour you expect.

discussing their favourite words and phrases

Personal log A

Purpose: for children to keep a personal reading, writing and thinking log in order to record thoughts and ideas for their own writing

- Ask the children to turn to p.18 in Anthology 2 Book 1 and to TTYP to decide which is their favourite kenning from the poem 'Tiger'. Tell them to think about why they have chosen that particular kenning and TTYP to explain their choice.

- Take feedback from a few sets of partners and write some of their responses on the board or a flipchart. Write the prompts: *My favourite kenning is…* and *because…* on the board.
- Ask the children to write their chosen kenning into their Personal log, explaining their choice. Remind the children to write a full sentence using the prompts on the board and to say their sentence to their partner before they write it down.

Curriculum link: participate in discussion and consider the opinions of others

Big Question (CD)

Purpose: for children to develop their skills of argument and discussion through a mini enquiry session based on a philosophical question relating to the work of the day

- Display today's Big Question on **CD (file 3.6)**:

  Are animals as important as humans?
- Follow the process as explained on Day 1.

DAY 4

checking the text makes sense as they read, making inferences, discussing sequence of events

Secret poem 3 (CD)

Purpose: for children to listen to a new poem and think about the imagery used in it

- Tell the children that it is time for another Secret poem. Wear or point to your Poetry star.
- Display **CD (file 4.1)** to show the Secret treasure chest. Click the chest to start the animation and the audio of the poem 'River' by June Crebbin.
- Ask the children to listen to the poem a second time with their eyes closed and make pictures in their mind as they hear the poem. Say that you want them to listen for the sound that is repeated at the end of every line in the poem. If necessary clarify that 'er' is used at the end of each line. Ask: '*How does the rhythm of the poem make you feel? Is it a sleepy rhythm, or a very sharp, regular rhythm?*'
- Ask the children to TTYP and choose a kenning from the poem that they particularly liked. Take feedback from a few sets of partners and encourage the children to explain their choices.

read accurately and fluently; listening to and discussing a wide range of poetry

Read a poem 2 (CD) (A)

Purpose: for children to see the poem for the first time and to read it with intonation and expression to show understanding

- Tell the children that you found another scroll in the Secret treasure chest. Display **CD (file 4.2)** to show the scroll.
- Navigate to the next slide to show the poem 'River' written on the unrolled scroll.
- Have fun reading the poem out a few lines at a time, using MT/YT, and really feeling the rhythm of the words (you could tap out the recurring 'one, two' stress/rhythm). Really draw out the long sounds, e.g. *stone-smoother* and *sun-seeker*.
- Draw the children's attention to the last line and read the words *sea-seeker* again. Ask: '*What sound do you hear twice in this line?*' Take feedback and clarify if necessary. Say that the 'ee' is a long stretchy sound, so it might make us think about a long journey to the sea, or maybe it's a relaxing sound because it's quite long and sleepy.
- Ask the children to turn to p.19 in Anthology 2 Book 1 and to take turns to read the poem to their partner, using lots of expression to make the reading exciting.
- Explain that you will be listening in and hoping to hear some star poetry readers.
- Give feedback to the whole class to model the skills and behaviour you expect.

Repetition, rhythm and rhyme

Purpose: for children to identify repetition in two of the poems they have read and to look at the effect it has on rhythm and rhyme

- Tell the children that they are going to look again at the poems 'Tiger' and 'River'. Say that both poems have been written using kennings and that sounds have been repeated in some of the kennings to create rhythm and rhyme in both poems.
- Ask the children to turn to pp.18–19 in Anthology 2 Book 1 and to TTYP to take turns to read each of the poems again.
- When they have finished, say you want them to find kennings in each of the poems that use words with the same initial sound/letter to create alliteration *(stone-smoother)* or that repeat the same sound at the end to make a rhyme *(bouncer* and *pouncer)*.
- Model reading through the poems and finding a few examples. Write your examples on the board or a flipchart. Encourage the children to notice that in both of the poems all of the lines end with the 'er' sound, and that this helps to create a rhythm.
- Use TTYP to build up a bank of words and phrases from the poems to put on the Poetry wall.

Curriculum link: expressing views about a wide range of poetry

Personal log

Purpose: for children to keep a personal reading, writing and thinking log in order to record thoughts and ideas for their own writing

- Tell the children that the poem 'River' has been written in a special way so it looks like a river. Say that this is called a *shape poem* (also known as a *concrete poem* but the term *shape poem* should be used with the children).
- Display 'River' by June Crebbin and 'Rhinos and Roses' by Gina Douthwaite on **CD (file 4.3)**. Explain that these are both shape poems.
- Read the poems chorally with the children and ask them to TTYP to decide which is the most effective as a shape poem, and why. Take feedback, encouraging them to give reasons for their choices.
- Ask them to write a sentence in their Personal log, explaining why their chosen poem is the most effective. Remind them to say their sentence to their partner before writing it down.

participate in discussion and consider the opinions of others

Big Question

Purpose: for children to develop their skills of argument and discussion through a mini enquiry session based on a philosophical question relating to the work of the day

- Display today's Big Question on the **CD (file 4.4)**:

  Are the words in a poem the most important thing?

- Follow the process as explained on Day 1.

DAY 5

read accurately and fluently; listening to and discussing a wide range of poetry

Read a poem 3

Purpose: for children to read a new poem with appropriate intonation and expression to show understanding

- Ask the children to turn to p.20 in Anthology 2 Book 1 and look at the poem 'Don't Call Alligator Long-Mouth Till You Cross River' by John Agard. Read the poem aloud, using appropriate intonation and expression to convey meaning.
- Tell the children that this poem has kennings in it too, but that they are used as insults.

- Ask them to TTYP to read the whole poem to each other, using lots of expression and then decide which line gives the best description of the alligator.
- Now ask them to think back to the poem *The Fish Who Could Wish* and ask if they can think of any kennings to describe the fish, e.g. *water-explorer, colour-flasher, ocean-gulper, bubble-singer, shark-dinner*.
- Now play **CD (file 5.1)** and ask the children to listen to the poem 'Don't Call Alligator Long-Mouth Till You Cross River' being read. Ask them to discuss their impressions of the reading. Did it sound any different to when they read it to their partners? Did it sound interesting and exciting? Take feedback.

Performance

Purpose: for children to develop their performance of a poem to include movement and actions

- Tell the children that most poems have the greatest impact when they are performed. Ask them to turn to pp.18–20 in Anthology 2 Book 1 and to TTYP to read the poems 'Tiger', 'River' and 'Don't Call Alligator Long-Mouth Till You Cross River' again.
- Ask the children to choose which poem they would like to perform and then group them according to their choices. They will perform the poem as a group.
- Display **CD (file 5.2)** and discuss the prompts with the children to help them develop their performance.
- You may want to give the children time to learn their lines off by heart so that they can really get into their performance.
- As they are practising, walk around, offering praise and encouragement.
- When the children are ready, they should share the performances with each other and perhaps another class.

Discuss a performance

Purpose: for children to evaluate their own and others' performances

- After the performance, ask the children to TTYP to share one thing they enjoyed about their own performance and one thing about another group's performance. Take feedback and say what you enjoyed about their performances.
- Ask the children to turn to p.16 in their Pupils' Book and look at the Discuss a performance activity. Ask them first to think back to their own performances and to TTYP to read and discuss the first set of prompts. Tell them to answer the questions using full sentences and to use the poetic terms on the Poetry wall where appropriate *(repetition, adjective, stanza, line, alliteration, kenning)*.
- Now ask the children to think back to another group's performances and to TTYP to read and discuss the second set of prompts. Remind them to answer the questions using full sentences and to use the poetic terms on the Poetry wall where appropriate.

Class log

Curriculum link: participate in discussion

Purpose: for children to share the process of keeping a class reading, writing and thinking log to record responses to texts and activities in a variety of forms

- Give each set of partners two sticky notes. Tell them to TTYP to decide which part of their performance they thought was best.
- Ask them to write their answers on their sticky notes and come up to the front to stick them in the Class log.
- Pick out a few sticky notes and ask the children to explain their choices.

Curriculum link: participate in discussion and consider the opinions of others

Big Question

Purpose: for children to develop their skills of argument and discussion through a mini enquiry session based on a philosophical question relating to the work of the day

- Display today's Big Question on the **CD (file 5.3)**:
  Is it always wrong to think bad thoughts about someone?
- Follow the process as explained on Day 1.

WRITING FICTION

DAY 6

Poetry makers

Purpose: for children to develop their understanding that poems are made by poets and that we can all become poets

- Show the children your Poetry star. Explain that this is to show that this week they are going to find out more about how the poems they have enjoyed so far are made.
- Ask the children to TTYP to share one or two ideas about what makes a good poem. Collect feedback and write some of their ideas on the board. Remind them that not all the poems you looked at in the Reading week rhymed, but they all had great images, repetition and rhythm. Copy some of their ideas on to card or paper and display on your Poetry wall for this Unit.
- Say that you are going to look in more detail at some of these features.

Follow me

Purpose: for children to work as a class to use kennings to extend a poem

- Display **CD (file 6.1)** to show the poem 'Don't Call Alligator Long-Mouth Till You Cross River' by John Agard. Read the poem together chorally.
- Remind the children that the kennings in this poem have been written as insults. If necessary, remind the children what a kenning is. Say that you are going to work together to add some more insults to 'Don't Call Alligator Long-Mouth Till You Cross River'.
- Display **CD (file 6.2)** to show the alligator from the poem and a list of words. Point to the alligator's head and say that you think *scaly* would be a good word to use to describe his head. Drag the word *scaly* into the first focus box and *head* into the second to create the insult *scaly head*.
- TOL as you repeat the process for *long back* and *pointy teeth*. Draw the children into the activity using MT/YT and TTYP as you play around with the words.
- Now tell the children to TTYP to orally compose their own insult. Tell them that they can use the words on screen or think of some of their own.
- Ask two or three sets of partners to share their insults. TOL as you orally improve a few of their ideas by using words that begin with the same sound (alliteration). Then use your comments as you TOL to orally improve your own ideas e.g. *humpy head, bumpy back, terrible teeth.*
- Ask the children to TTYP to improve their own insults using alliteration. Then ask them to practise saying them with the stem *call alligator…* Make sure they say their line confidently and clearly.

- Say that as a class you are going to put your ideas together to extend the poem. Explain that you will read the poem on **CD (file 6.1)** and stop after...*bumpy-bum*. Then you will point to each set of partners and they will add their line. When each set of partners has said their line everyone will say the final lines *call alligator all dem rude word but better wait till you cross river.*
- You may wish to record the class poem and play it back to the children.

Curriculum link: Year 2 Grammar learning how to use punctuation correctly, including commas for lists

Grammar: commas in lists

Purpose: for children to develop their understanding of the use of commas in lists

- Tell the children that poets often break writing rules because poetry is very special. Remind them that poems have lines rather than sentences and punctuation might not always be used exactly as we expect it to be.
- Remind the children of the poem they heard, 'Don't Call Alligator Long-Mouth Till You Cross River' by John Agard. Say that this poem gave a list of insults, so you decided to have a go at using this idea to describe a lion.
- Display **CD (file 6.3)** to show the list of insults that you thought you could use in your poem. Say that you have used line breaks instead of commas.
- Navigate to the next slide to show your description written out as a sentence.
- Ask the children to TTYP to identify what punctuation is used in the description. Invite them to Popcorn their answers. Clarify if necessary that there is just a *capital letter* at the beginning and a *full stop* at the end. Remind the children that usually, we use *commas* to separate ideas in a list.
- Revise or teach the *twist a wrist* punctuation mime for a comma (see the Extras section of the Software).
- Click 'Commas' to show the description written out again with commas inserted. Tell the children to look out for the commas as you read the description and to perform the mime when appropriate.
- Explain that, in writing that isn't poetry, it is important to stick to the rules for using commas in lists because it can be confusing for the reader without them.
- Navigate to the next slide to show a sentence which doesn't have any commas. Use MT/YT to read the sentence and then click 'TOL' to display some think bubbles. Use these to talk about the effect of the missing commas.
- Navigate to the next slide to show the sentence punctuated correctly. Use MT/YT to read the sentence aloud. Ask the children to think of reasons that they might need to make a list. Tell them to Popcorn their answers.
- Say that Peter the poet needs to get some shopping. Navigate to the next slide to show Peter's shopping list. Read the list aloud using MT/YT.
- Leave the shopping list displayed on the board. Ask the children to turn to p.17 in their Pupils' Book and look at the Grammar: commas in lists activity. Ask the children to TTYP to read the note and discuss where the commas should go. This is just an oral activity. The children don't need to write anything down.
- Choose a few sets of partners to share their answers.

Homework Book p.8 provides further practice on commas in lists.

making inferences on the basis of what is being said and done

What if not...?

Purpose: for children to explore unusual imagery in poetry

- Tell the children that imagery is very important in poetry. Say that the images that you create in your mind when you read a poem help to bring the poem to life.
- Display **CD (file 6.4)** to show the cover of *The Fish Who Could Wish*. Ask: '*What if not* a sea creature? *What if* a farm animal *came to live in the sea?*'

- Remind the children of the lines from *Underwater Farmyard* that they heard during the Reading week. Navigate to the next screen and click on the treasure chest to hear the poem being read.
- Say that when you heard this poem it made you imagine lots of different farm animals living under the sea. Tell them that you thought about cows floating about slowly and goats nibbling at a shipwreck. Ask the children to TTYP to think about what they imagined when they heard the poem. Take feedback.
- Ask: '*What if not* a sea creature? *What if there was* a wildlife park under the sea?'
- If necessary remind children what a wildlife park is and ask them to TTYP to think of some animals that they might see at a wildlife park. Take feedback and write some of their ideas on the board or a flipchart.
- Display **CD (file 6.5)** to show some photographs of some animals at a wildlife park. Stop on slide 4.
- Now ask the children to turn to p.17 in their Pupils' Book and look at the What if not…? activity. Ask the children to read the What if not…? question again and then to TTYP to think of some animals and talk about the question prompts. Take feedback and ask questions to expand on ideas where appropriate.
- Return to **CD (file 6.5)** and navigate to the final slide to show an underwater scene with some animals you might find at a wildlife park.

Word play 1 CD PB

Purpose: for children to build on the bank of words that they use in their poetry

- Display **CD (file 6.6)** to show the children pictures of some of the animals that they may have talked about in the previous activity and two Word banks.
- Say that you are going to choose an animal (don't tell them which animal) and think about what it looks like and how it moves to create a kenning to describe it. Model choosing a word from under the heading *What it looks like* and drag it into the first focus box and then choose a word from under the heading *How it moves* and drag it into the second focus box.
- Read your kenning to the children and ask them to TTYP to decide which animal the kenning is about. Repeat a few times.
- Now ask the children to turn to p.18 in the Pupils' Book and look at the Word play 1 activity. Ask them to TTYP and take it in turns to pick an animal and to choose two words to create a kenning to describe it.
- Choose a few sets of partners to share their kennings and ask the other children to guess which animal they are describing.
- Ask the children to write their kennings into their Personal log.

Curriculum link: writing down ideas and/or key words

Personal log

Purpose: for children to keep a personal reading, writing and thinking log in order to record thoughts and ideas for their own writing

- Ask the children to TTYP to think about what their favourite wild animal is. Say that you want them to think of reasons why this is their favourite animal and TTYP to discuss.
- Choose a few sets of partners to share their ideas with the rest of the class, drawing out why they have chosen their animal.
- Ask them to write the name of their animal in their Personal log and to list things they like about the animal. Remind the children that they can just write short notes; they don't have to write full sentences.

Curriculum link: participate in discussion and consider the opinions of others

Big Question

Purpose: for children to develop their skills of argument and discussion through a mini enquiry session based on a philosophical question relating to the work of the day

- Display today's Big Question on the **CD (file 6.7)**:

  Does everyone's voice deserve to be heard?
- Follow the process as explained on Day 1.

DAY 7

understand, through being shown, the skills and processes essential to writing

Build a poem 1

Purpose: for children to work together to create strong visual imagery to use as inspiration for their poetry

- Display **CD (file 7.1)** to show an image. Tell the children that this image is based on a kenning from the poem 'Don't Call Alligator Long-Mouth Till You Cross River'.
- Ask the children to TTYP and talk about what the image shows and how it makes them feel. Ask them if they can think back to when they heard the poem yesterday and remember which kenning it might show. Take feedback.
- Click 'Reveal' to show the kenning *scissors-mouth*. Navigate to the next slide and repeat the process for the next image *(saw-mouth)*.
- Tell the children that you have invented a new sea creature. Navigate to the next slide to reveal the image of the sea lion. Ask the children to TTYP to discuss what is strange about this combination. Say that to survive under water, a lion would have to change how it moves, what it eats and where it lives.
- Display **CD (file 7.2)** to show a coral reef and a selection of animals. Choose the lion and drag and drop it into the coral reef. TOL about how the animal might behave in its new environment, e.g. *'The sea lion would hide behind coral and pounce on its prey. Its prey could be zebra fish. It might make a lair in the dark sea caves.'*
- Choose a few children to suggest other animals to drag and drop into the setting. Ask the rest of the class to TTYP to describe how each animal would move, what it would eat, and where it would live. Take feedback. (All animals must have been dragged onto the coral reef before you can move onto the next screen.)
- Navigate through the screens and repeat the process for the other settings.

planning or saying out loud what they are going to write about

Write a poem 1

Purpose: for children to develop the first stage of their poem

- Before the lesson, print off a Strange combinations grid from **CD (file 7.3)** for each child.
- Explain to the children that they have already begun to collect the 'ingredients' they need to create their own kennings about a new sea creature.
- Give each child a Strange combinations grid from **CD (file 7.3)**.
- Remind the children of the Personal log activity they completed at the end of yesterday's session, where they wrote down ideas about their favourite animal.
- Tell the children that they are now going to create a new sea creature just like you did with the sea lion. Say that they can base their new creature around their favourite animal or one of the animals listed at the top of the grid.
- Read through the questions in each of the boxes in the grid using MT/YT.
- Ask the children to TTYP to talk about the questions and think about what their new sea creature is going to be like. Tell them to complete each box and tell their partner what they are going to write before they record it on the grid.
- Model building up information for one of the sea creatures on the grid using the following TOL and your own ideas.

I have chosen a lion. It will hunt in the coral. The coral will be like a jungle for it to roam through. The sea lion hunts alone. It hides in the coral and pounces on passing shoals of zebra fish. It thrashes about when it chases its prey and its mane waves about in the sea current.

- Take feedback from some of the children about their new sea creature and use this opportunity to TOL about what some their animals and settings will be like.
- Ask the children to add some more detail to their grids in the Notes section using the question prompts on p.19 of their Pupils' Book.
- Move around the class quietly as the children write their ideas down. Stop the class to share good ideas to give children some further inspiration.

Word play 2 (CD)

Purpose: for children to build powerful images to use in their poetry

- Remind the children that in yesterday's session they had a go at creating some kennings to describe animals that they might find at a wildlife park.
- Display **CD (file 7.4)** to show two lists of words, one to describe the animals and one to describe how the animals might move under water. Tell the children that they are now going to focus on creating kennings to describe their new sea creature in its underwater environment.
- Drag a word that could be used to describe your new creature into the first focus box, then drag a word to describe how it moves under water into the second focus box. TOL to explain your choices, e.g. *'The sea lion roars loudly and it glides through the water so I'm going to use the words* roaring *and* glider *to create the kenning* roaring glider.'
- Ask some of the children how they might use the words to create a kenning to describe how their new sea creature moves under water and use the drag and drop to experiment with some of the combinations.

Curriculum link: writing down ideas and/or key words

Personal log (CD)

Purpose: for children to keep a personal reading, writing and thinking log in order to record thoughts and ideas for their own writing

- Leave the Word banks from **CD (file 7.4)** on display.
- Ask the children to use their Strange combinations grids and TTYP to think of some ideas for two or three kennings to describe their new sea creature, thinking about what it looks like, how it behaves and how it moves under water. They can use the words in the Word banks or think of some of their own.
- Tell them that before they write their kennings, they can record their ideas in their Personal log. They may like to use mind maps or annotated pictures.
- Take feedback and TOL about some of the children's ideas.
- Ask the children to write their kennings into their Personal log. Remind them to say their kennings aloud to their partner before they write them down.

participate in discussion and consider the opinions of others

Big Question (CD)

Purpose: for children to develop their skills of argument and discussion through a mini enquiry session based on a philosophical question relating to the work of the day

- Display today's Big Question on **CD (file 7.5)**:

  Is something strange because *you* think it is?
- Follow the process as explained on Day 1.

DAY 8

Curriculum link: understand, through being shown, the skills and processes essential to writing

Build a poem 2

Purpose: for children to explore poetic techniques to use in their poems

- Point to your Poetry wall and remind the children of the poetry terms that you looked at during the Reading week. Explain that today you will be using some of these techniques to create some more kennings about their new sea creatures.
- Display **CD (file 8.1)** to show some kennings from the poems they looked at in the Reading week.
- Remind the children that some of the poems had words that repeated the same initial sound. This is called *alliteration*.
- Use MT/YT to say the kennings *stone-smoother*, *sun-sparkler and sea-seeker*. Explain that the repetition of the long 's' sound in these kennings makes them sound peaceful, like water flowing.
- Ask the children to say *bad biter* and *strong striker*. In contrast, the repetition of the short, sharp 'b' and 'st' sounds in the kennings make them sound strong and fierce.
- Navigate to the next slide to show some kennings that use rhyme. Share the rhyming couplets using MT/YT. Say that when poets use rhyme, it helps to give the poems rhythm.
- Tell the children that you are going to create some kennings to use in your poem which use repetition, alliteration and rhyme to create rhythm.
- Display **CD (file 8.2)** to show some kennings. Read the first kenning using MT/YT and then click 'TOL' to show a think bubble about how you could improve the kenning. Click 'Develop' to show your improved kenning.
- Repeat for the other kennings on the slide. Read your final kennings out when you reach the end of the slide. Navigate through the slides, repeating the process.
- Print the kennings from **CD (file 8.3)** and add them to your Poetry wall.

encapsulating what they want to say before beginning

Write a poem 2

Purpose: for children to create a bank of kennings to use in their final poem

- Ask the children to use the ideas they have written in their Personal log and their Strange combinations grid, and the words and kennings on the Poetry wall to write some more kennings to describe their new sea creature. They should think particularly about where their sea creature lives and what it likes to eat, and should aim to write at least four more kennings.
- Ask the children to TTYP to share each of their ideas before writing them down in their Personal log.
- At the end of the activity ask each child to share their favourite kenning and to explain their choice. Give lots of positive feedback about each kenning and explain what you like about them.
- Choose a few of the children's kennings to write into the Class log.

Layout

Purpose: for children to begin to consider how to lay out and organise their poem

- Remind the children that during the Reading week they looked at the shape poems 'River' and 'Rhinos and Roses'. Ask them to turn to p.19 in Anthology 2 Book 1 to look again at 'River' and to TTYP to read it aloud.
- Say that before you start to order the kennings that you have written you want to think about what shape you are going to use to lay out your poem.

- Explain that if you can imagine a shape for your poem it will help you start to think about a rhythm for your poem which links to the shape. Remind them that some of the long sounds in 'River' reminded you of a long journey to the sea and made you feel relaxed and sleepy. Say that this matched the shape of the river.
- Display **CD (file 8.4)** to show your kennings. Click 'Layout' to show the kennings laid out in the shape.

Curriculum link: think aloud as they collect ideas

Personal log

Purpose: for children to keep a personal reading, writing and thinking log in order to record thoughts and ideas for their own writing

- Ask the children to look back at the kennings they wrote in their Personal log and to TTYP to share them.
- When they have finished, ask them to TTYP to talk about which shapes they could use to lay out their poems.
- Ask them to sketch their ideas into their Personal log.
- Choose some children to read their kennings to the rest of the class and share their ideas about which shapes they think would work well for their poems.

participate in discussion and consider the opinions of others

Big Question (CD)

Purpose: for children to develop their skills of argument and discussion through a mini enquiry session based on a philosophical question relating to the work of the day

- Display today's Big Question on **CD (file 8.5)**:

  Can a whole person be summed up in a poem?

- Follow the process as explained on Day 1.

DAY 9

understand, through being shown, the skills and processes essential to writing

Build a poem 3 (CD)

Purpose: for children to see an example of a finished poem that will provide a model for their own writing

- Display **CD (file 9.1)** to show some of your kennings and some additional kennings. TOL as you drag them into the box on the right hand side of the screen, playing around with the order to use rhyme, repetition and alliteration to create rhythm. Use the TOL below and your own ideas as you experiment.

  My kennings show two different sides to my sea lion: the silent hunter and the angry fighter. I think I'm going to start my poem using the kennings that describe its sleek, silent side as it hunts its prey and then finish the poem with the strong, powerful kennings as it pounces on its prey. I want to use the kenning sudden springer *to show the point where the sea lion moves from a silent hunter to an angry fighter.*

- Read your kennings aloud as you order them to check the rhythm. When you are happy, share the whole poem with the children using MT/YT to read two kennings at a time.
- Remind the children that you do not have to use all the kennings you have created.
- Copy your poem onto the board or a flipchart. TOL as you model making any final changes to improve the rhythm and imagery, e.g.

  I really like my poem but I don't have any rhyming pairs. I think I'm going to add in seaweed sneaker *to create a rhyming pair with* coral creeper; *and* savage splasher *to create a rhyming pair with* deadly thrasher.

- Draw the children into the modelling using MT/YT and TTYP, and ask them to give their feedback on changes they think you could make to your poem.

Curriculum link: develop stamina for writing by writing poetry

Write a poem 3 PB

Purpose: for children to create their own poem about their new sea creature

- Tell the children that they are going to write their own poem about their strange new sea creature using their Strange combinations grids, and the shapes and kennings they have recorded in their Personal log.
- Remind them how you ordered the kennings to write your poem. Say that you rehearsed your ideas by thinking out loud and that you kept on reading your poem aloud as you wrote.
- Ask the children to turn to p.19 in their Pupils' Book and look at the Write a poem 3 activity. Ask them to read the Top Tips for ordering their poem and TTYP to discuss.
- Tell the children that they can add new kennings and borrow ideas from the Poetry wall. Say that it's better to have too many ideas because it gives you more choice.
- Remind the children that commas can be used to separate items in a list, and that they may like to include commas to separate their kennings, or to tell the reader when to pause. Tell the children to write their finished poems in their Personal log when they are happy with them.

make simple additions to their own writing; read aloud what they have written

Personal log

Purpose: for children to keep a personal reading, writing and thinking log in order to record thoughts and ideas for their own writing

- Remind the children that, although you were happy with your poem, you decided to create some new kennings to make sure that you included some rhyming pairs to strengthen the rhythm in your poem.
- Ask the children to TTYP to share their poem so far.
- Tell them that you want them to add in at least two new kennings to create some rhyming pairs. Some children may need some support to think of rhyming words.
- Choose a few children to share their rhyming pairs with the rest of the class. Write them onto strips of card or paper and add them to your Poetry wall as inspiration for the rest of the class.

DAY 10

develop stamina for writing by writing poetry

Write a poem 3 (continued)

Purpose: for children to create their own poem about their new sea creature

- It is important that all the writing that the children do at this stage is in draft form and that they feel able to play around with the words and order of the poem. When they start to think about the layout of their poem, encourage them to draw the shape they want first rather than writing the whole poem out.
- Ask children to write a full draft of their poem and think about how they might like to set it out. Monitor them as they write.

evaluating their writing with the teacher and other pupils; make simple additions, revisions and corrections

Evaluate and edit PB

Purpose: for children to evaluate their own and their partner's work against specific criteria and then discuss how they could improve their work

- Ask the children to turn to p.20 in their Pupils' Book and look at the Evaluate and edit activity. Ask them to TTYP to read through the question prompts.
- As a model, select an example of work where the writing has met the criteria, and share this with the other children, explaining why it works well.
- Tell the children to take turns to read their partner's writing in pairs and discuss together how well each piece of writing has met the criteria.
- Ask children to discuss at least two changes they could make to improve their work.

Curriculum link: proofreading to check for errors in spelling, grammar and punctuation

Proofread

Purpose: for children to proofread their work and make changes to improve the accuracy of their grammar, punctuation and spelling

- Now ask the children to proofread their work. If you have noticed that several children need to improve on a particular aspect of spelling, grammar or punctuation, use this as a focus for the Proofread activity. Write an example which includes common errors from the children's writing and use this as a model.
- The children should always be checking for standard use of punctuation and correct spelling of common exception words.
- The following point would be relevant as the particular focus for this Unit:
  - where appropriate, using commas correctly to separate items in a list.

read aloud what they have written, with appropriate intonation to make the meaning clear

Performance

Purpose: for children to practise reciting, performing or reading their poem with feeling

- Remind the children of when they performed the poem in the Reading week. Say that using expression and movement made the poems sound exciting.
- Choose a poem by one of the children, or you can use your poem (Build a poem 3) and perform it, using lots of expression and exaggerating the alliteration, rhythm and rhyme. Make sure you use exaggerated hand and body gestures, and facial expressions, as well as intonation to convey meaning and impact.
- Tell the children that you want each one of them to practise performing their poem. Give them plenty of time to practise and then ask them to take turns performing their poems to their partners or in small groups.
- You may wish to take photographs of the poetry performances to paste into the Class log or to use them for display.

Further activity

- Publish: ask the children to type up their poems, making any changes from the Evaluate and edit, and Proofread activities, and print them off. Use them to make a class Poetry book.

READING AND WRITING NON-FICTION

The Non-fiction week continues the theme of the underwater world through exploring a non-chronological text about oceans.

See p.48 for the daily timetable for the Non-fiction week.

Non-fiction

Reading

Children will:

- find answers to their questions about oceans by reading a non-chronological text
- identify how non-chronological texts are structured to help the reader find information, using key features such as headings and subheadings
- use mind maps to organise notes and decide whether information is useful to the reader.

Writing

Key writing purpose to be shared with the children:

To write a well-structured non-chronological text about shipwrecks.

Writing evaluation to be shared with the children

My text about shipwrecks:

- uses features like *headings*, *subheadings* and *pictures* to make it easy for the reader to find information
- includes interesting information from my notes
- includes facts, not opinions.

Grammar:

- includes correct use of -*er* and -*est* suffixes if comparisons are made.

See the Planning section of the Software ('Timetables' tab) for a printable version of the Writing purpose and evaluation.

DAY 11

Curriculum link: pupils should be guided to participate in discussion

Think and link

Purpose: for children to develop an interest in non-chronological texts via one of the Big Questions they have explored

- Display the Big Question from Day 2 on **CD (file 2.5)**:
  Will there always be new things to find?
- Ask the children to TTYP to recall some of the ideas they discussed when they looked at the question for the first time and take feedback.
- Remind the children of the poem *Underwater Farmyard* that they heard in the Reading week and the poems they wrote in the Writing week. Share some of the funny names they made up for their sea creatures.
- Display **CD (file 11.1)** and navigate through the slides to show some real sea creatures based on some strange combinations, e.g. *sea lion, sea cow (manatee), dogfish, seahorse, zebra fish, tiger fish, goatfish*. Click 'Reveal' on each slide to show what each of the sea creatures are called. Pause at the end of each slide and ask the children to TTYP to talk about how they think each creature got its name.

asking questions

Introduction

Purpose: for children to understand why we read non-chronological texts

- Tell the children that you are interested in finding out more about the different plants and animals that live in oceans around the world. Explain that you are going to look at an information text about the world's oceans. Say that before you read the text you want them to help you to write some questions, so that they can use the text to be *detectives* and find out the answers.
- Display **CD (file 11.2)** to show an image of the shallows. Model composing a question around the image, e.g. '*I would like to know if any dangerous creatures live in the shallows.*' TOL as you write your question: *Are there any dangerous animals in the shallows?* onto the board or a flipchart under the heading *The Shallows*.
- Ask the children to TTYP to compose a question of their own based on the image of the shallows. Take feedback and orally improve some of the children's questions. Choose a few questions to write onto the board or flipchart.
- Navigate through the slides and repeat the process for each of the images and subheadings. You will need to keep the questions on display for the next activity.

Non-chronological detectives

Purpose: for children to use the questions they have composed to gather information from the Anthology text

- Tell the children that you have a non-chronological text that you hope will answer some of their questions (it doesn't need to answer all of them).
- Ask the children to turn to pp.21–24 in Anthology 2 Book 1 and look at the text 'Journey to the Deep'. Review your questions before you read the first section. Ask the children to be *detectives* and listen for any clues to help them find the answer to the first question: *Are there any dangerous animals in the shallows?*

- Read the first section of the text, 'The Shallows', aloud to the children. TOL as you explain what key words you are looking for in order to answer your first question. Draw the children's attention to the 'Look out!' box on p.23. Explain that you think the word *deadly* is a clue because it means *dangerous*. Ask the children to TTYP to read the 'Look out!' box and to discuss which creatures are *deadly*.
- Use TTYP and MT/YT to build up an answer to the question, and repeat for the next question under the heading *The Shallows*, followed by the questions for *Deeper Down* and *The Deep*.

Curriculum link: listening to, discussing and expressing views about a wide range of non-fiction

Class log

You will need to have collected some examples of non-chronological texts for this activity. (These do not need to be linked to the sea.)

Purpose: for children to share the process of keeping a class reading, writing and thinking log to record responses to texts and activities in a variety of forms

- Review the list of questions from the previous activity and discuss the ones that could not be answered using the Anthology text. Ask the children to TTYP to talk about where else they could find out the answers to the remaining questions.
- Show them some examples of non-chronological texts from books and various websites (use print outs) and discuss whether they might be useful, and why. (The texts do not necessarily need to answer the questions.)
- Explain that you are going to add a non-chronological text section to the Class log and paste in some of the examples you brought in. Tell the children to bring in some examples from home to paste into their Personal log.

being introduced to non-fiction that is structured in different ways

Zoom in on non-chronological texts A CD

Purpose: for children to become familiar with some of the key features associated with non-chronological texts

- Ask the children to have p.21 of Anthology 2 Book 1 open in front of them.
- Display **CD (file 12.1)** to show the first key feature and read it aloud using MT/YT. Click 'Reveal' to show an example from the Anthology text 'Journey to the Deep'.
- Navigate to the next slide and click 'Reveal' to show an example. Ask the children to TTYP to find another example of the key feature in the Anthology text. Take feedback from a few sets of partners. Repeat for the rest of the slides.

discussing how items of information are related

Non-chronological texts 1 CD

Purpose: for children to understand how to group information

- Display **CD (file 12.2)** and tell the children that you have found the author's notes for the Anthology text 'Journey to the Deep' but all of the information has been jumbled up. Explain that they need to group all of the information under the correct subheadings and decide which notes are useful.
- Read the subheading *The Shallows* aloud using MT/YT. TOL as you model dragging the first note, *shallow water is warm*, into the first box under the heading.
- Continue to focus on the same subheading and ask the children to TTYP to decide which of the notes should go under it. Take feedback and drag the notes into position, using MT/YT to read each of the notes aloud.

- Point to the note *swimming in the sea is so much fun*. Ask the children whether they think this would be a useful note to add under this heading. Explain that this is the author's opinion and does not really give any information so it would not be very useful in this context.
- Navigate to the next screen and repeat the process for *Deeper Down*.
- Make sure you point out the note *fish are really cool* to reinforce the point about checking that the notes are useful for this purpose.

Curriculum link: writing down key ideas and/or words, including new vocabulary

Write 1

Purpose: for children to learn how to group notes using a mind map

- Before the lesson, print a copy of the mind map and the notes from **CD (file 12.3)** for each child or set of partners. Cut out the notes.
- Say that a mind map is a useful way of organising notes and planning what you are going to write. The children need to help by sorting the author's notes for 'Journey to the Deep' using a mind map.
- Give each child or set of partners a copy of the mind map and notes from **CD (file 12.3)**. Tell them that you have already added the notes for *The Shallows* but they will need to use the mind map to organise the notes for *Deeper Down* and *The Deep*.
- Ask the children to TTYP to take turns to read the two subheadings and the notes and to decide which notes need to be organised under each of the subheadings on the mind map. Remind them that they do not have to include all of the notes because they may not think that all of them are useful. Take feedback from a few sets of partners.
- Ask them to complete the activity orally before pasting the notes under the correct subheadings on the mind map.
- Ask the children to paste their mind map into their Personal log. (If the children had one mind map between partners, you may wish to copy them so they each have a copy for their Personal log.)

discussing and expressing views about a wide range of non-fiction

Class log

Purpose: for children to share the process of keeping a class reading, writing and thinking log to record responses to texts and activities in a variety of forms

- Before the lesson, print out a copy of each text from **CD (file 12.4)**.
- Tell the children that you have some other non-chronological texts to share with them. Display **CD (file 12.4)**. Each slide shows one text.
- Draw their attention to the different ways the texts have been laid out and the different types of organisational features that have been used, e.g. *subheadings, pictures, captions, labels*.
- Tell the children to look carefully at the layout of the texts and to TTYP to discuss which of them they find the easiest to read and find information in.
- Collect feedback, clarifying where necessary.
- Give each set of partners a sticky note and ask them to write one reason why they think their chosen text is the clearest.
- Print out and paste a copy of each text onto separate pages in the Class log. Ask each set of partners to come to the front of the class and paste their sticky note next to the appropriate text in the Class log.

DAY 13

Curriculum link: Year 2 Grammar learning the grammar of word structure

Grammar: suffixes 1 *-ing*

Purpose: for children to identify root words and word endings

- Tell the children that in their writing they might need to use some words to describe marine life that use the suffix *-ing*.
- Display **CD (file 13.1)** to show the word *drift*. Remind the children what a root word is and explain that *drift* is the root word of *drifting*.
- Click 'Definition' to show a definition for the root word *drift*. Use MT/YT to say the word and its definition.
- Click 'Ending' to show the root word and the ending *-ing*.
- Click 'Sentences' to display sentences for *drift* and *drifting* and read them aloud using MT/YT.
- Navigate to the next slide and repeat the process for the root word *bubble*.
- Ask the children to TTYP to share what they noticed about the 'e' in the root word. Take feedback. Explain that words that end in 'e' drop the 'e' when you add *-ing*, because *you cannot have an 'e' and an 'i-n-g'*.
- Navigate through the slides, repeating the process for each of the root words.
- Print off the words from **CD (file 13.2)** and display them on your Non-chronological texts wall.

Questions

Purpose: for children to build questions around photographs as a starting point for their own writing

- Explain that there is another section of 'Journey to the Deep' that still needs to be written. Say that the new section will be called *Shipwrecks*. Before you write it, you are going to ask the children to help you write some questions.
- Ask children to turn to p.21 in their Pupils' Book and look at the Questions activity. Look at the photographs of a shipwreck and some examples of creatures that might live in shipwrecks and model composing a question around the pictures, e.g. *I would like to know what dangerous creatures live in shipwrecks*. TOL as you compose your question, *What dangerous creatures live in shipwrecks?* and write it on a large sheet of paper or a flipchart.
- Ask the children to TTYP and compose a question of their own based on the pictures. Take feedback and orally improve some of the children's questions. Choose a few questions to write on the board or flipchart.
- You will need to keep the questions to use on Day 15.

discussing the sequence of events; discussing how items of information are related

Non-chronological texts 2

Purpose: for children to learn how to order notes under headings

- Tell the children that you have found the notes from the author for the new section of 'Journey to the Deep' called *Shipwrecks*. Say that the notes need to be organised so that they make more sense.
- Display **CD (file 13.3)** to show a list of notes and the subheading *Dangerous Creatures*. Model dragging the note *lionfish can sting you with their venom* into one of the boxes under the heading. Say that this sounds dangerous so you think it belongs under this heading.
- Ask children to TTYP to discuss which other notes should come under the subheading *Dangerous Creatures*. Take feedback and drag the correct notes into the boxes underneath the heading.

- Point to the notes *I have a shipwreck in my fish tank* and *shipwrecks are great.* Ask the children whether they think these would be useful notes to add under this subheading. Explain that these notes are the author's opinions but do not really give any information.
- Repeat the process on the next screen, reinforcing the point about including opinions in information texts.

Curriculum link: planning or saying out loud what they are going to write

Write 2

Purpose: for children to organise notes onto a mind map to create a plan for their own writing

- Before the lesson, print out a copy of the mind map and notes from **CD (file 13.4)** for each child and cut out the statements on the second page.
- Explain that the children need to organise the author's notes under the correct subheadings using a mind map so they have a plan for their writing.
- Give each child a copy of the mind map and notes from **CD (file 13.4)** and read the notes that are already in place under the subheading *Dangerous Creatures* using MT/YT. Say that you want them to organise the notes for *At Night* and *A Habitat.*
- Ask the children to TTYP to take turns to read the two subheadings and the notes and to decide which notes need to be organised under each of the subheadings. Remind them that they do not have to include all of the notes because they may not think that all of them are useful. Take feedback from a few sets of partners.
- Ask them to complete the activity orally before placing the notes under the correct headings on the mind map.
- When the children have completed the task, explain that they are now going to review what they have done.
- Display the completed mind map on **CD (file 13.5)** at the front of the class on the board or a flipchart. Talk through the mind map with the children and encourage them to move any notes they have placed under the incorrect subheading.
- Ask them to paste the notes under the correct headings, then paste their mind maps into their Personal log.

writing for different purposes

Personal log

Purpose: for children to keep a personal reading, writing and thinking log in order to record thoughts and ideas for their own writing

- Ask the children to turn to p.21 in their Pupils' Book and look again at the photographs of a shipwreck and the kind of creatures that live in shipwrecks. Ask the children to TTYP to decide which images they would use with each of the subheadings. Take feedback from a few sets of partners and talk about their choices.
- Ask children to write in their Personal log which pictures they would choose and why.

DAY 14

Curriculum link: Year 2 Grammar learning the grammar of word structure

Grammar: suffixes 2 *-er* and *-est*

Purpose: for children to identify root words and word endings

- Remind the children of the subheadings used in 'Journey to the Deep': *The Shallows, Deeper Down, The Deep*. Say that these subheadings describe and compare the different parts of the sea.
- Explain that they will find these comparisons useful when they begin their own writing.
- Display **CD (file 14.1)** to show the root word *deep*. Click 'Comparison' to show how adding the suffix *-er* to the word means that it can be used to compare something. Click 'Comparison' again to show how adding the suffix *-est* to the word provides another way of changing the root word to compare something. Explain that *deepest* is the most powerful word as it means *most deep*.
- TOL as you model building up three sentences using *deep, deeper* and *deepest*. Write your sentences on the board or a flipchart and read them aloud using MT/YT. Make sure that you explain when you are using the root word and when you are using words that have had suffixes added.

  The sea is deep. As it gets deeper it gets colder. At its deepest it is freezing and pitch-black.

- Navigate through the slides and repeat the process for the words: *dark, darker, darkest; quick, quicker, quickest.*
- Ask the children to turn to p.22 in their Pupils' Book and look at the Grammar: suffixes 2 *-er* and *-est* activity. Say that you want them to TTYP to compose some sentences using the comparison words they have just looked at.
- Ask the children to say each of their sentences aloud to their partner before writing them into their Personal log. Tell them to write the root words and the suffixes in different colours.
- Challenge children who find this activity easy to write a sentence using as many of the words as they possibly can.
- Print off the words from **CD (file 14.2)** and display them on your Non-chronological texts wall. Children might use these later in their own writing.

***Homework Book p.9 provides further practice on the suffixes* -er *and* -est.**

understand, through being shown, the skills and processes essential to writing

Non-chronological texts 3

Purpose: for children to participate in the process of writing a section of a non-chronological text

- Before the lesson, print out a single copy of the TOL notes from **CD (file 14.5)**.
- Tell the children that you are going to work together to write the first section of *Shipwrecks*. Explain that you are going to write an opening sentence to tell the reader what this section is all about.
- Display **CD (file 14.3)** to show your first attempt at an opening sentence. Read the first think bubble and then read the sentence using MT/YT. Say that you think the sentence could be improved. Click 'TOL' and use the think bubble to discuss how you could improve the sentence. Then click 'Improve' to show how the sentence has been improved.

- Navigate to the next slide and repeat the process. Use TTYP to draw the children into the process of improving the sentence.
- Copy your finished sentence onto the board or a flipchart. Tell the children to TTYP to orally compose their own opening sentence. Say that they can use yours as an example but that they should try to add some of their own ideas. Once they have orally composed their sentence, ask them to write it down in their Personal log.
- Now tell the children you have chosen to write some information under the subheading *A Habitat*. Say that before you start writing you need to look back over your notes and think about which order you want to put them in.
- Display **CD (file 14.4)** to show a list of notes for the heading *A Habitat*. TOL as you drag and drop the notes into the order that you will use them in the first paragraph. Once you have your order you can print out your notes to use for your modelled writing.
- Use the TOL notes from **CD (file 14.5)** and your own ideas to model writing your first paragraph on the board or flipchart underneath your opening sentence. Make sure you model crossing things out and making changes to show that it is all right for the children to improve their own work in this way.
- Ask the children to TTYP to evaluate your first paragraph. Tell them to consider the following: '*Does it make sense? Have you included enough information? Is it easy to understand?*' Collect feedback and make changes based on the children's evaluations and your own ideas.

Write 3

Curriculum link: develop stamina for writing; encapsulating what they want to say, sentence by sentence

Purpose: for children to write a section of a non-chronological text independently

- Before the lesson, print an appropriate writing frame for each child from **CD (file14.6a, b** or **c)**; **a)** gives the least support and **c)** gives the most.
- Ask the children to use their mind map from **CD (file 13.4)** to help them to write a paragraph for one or two of the subheadings, depending on which writing frame you give them. Remind them that you ordered your notes before you began writing and that they should use conjunctions (*because, so,* etc.) to make connections between the sentences.
- Remind them that they can look at the photographs on p.21 of the Pupils' Book to give them some ideas.
- Give each child a copy of their own (appropriate) writing frame from printable **CD (file14.6a, b** or **c)**.
- Remind them to use their mind maps and to decide on the order of their notes before they write. If possible, they should try to include some comparisons in their writing by using the suffixes -*er* and -*est*.
- Guide the children through the process of writing their own non-chronological paragraph/s as independently as possible but give support where necessary.
- You might need to give children time to finish writing their paragraphs at the beginning of the next session.

Curriculum link: writing for different purposes

Personal log

Purpose: for children to keep a personal reading, writing and thinking log in order to record thoughts and ideas for their own writing

- Before the lesson, print out copies of the photographs on **CD (file 14.7)**. Then give children copies of the photographs they chose on Day 13. Model writing a caption for one of the pictures.
- Ask the children to TTYP to orally compose their own caption. When they are happy with their captions, ask the children to write them in their Personal log and paste the photograph next to it.
- Take feedback from a few sets of partners and write some of the captions onto the board or a flipchart.

DAY 15

develop stamina for writing; encapsulating what they want to say, sentence by sentence

Write 3 (continued)

Purpose: for children to write a section of a non-chronological text independently

- You may need to allow time at the beginning of the session for the children to complete their paragraph/s. Some children may wish to write an additional paragraph. Monitor the children as they complete their writing.

evaluating their writing with the teacher and other pupils; make simple additions, revisions and corrections

Evaluate and edit

Purpose: for children to evaluate their own and their partner's work against specific criteria and then discuss how they could improve their work

- Display the questions that the children wanted to find answers to on Day 13.
- Now ask the children to turn to p.22 in their Pupils' Book and look at the Evaluate and edit activity. Ask them to TTYP to read through the prompts.
- As a model, select an example of work where the writing has met the criteria, and share this with the other children, explaining why it works well.
- Tell the children to take turns to read their partner's writing in pairs and discuss together how well each piece of writing has met the criteria.
- Ask children to discuss at least two changes they could make to improve their work.

proofreading to check for errors in spelling, grammar and punctuation

Proofread

Purpose: for children to proofread their work and make changes to improve the accuracy of their grammar, punctuation and spelling

- Now ask the children to proofread their work. If you have noticed that several children need to improve on a particular aspect of spelling, grammar or punctuation, use this as a focus for the Proofread activity. Write an example which includes common errors from the children's writing and use this as a model.
- The children should always be checking for standard use of punctuation and correct spelling of common exception words.
- The following points would be relevant as the particular focus for this Unit:
  - checking suffixes have been correctly added to the end of root words and these words have been used appropriately, e.g. *deeper, deepest, darker, darkest.*
  - checking their spelling of technical (subject specific) vocabulary, e.g. *seaweed, coral, predators.*

Publish (CD)

Purpose: for children to choose the organisational features they want to use to lay out and publish their writing

- Remind the children about the two texts you printed on Day 12 from **CD (file 12.4),** drawing attention to the layout, use of diagrams, pictures and captions. TOL as you describe how the information is broken up and the pictures are used to give information too.
- Tell the children that they can use their pictures and captions, and draw diagrams to organise and publish their page.
- You may want to give them the opportunity to use ICT to publish their texts.

Fiction: Playscripts
Non-fiction: Persuasive writing

Timetable

WEEK 1 Reading fiction Playscripts *Oh, Gnome!*

Day 1	Day 2	Day 3	Day 4	Day 5
The story store 🖨	Dramatic reconstruction 1 🖨	Word power 2 🖨	Who's the most important?	Think and link
Word power 1 🖨	Secret script 1	Read a script	Role on the wall 🖨	Special effects 🖨
Show me the story	Secret script 2	Say it, show it	Class log	Dramatic reconstruction 2
Personal log	Secret script 3	Grammar: sentences with different forms	Big Question	Personal log
Big Question	Class log 🖨	Personal log		Big Question
	Big Question	Big Question		

WEEK 2 Writing fiction Playscripts *Oh, Gnome!*

Day 6	Day 7	Day 8	Day 9	Day 10
Script makers	Zoom in on endings	Write a script 1	Write a script 2 🖨	Build a script 3 (continued)
What if not…?	Build an ending	Build a script 2	Build a script 3	Write a script 3
Step into the script 🖨	Build a script 1	Class log	Class log	Special effects
Personal log	Personal log	Big Question		Evaluate and edit
Big Question	Big Question			Proofread

WEEK 3 Reading and writing non-fiction Persuasive writing

Day 11	Day 12	Day 13	Day 14	Day 15
Think and link	Grammar: adjectives and nouns	Adverts 2	Adverts 3	Dramatic reconstruction
Word power 🖨	Adverts 1	Write 2 🖨	Write 3 🖨	Evaluate
Say it	Write 1 🖨	Class log	Proofread	Personal log
Role-play	Personal log		Class log	
Class log				

🖨: shows that a file should be printed out from the Software

Overview of the Unit

This Unit uses a picture book, *Little Croc's Purse* by Lizzie Finlay, and a playscript, *Oh Gnome!* by Lou Kuenzler to explore themes of honesty, friendship and persuasion or influence.

The Non-fiction week looks at persuasive texts in a variety of forms, including adverts, posters, leaflets and trailers. For more information about the Non-fiction week and the Non-fiction writing evaluation criteria, see p.97.

Where appropriate, the children will be encouraged to develop an awareness of audience and purpose in relation to the fiction and non-fiction texts they are reading and writing.

Teacher modelling is provided in the teaching notes and the Software, supporting the children's writing at every stage in the Fiction and Non-fiction weeks.

The Homework Book provides a homework activity related to the content of this Unit for each of the three weeks.

Fiction

Reading

Children will:

- connect and explore the central themes of honesty, friendship and persuasion in *Oh, Gnome!* by drawing links between texts
- explore characters' thoughts and feelings throughout *Oh, Gnome!* and discuss what their actions show about them
- discuss the importance of specific characters and moments
- understand the impact of sound effects in playscripts.

Writing

Key writing purpose to be shared with the children:

To write some new scenes for a play.

Writing evaluation to be shared with the children

My new scenes:

- use key features of playscripts, e.g. *names before speech, stage directions* and *scene descriptions*
- include interesting dialogue, which reveals something about my characters' personalities.

Grammar:

- includes correct use of exclamation marks or full stops to show a command
- includes correct use of question marks to show a question.

See the Planning section of the Software ('Timetables' tab) for a printable version of the Writing purpose and evaluation.

READING FICTION

Resources

PB Pupils' Book, pp.23–35
A Anthology 2 Book 2, pp.2–13
CD CD on interactive whiteboard, Unit 3
GB Grammar Bank on CD
HB Homework Book, pp.10–13

DAY 1

Curriculum link: participate in discussion about books, becoming familiar with a wide range of books

The story store

Purpose: for children to hear and enjoy a picture book story that introduces themes to be explored in the Anthology text

- Before the lesson, print out a copy of the TOL (Think out loud) points from **CD (file 1.2)**. In addition to this, make yourself a simple badge with a star to use as a Story star.
- Show the children your Story star. Explain that when they see this star it means that they are going to hear a wonderful story.
- Use the **CD (file 1.1)** to show the front cover of *Little Croc's Purse* by Lizzie Finlay. Ask the children to read the title and look at the picture and then TTYP (Turn to your partner) to share what they think the story might be about. Collect feedback and use praise to show how much you value their ideas.
- Navigate through the pages by clicking on the forward arrow or the corners of the pages. Read the story aloud to the children with great enthusiasm and obvious pleasure. Use TTYP to explore a few aspects of the story as they arise, emphasising the themes of honesty, friendship and generosity.
- Tell the children that they are going to help you to re-read the story.
- Navigate to the beginning of the story again. Use MT/YT (My turn/Your turn) to re-read the first page.
- As you re-read the story with the children, use the TOL points you printed from **CD (file 1.2)** and your own ideas and TTYP to explore the connections between the words and the pictures. Focus on small but significant details in the pictures. Draw children's attention to the effect of changes in font size and style on relevant pages.
- When you have finished re-reading the story, tell the children that on p.5 there is a Special phrase that you like: *Everyone gasped.*
- Encourage the children to use the phrase during the day, both at school and at home.

discussing their favourite words and phrases, new vocabulary

Word power 1

Purpose: for children to learn the meaning of specific vocabulary used in the story and increase their knowledge of synonyms

valuable embarrassing jeered

- Tell the children that there were some words in the story that they may not hear all the time.
- Display **CD (file 1.3)** to show the Power words *valuable, embarrassing* and *jeered* and their definitions. Look at the words with the children and then use MT/YT as you read the sentences to them, putting special emphasis on the relevant words.
- Explain that the writer could have chosen different words that mean the same thing. Navigate to the next screen, showing the first word and its synonyms. Drag and drop the synonyms into the first sentence and use MT/YT to read it aloud after each substitution.
- Ask the children to TTYP to share which word they liked best.
- Navigate through the screens and repeat the process for the other sentences.

- These words, their synonyms and definitions can be printed from **CD (file 1.4)** to display on your Playscript wall for this Unit. Let the children hear you using them in your conversation and teaching throughout the day in an exaggerated fashion, e.g. *'OK, I will lend you my most* valuable *pencil, as long as you look after it!'*
- Ask the children to create mini-mimes when you say to them: '*Show me* valuable! *Show me* embarrassed! *Show me* jeered!'

Show me the story (CD)

Purpose: for children to show their understanding of the story through drama

- Explain to the children that you are going to read some pages from *Little Croc's Purse* but that they will not be able to see the pictures because you are not going to display it on the board. Tell the children that you want them to 'be' the pictures.
- Without displaying it on the board, navigate to pp.3–4 ('Excited crocodiles...') of **CD (file 1.1)**. Read the words, then model how you want the children to create a dramatic mini-mime to *illustrate* the pages. Ask them to practise their mini-mimes.
- Ask them to stand up as you read p.13 ('...Murdock !') with great enthusiasm and appropriate intonation. Stop to allow them to show you their mini-mimes.
- Repeat for p.18 ("That's my dear...") and p.23 ('Little Croc found...'), reminding the children they need to try and mime both actions and feelings.

Curriculum link: writing for different purposes

Personal log

Purpose: for children to keep a personal reading, writing and thinking log in order to record thoughts and ideas for their own writing

- Ask the children to TTYP to recall what Little Croc wrote on the front of his three envelopes. Take feedback and ask children to TTYP to recall what he bought for himself. Ask two or three sets of partners to feed back their answers.
- Repeat the process for what he shared and what he was going to save for.
- Give each child an empty envelope and tell them to imagine they have been given £20 as a reward for honesty. They can decide whether they want their envelope to be a *spend*, a *share* or a *save* envelope.
- Give them some time to think and then ask them to TTYP to discuss how they would spend their money, or what they would save for or share, and why.
- Explain that you want them to write down their ideas and reasons on a piece of paper and pop it in the envelope and then write *Spend, Save* or *Share* on the front.
- Ask them to use a paper clip to fasten their envelope to a page of their Personal log.

participate in discussion and consider the opinions of others

Big Question (CD)

Purpose: for children to develop their skills of argument and discussion through a mini enquiry session based on a philosophical question relating to the work of the day

- Display today's Big Question on **CD (file 1.5)**:

  How do you know something is valuable?

- Ask the children to TTYP to talk about this question. Collect feedback and write some responses on the board.
- Click 'Prompts' to show some statements that may help to encourage discussion.

DAY 2

Curriculum link: drama techniques to help pupils identify with and explore characters

Dramatic reconstruction 1

Purpose: for children to see and experience parts of the same story reconstructed as a script

- Before the lesson, print a copy of the script conventions from **CD (file 2.2)**.
- Remind the children that they created some mimes showing parts of the story, *Little Croc's Purse*. Say that you think the story would make a great play and so you are going to turn some of the story into a script.
- Display **CD (file 2.1)** to show a short section of the story. Read the section using MT/YT. Say that you need to sort out what each character is saying. Click 'Highlights' to highlight the dialogue and say that we call this *dialogue*.
- Navigate to the next slide to show the same section of the story, in script form.
- Use your own TOL to draw attention to the basic conventions of scripts, e.g. short description of setting, name of character speaking, stage directions to show actions or how to speak.
- Use MT/YT to read through the short script, demonstrating the different voices of the characters.
- Hold up the script conventions from printable **CD (file 2.2)** and use MT/YT to say the words. Check that children understand the words and display them on your Playscript wall. Say you have a new story, in the form of a playscript.

making inferences, answering and asking questions, predicting

Secret script 1

Purpose: for children to be excited and motivated to 'unlock the secrets' of a new story in playscript form, and to make connections between the new story and the picture book story they have read

- Tell the children that it is time for the Secret script. Wear or point to your teacher's Script star.
- Explain that you have found a basket of props behind a stage and you are hoping that it contains some clues about the Secret script.
- Show your own eagerness and enthusiasm and draw the children into your excitement about the contents of the basket. Try to include some Power words from *Little Croc's Purse*, e.g. '*There could be something* valuable *in the props basket!*'
- Display **CD (file 2.3)** to show the Secret script props basket. TOL as you show your curiosity and interest about the contents of the basket.
- Click 'Secret'. One picture, word or phrase will emerge from the basket. Click 'TOL' to show a think bubble. Use this and your own ideas and TTYP to speculate on the significance of the contents.
- Navigate through the slides, revealing a different secret on each one.
- Make sure you do not reveal the title, any surprises or the ending of the script at this stage!

making inferences, answering and asking questions, predicting

Secret script 2

Purpose: for children to hear more about the new script, to make links with their own experiences and make predictions. For children to become more familiar with what they know about the script so far before they hear the full version

- Tell the children that there was one more item hidden away right at the bottom of the Secret script props basket. Display **CD (file 2.4)**. Do not navigate past the first slide at this stage.
- Say that you are really excited about what might be written on the scroll as it could tell us more about the Secret script.

- Navigate to the next slide to show the unrolled scroll and then click 'Audio' to hear the contents read out by a narrator.
- On the next slide, click 'Audio' to hear the first section again. Ask the children to TTYP to discuss the question the narrator poses and then take feedback.
- Repeat the process for the next two sections.
- Navigate to the next slide and click 'Audio' to hear the narrator's final message.
- Finally, navigate to the last slide to show the scroll rolling up again.

Curriculum link: checking the text makes sense as they read, making inferences, discussing sequence of events

Secret script 3

Purpose: for children to hear and enjoy the full version of the script for the first time

- Tell the children that they are now going to hear the whole playscript for the very first time. TOL about which parts you cannot wait to hear about.
- Tell the children to TTYP to share what they are looking forward to.
- Remind the children to listen out for the Special phrase *Everyone gasps*.
- Open **CD (file 2.5)** to hear the playscript read by actors.
- At the end of the script, ask the children to look at the Secret script 3 activity on p.23 in their Pupils' Book and TTYP to read and discuss the questions. Encourage the children to give their own ideas and opinions, as well as thinking about the events in the story. Take feedback from a few sets of partners.
- The children may find it useful to find out a bit more about gnomes now that they have heard the playscript. Open **CD (file 2.6)** and navigate through the slides, discussing the gnome facts as you read them. Provide the children with opportunities to TOL about whether they have come across a gnome before.

discussing and expressing views; consider the opinions of others

Class log

Purpose: for children to share the process of keeping a class reading, writing and thinking log to record responses to texts and activities in a variety of forms

- Tell the children that today is the day they are going to start making their Class log for Playscripts. Show them the title page with just the heading *Playscripts* written on it.
- Ask the children to turn to the Class log activity on p.24 in their Pupils' Book. Explain that they should look at the posters advertising *Oh, Gnome!* and TTYP to discuss which is the best advert for the play, and why. Ask: '*Which picture matches the play best of all? Is the information on time, date and place clear and easy to read? Which one is most likely to make someone buy a ticket?*'
- Ask for feedback and take a vote for the best poster. Before the next lesson, print their chosen poster from **CD (file 2.7)** and paste it onto the *Playscripts* title page in the Class log.
- Tell the children that they can bring in things to paste into the Class log, e.g. pictures of gardens or garden gnomes; a cricket bat from a catalogue; a recipe for Grandma's pizza; adverts for a play. Make sure you bring in anything that could be relevant as well: theatre programmes, theatre tickets, etc.

participate in discussion and consider the opinions of others

Big Question

Purpose: for children to develop their skills of argument and discussion through a mini enquiry session based on a philosophical question relating to the work of the day

- Display today's Big Question on the **CD (file 2.8)**:

  Should we always tell the truth?

- Follow the process as explained on Day 1.

DAY 3

Curriculum link: discussing their favourite words and phrases, new vocabulary

Word power 2

Purpose: for children to use their phonic knowledge to decode multi-syllabic words and increase their understanding of rarer vocabulary they will encounter in the text

triumphantly lethal fragile appreciates

- Tell the children that there were some words in the script they heard yesterday that are unusual because we do not hear them very often.
- Display **CD (file 3.1)** to show definitions of some multi-syllabic Power words that are in the script: *triumphantly, lethal, fragile, appreciates.*
- Discuss any tricky graphemes in the words and use the *Read Write Inc.* Complex Speed Sounds chart on the CD to explain where they would be on the chart. The chart can be called up by opening the 'Complex Speed Sounds chart' from the top of the resources list for Day 3. The words and definitions can be printed from **CD (file 3.2)** to display on your Playscript wall for this Unit. Let the children hear you using these words throughout the day, *e.g.* '*Your new classmate* appreciates *you for making them feel welcome.*' Remember to praise them if they use one of the words.

checking that the text makes sense to them as they read and correcting inaccurate reading

Read a script

Purpose: for children to gain a deeper understanding of the script and to see the full text for the first time

- Let the children follow their own copy of the text on pp.2–11 of Anthology 2 Book 2 as you read the full version of the script (including stage directions) aloud with great enthusiasm. Put special emphasis upon the Power words.
- Now tell the children that they are going to read the script without you. Tell Partner 1s that they are going to be Katie and Jerome and Partner 2s that they are going to be Oliver and Grandma. Say that both partners will read the cast list, scene descriptions and stage directions together.
- Explain that you will be listening in and hoping to hear some star actors.
- Give feedback to the whole class on good reading partners to model what skills and behaviour you expect. Choose partners who use lots of expression or who are good listeners, remembering to provide examples when you praise them.

Say it, show it

Purpose: for children to be able to summarise parts of a script orally and use drama techniques to communicate ideas and show understanding

- Join two sets of partners together to make groups of four. Tell the children that you have chosen one section of the play to *pause* or *freeze*. Display **CD (file 3.3)** to show one section of *Oh, Gnome!*
- Read it aloud chorally with the children. Click 'Hide' and ask the children to TTYP to summarise that part of the script in their own words. Take feedback and share two or three summaries.
- In their groups, tell them to create a freeze-frame to show that part of the script. Give them time to discuss and practise their freeze-frames.
- After practising, tell them you want them to walk around very slowly with their group and when you say '*freeze*', to stop and show you their freeze-frames.
- Tell the children to relax and then say that you want them to *rewind* and TTYP to discuss what happened just *before* that part of the play.
- Take feedback, compare ideas and clarify if necessary, then ask them to create another freeze-frame to show that part of the play.

- Repeat the process, telling the children to *fast forward* and TTYP to discuss what happened just *after* the part of the play shown on the board. They should create another freeze-frame to show this.
- Say to the children that you now want them to show each freeze-frame individually, in the order they occur in the play. Explain that they need to show a different freeze-frame each time you say '*One… two… three… freeze*'. Take photographs of the freeze-frames. Print them to paste into the Class log, to be used on Day 4.

Curriculum link: Year 2 Grammar
learning how to use sentences with different forms

Grammar: sentences with different forms

Purpose: for children to develop their ability to recognise different sentence forms

- Explain that each time you told the children to *freeze* you were giving them a *command*. Say that when we give a command in *spoken form,* we often say it quite forcefully. Use MT/YT to say '*Freeze!*' in a very commanding voice.
- Display **CD (file 3.4)** to show a definition for the word *command*. Read the definition out to the children and then use MT/YT to read the example sentence with exaggerated intonation and appropriate emphasis.
- Point out the exclamation mark at the end of the dialogue and say that when a command is given in written form, we sometimes use an exclamation mark instead of a full stop to give the command authority and emphasis.
- Teach or revise the punctuation mime for an exclamation mark (see the Extras section of the Software) by making a downward action as you say '*wiiiith*' and punch as you say '*feeling*'. Ask the children to join in chorally with the sentence '*Do it immediately!*' and copy the mime. Ask them to TTYP and say it to their partner.
- Explain that when we write a sentence that we know is a command, we can say it like that in our heads to remind ourselves that we have the choice whether to use a full stop or add an exclamation mark at the end.
- Explain that exclamation marks can be used in other kinds of sentences to show strong feelings like anger, excitement, astonishment or shock. Click 'Next' to show a definition for the word *exclamation*. Read the definition aloud.
- Now use MT/YT to read the following example sentences with exaggerated intonation and appropriate emphasis: '*Oh, you naughty puppy! I can't wait to go on that rollercoaster! I can't believe you did that! That is terrible!*'
- Ask the children to turn to p.25 in their Pupils' Book and look at the Grammar: sentences with different forms activity. Tell them to TTYP to read the sentences and decide which ones are commands. Remind them that not all commands have an exclamation mark. Tell them that they just need to complete this activity orally.

Homework Book pp.10–11 provides further practice of sentences with different forms.

writing for different purposes

Personal log

Purpose: for children to keep a personal reading, writing and thinking log in order to record thoughts and ideas for their own writing

- Ask the children to look at the Personal log activity on p.25 of their Pupils' Book. Tell them to TTYP to identify which part of the playscript the story squares show. Take feedback and clarify if necessary.
- Now ask them to choose a character from one of the story squares, then TTYP to discuss what that character might be saying or thinking at that moment.
- Model on the board how you want them to write their dialogue in their Personal log in the form of a mini playscript.
- Choose sets of partners to share their dialogue, in role, with the group.

Curriculum link: participate in discussion and consider the opinions of others

Big Question

Purpose: for children to develop their skills of argument and discussion through a mini enquiry session based on a philosophical question relating to the work of the day

- Display today's Big Question on the **CD (file 3.5)**:

  Would it be a good thing if we could freeze, fast forward or rewind real life?
- Follow the process as explained on Day 1.

DAY 4

making inferences based on what is being said or done

Who's the most important?

Purpose: for children to explore the importance of individuals and events in the context of the script

- Tell the children that all the characters are important to the playscript, but they might think that some are more important than others.
- Display **CD (file 4.1)** to show one section from *Oh, Gnome!* Ask the children to read it aloud chorally. Remind them to use appropriate intonation and expression to show understanding.
- Click 'TOL' to show think bubbles and use them and your own ideas to discuss who seems to be the most important character in this part of the play. Make sure you use discursive language, e.g. *on the other hand... it could be... but...*
- Draw the children into the TOL and then ask them to TTYP to discuss who they think is the most important character in this section of the play, and why. Take feedback and make sure the children can support their ideas.
- Now ask them to look at the Who's the most important? activity on pp.26–27 of their Pupils' Book. Explain that you want them to TTYP to read the section of the script on p.26 and then discuss which character is most important in this section. Make sure they understand that there is not a right answer, you are just asking for their own ideas and opinions.
- Take feedback and give praise when they show they can use discursive language in the way you modelled.
- Now ask children to look at p.27 in the Pupils' Book and TTYP to read the statements about the most important moment in the whole play. Tell them to discuss which statement they agree with the most, and why.
- Collect feedback and lead a short class discussion based on their responses.

drama techniques to help pupils identify with and explore characters

Role on the wall (teacher only)

Purpose: for children to think more deeply about characters in the script and to record their ideas

- Before the lesson, print off a blank body outline and character Word bank for each set of partners from printable **CD (file 4.2)**.
- Display **CD (file 4.3)** to show a blank body outline and explain that this represents the character of Katie in the play. Drag and drop her name onto the body.
- Explain that you want to think about what kind of person Katie is and you have lots of words to choose from to describe her.
- Remind the children that we could all be described in different ways at different times, e.g. sometimes we could be described as kind and sometimes as unkind, depending on the situation.
- TOL as you select words and phrases to describe the character of Katie, referring, where appropriate, to the Anthology text, *Oh, Gnome!* to support your choices.
- Draw the children into the TOL and drag and drop the words onto the body. Click on the Reset icon and repeat the process for the character of Grandma.

- Give each set of partners one blank body outline and characteristics Word bank. Ask the children to TTYP to complete the Role on the wall activity for either Oliver or Jerome by writing the words onto the body. Them them to keep the words and tuck them into their Personal log for use on Day 5.

Curriculum link: drama techniques to help pupils identify with and explore characters

Class log

Purpose: for children to share the process of keeping a class reading, writing and thinking log to record responses to texts and activities in a variety of forms

- Make sure you have chosen at least three photographs from yesterday's drama activities, and pasted them into the Class log.
- Show the children one of the photographs and ask them to suggest what part of the play the group were showing. Ask the children in the photograph to clarify (you may need to prompt them to help them to clarify).
- Now ask all of the children to TTYP to say what any of the characters might be *thinking* at the moment shown in the freeze-frame and take feedback.
- Write one or two of their responses in a think bubble or on a sticky note and attach it to the photograph.
- Repeat the process for the other two photographs but use a *feeling* bubble for the second one and a *saying* speech bubble for the third one.
- Display other photographs on the Playscript wall for this Unit and add some laminated *thinking, feeling* and *saying* bubbles for children to write in with board markers at any time during the reading and writing weeks.

participate in discussion and consider the opinions of others

Big Question (CD)

Purpose: for children to develop their skills of argument and discussion through a mini enquiry session based on a philosophical question relating to the work of the day

- Display today's Big Question on **CD (file 4.4)**:

  What makes someone important?

- Follow the process as explained on Day 1.

DAY 5

answering and asking questions

Think and link (CD)

Purpose: for children to develop their lateral thinking skills to explore the text

- Remind the children of the Secret script props basket they looked at on Day 2. Say that the basket has been re-filled and you are going to show them how to play Think and link with the new items.
- Display **CD (file 5.1)** to show the Secret script props basket. Click 'Secret' to reveal the first item, then click 'TOL' to reveal the think bubble. The items will not have obvious links as they are intended to develop the children's lateral thinking skills to deepen their understanding of the text. TOL using the bubble and your own ideas.
- Navigate through the slides and repeat the process for each item. When you reach the final item (the heart), tell the children that they are going to have a go themselves. Click 'TOL', then ask them to TTYP to Think and link the item to the script. Take feedback and type one or two ideas in the empty think bubble.

Special effects (CD)

Purpose: for children to develop their awareness of how mood and atmosphere are created in live or recorded performances

- Tell the children that plays and films have *special effects* that help to create the right *mood, feelings, atmosphere* and *images*.

- Write these words on the board or flipchart and use MT/YT to say them: *special effects, visual, sound, mood, feelings, atmosphere*. They can also be printed from **CD (file 5.2)** to display on your Playscript wall for this Unit.
- Explain that special effects can be *visual*, e.g. smoke, mist, different colour lights, slow motion. Ask the children to TTYP to discuss when slow motion was used in *Oh, Gnome!* and why they think it was used. Take feedback.
- Now explain that special effects are also created through *sound*, and that these are known as *sound effects*. Say that if scripts are performed on the radio rather than on stage or in a film, the audience cannot see anything and so sound effects are even more important to help the audience to understand and imagine events.
- Display **CD (file 5.3)**. Click on the first sound effect icon to play the first sound. Ask the children to TTYP to say what images and feelings it created for them. Choose two or three sets of partners to share their answers.
- Repeat the process for four more sounds, focusing on the *mood, feelings, atmosphere* and *images* the sounds create, not simply what they are. (These sounds are not connected to the playscript.)
- Ask the children to look at the beginning of the *Oh, Gnome!* script on p.2 of Anthology 2 Book 2. Draw their attention to the fact that the scene is set in summer. Ask the children to TTYP to discuss which sounds would let radio listeners know that it is a lovely summer's day, e.g. *birdsong, trees rustling, a lawnmower.*
- Collect feedback and add your own ideas. Ask children to write some answers in their Personal log.

Curriculum link: read accurately and fluently

Dramatic reconstruction 2 A CD

Purpose: for children to create mood and atmosphere using sound effects in a performance

- Join two sets of partners together. Tell them to turn to p.2 of Anthology 2 Book 2 and perform the beginning of *Oh, Gnome!* (from 'Katie is amongst the neat flower beds …' to 'We need to be careful, though.'), with sound effects.
- Explain that three children in the group will read the parts of Katie, Oliver and Jerome and the other child will create the sound effects with their voice, hands and feet. Give the groups time to allocate roles and practise their performances.
- Decide whether you want each group to perform in turn to the others or have them all perform at once as you walk around and watch each one.
- Make sure they receive feedback from you and the rest of the group about their performance and the sound effects. You should praise co-operation, effective group planning and impressive performances.
- Now ask the children to look at p.6 of Anthology 2 Book 2. Remind them that if this was recorded for a radio show, it would be useful to add sound effects to help the audience to visualise the scene. Explain that you have a radio version of this part of the script with sound effects added. Play **CD (file 5.4)**.
- Play it again and ask the children to TTYP to identify as many sounds as possible. Ask them to Popcorn (see Introduction p.17) their answers. Now ask them to TTYP to evaluate how effective the sound effects were.

drama techniques to help pupils identify with and explore characters

Personal log

Purpose: for children to keep a personal reading, writing and thinking log in order to record thoughts and ideas for their own writing

- Remind the children that they created a Role on the wall for the characters in *Oh, Gnome!* Explain that you now want them to create one for themselves. Tell them to draw a simple body outline in their Personal log.
- Model how you want them to use the Word banks from Day 4 to identify aspects of their own character and write them inside the body outline.

- When they have finished, they can paste the shape in their Personal log.
- Use TTYP and feed back to share some aspects of their personal Roles on the wall.
- Ask the children to TTYP to say which character in the play they think they are most like, and why. Tell them to record it in their Personal log using a full sentence.

Curriculum link: participate in discussion and consider the opinions of others

Big Question (CD)

Purpose: for children to develop their skills of argument and discussion through a mini enquiry session based on a philosophical question relating to the work of the day

- Display today's Big Question on **CD (file 5.5)**:

  Is it only actors who pretend to be someone else?

- Follow the process as explained on Day 1.

WRITING FICTION

DAY 6

Script makers (CD)

Purpose: for children to develop their understanding of how scripts are created by writers and to learn that we can all become writers

- Show the children your Script star. Explain that it shows that we are going to find out more about writing scripts.
- Remind them that a script or a play is still a story; it is just presented in a different way because it is written to be performed as well as read.
- Tell them that if we can find the secret to making great scripts, we can all call ourselves Script makers.
- Display **CD (file 6.1)** to show the beginning of *Little Croc's Purse* as a script. This version will have some additional features to the section shown on Day 2.
- Ask the children to TTYP to discuss how they can tell this is part of a script. Collect feedback and clarify where necessary to make sure they recall features such as *names of characters before speech, stage directions* and *scene descriptions*. Note new ones such as a cast list.

making inferences on the basis of what is being said and done

What if not...? (CD)

Purpose: for children to understand how small changes can have big consequences in narratives

- Tell the children that if the writer decided to turn the whole of *Little Croc's Purse* into a playscript, they might want to change some of the story. For example, the writer might think: What if not *full of money?* What if *Little Croc found a purse that had no money in it?*
- Display **CD (file 6.2)** to show a section of the story re-written as a script again. Navigate to the next slide to reveal the same section with the What if not…? changes made. Read it aloud to the children.
- Click 'Highlights' on the final slide to show the changes. Note how the mood changes. Ask the children to TTYP to discuss what could happen next.
- Collect feedback and develop their responses into a TOL. Use your own ideas to guide discussion about possible effects the changes would have on other characters and events, e.g.

  Little Croc might have left the purse on the path or kept it because it didn't look valuable and Mrs Doolally might never have got her precious locket back, or… The money could have been stolen before Little Croc found it. When he returned the empty purse to Mrs Doolally, she might have accused Little Croc of stealing the money!

- Make sure the children understand that the whole story would be different if just one thing were changed, so every choice a writer makes is important and has an effect.

Step into the script

Purpose: for children to learn how to improvise dialogue in an imaginary setting

- Before the lesson, print a copy of the script for the new scene from **CD (file 6.4)** for each set of partners.
- Display **CD (file 6.3)** to show a script for the new scene. Point out that where the character is Partner 1 or Partner 2, there is no speech. Explain that they are going to take turns improvising or making up their own responses to Little Croc.
- Navigate to slide 3 to show an example of a possible improvisation. Read it aloud to or with the children. Explain that the children's improvisations can be different to this. Navigate to slides 5–6 to show another version. Ask the children to TTYP to say how they were different and take feedback.
- Give each set of partners a copy of the script that you printed from **CD (file 6.4)**. Now ask the children to TTYP to read through the scene without adding their own responses.
- When they have all read through the scene, ask them to begin improvising their speeches for the missing parts of the script. This is an oral activity only; the children do not need to write their dialogue.
- Choose two or three confident sets of partners to share their improvisations.
- Display the beginning of **CD (file 6.3)** again and write some of their improvised dialogue in the appropriate boxes. Do not make it look easy. TOL as you repeat what they have said to make sure it makes sense. Break their dialogue down into smaller chunks to show how it helps you to 'hold' the words in your head as you write them down.

Curriculum link: increase pupils' vocabulary; draw on and use new vocabulary

Personal log

Purpose: for children to keep a personal reading, writing and thinking log in order to record thoughts and ideas for their own writing

- Remind the children of how they added dialogue to some story squares last week (Day 3 Personal log).
- Explain that you now want them to create a two-square storyboard for the scene they have just read and improvised dialogue for. Tell them to use pencil only for the pictures and to add the dialogue in speech bubbles. Remind them that, because they are using speech bubbles, they will not have to use *he said, she replied,* etc. Explain that they should just select two pieces of dialogue for each story square.
- Tell them to TTYP to recall what dialogue they improvised, but encourage them to edit and make changes if they want to.

participate in discussion and consider the opinions of others

Big Question

Purpose: for children to develop their skills of argument and discussion through a mini enquiry session based on a philosophical question relating to the work of the day

- Display today's Big Question on **CD (file 6.5)**:

  How do people choose what to do? *

- Follow the process as explained on Day 1.

  ** This Big Question will be revisited on Day 11 – the first day of the Non-fiction week.*

DAY 7

Curriculum link: making inferences on the basis of what is being said and done

Zoom in on endings

Purpose: for children to develop their inferential thinking skills

- Ask the children to look at the *Oh, Gnome!* script on pp.2–11 of Anthology 2 Book 2.
- Tell them to re-read the script together. Tell Partner 1s that they are going to be Katie and Jerome and Partner 2s that they are going to be Oliver and Grandma. Say that both partners will read the cast list, scene descriptions and stage directions together.
- Display **CD (file 7.1)** and explain that you want to focus on the ending. Use MT/YT to read it aloud with the children. Ask the children to TTYP to summarise the ending. Choose one or two partners to feed back.
- Ask the children to TTYP to discuss if it tells you in the script whether Grandma is going to keep Jerome, now he has been damaged, or throw him away.
- Collect feedback. Ask children if they can find any evidence in the ending to support their view.
- Have a vote on whether Grandma should keep or get rid of the damaged gnome.
- Ask the children to Popcorn an answer to the question: '*What would you do with Jerome?*'

understand, through being shown, the skills and processes essential to writing

Build an ending

Purpose: for children to see and participate in the re-writing of an ending

- Say that you have had an idea about changing the ending. Display **CD (file 7.2)** to show the original ending.
- Explain that you thought about what Grandma might do next. Navigate to the slide which shows your notes. Ask the children to read the notes aloud chorally. Keep this slide on the screen, but don't click 'TOL' or 'Highlights' until the next activity.
- Now ask the children to look at p.10 of Anthology 2 Book 2 and TTYP to find out who mentioned car boot sales before and why. Collect feedback and clarify if necessary.
- Tell the children to Popcorn words that could describe how Jerome will feel when he finds out he is being sold at a car boot sale. Write some of their words and ideas on the board or a flipchart.
- Ask the children to write these words in their Personal log for use later on.
- Keep **CD (file 7.2)** on screen to use for the next activity.

understand, through being shown, the skills and processes essential to writing

Build a script 1

Purpose: for children to see a script grow through three stages of development that will provide a model and stimulus for their own writing

- Explain that, now you know what Grandma might *do* next, you need to use the notes to write what Grandma *says* next.
- Remind the children how they saw part of *Little Croc's Purse* as a script yesterday.
- Explain that you are going to use your notes to write the speech for the actor playing Grandma.
- Return to the Notes screen on **CD (file 7.2)** and click 'TOL' to show the think bubble. Use this to explain how you are going to use the notes to create a script. Click 'Highlights' and explain that these are the words you are going to give to the actor playing Grandma.
- TOL as you model on the board or flipchart how to use the highlighted text to write Grandma's speech using the conventions of script form.

  Grandma I don't want to keep a broken gnome. Jerome will break again if a puff of wind blows him over. I'll sell him at a car boot sale.

- Navigate to the next slide to display Grandma's speech. Draw attention to the words you have added, *I* and *I'll,* and the punctuation you have added.

- Click 'Synonyms' to show some words from your script and their synonyms. Draw the children into a TOL as you try out different words orally. Leave these words and synonyms on the screen while the children complete the next activity.

Curriculum link: writing for different purposes

Personal log

Purpose: for children to keep a personal reading, writing and thinking log in order to record thoughts and ideas for their own writing

- On **CD (file 7.2)** click 'Hide' to hide your version of Grandma's speech and ask the children to write down their own version in their Personal log. Explain that they must keep the fact that Jerome is going to the car boot sale but they can:
  - use any of the synonyms they have looked at
  - change Grandma's reasons for getting rid of Jerome, e.g. she is fed up with him or he is old-fashioned.
- Remind them to discuss their ideas and say their first sentence to their partner before writing it down. Ask the children to make sure they write in script form.
- Walk around, supporting and guiding as they write. Note good examples to share with the whole class.

participate in discussion and consider the opinions of others

Big Question

Purpose: for children to develop their skills of argument and discussion through a mini enquiry session based on a philosophical question relating to the work of the day

- Display today's Big Question on **CD (file 7.3)**:

  Is getting rid of old possessions a good thing?
- Follow the process as explained on Day 1.

DAY 8

planning or saying out loud what they are going to write about

Write a script 1

Purpose: for children to develop the first stage of a script

- Tell the children that the new ending they looked at yesterday for *Oh, Gnome!* has given you a good idea for a third scene. You think an audience would enjoy seeing what happens to Jerome at the car boot sale and you would like them to help you write it.
- Remind the children that they wrote their own version of Grandma's shock news and display **CD (file 8.1)** to show your version again. Say that you need to think about what Oliver and Katie would say when they hear Grandma's decision.

Katie

- Remind the children about the Role on the wall they created for Katie last week. Tell Partner 1s that they are Grandma and Partner 2s that they are Katie. Ask them to Popcorn Grandma's characteristics and then Katie's.
- Now explain that you want Grandma to say the lines about sending Jerome to the car boot sale and Katie to improvise a response.
- Ask them to swap roles and to repeat the mini role-play, improvising a different response from Katie.
- Choose some partners to share their role-plays with the group.
- Using **CD (file 8.1)**, write an example of the dialogue as a model for the children, e.g.

  Katie Oh, but he was your pride and joy, Grandma! Please don't sell him. I'd miss little Jerome!
- Ask the children to add their version of Katie's speech as a response to the lines that they wrote for Grandma in their Personal log on Day 7. Remind them to TTYP to say their speech before they write it down.
- Now tell the children to look at the Write a script 1 activity on p.28 of their Pupils' Book.

Oliver

- Ask them to TTYP to read the different reactions from Oliver.
- Tell them to decide which prompt they want to use when they play Oliver in the role-play. Give them time to discuss this and make their decisions. Ask a few sets of partners to share their choice.
- They are going to continue their mini role-plays by adding Oliver's speech. Say that Partner 1s are going to be Katie and Partner 2s are going to be Oliver.
- Explain that Partner 1s will say Katie's lines from their Personal log and Partner 2s will improvise a response from Oliver based on the prompt they chose.
- Ask them to swap roles and repeat the mini role-play. Choose some partners to share their role-plays with the rest of the group.
- Ask the children to add Oliver's dialogue to Grandma and Katie's lines in their Personal log. Remind them to TTYP to say their speech before they write it down.
- Model by typing an example of Oliver's dialogue below Katie's lines on **CD (file 8.1)**, e.g.

  Oliver I won't miss him! Good idea, Gran. Can I help out at the car boot sale?

- Walk around, supporting and guiding the children as they write. Note effective examples to share with the whole class.

Build a script 2 A PB

Curriculum link: role-play and other drama techniques to help pupils to identify with characters

Purpose: for children to see a script grow through three stages of development

- Remind the children that they have been writing lots of *dialogue*. This means speaking with other people. There is another word, *monologue*, which means speaking alone. Explain that lots of scripts have a character speaking alone, sometimes to the audience.
- Ask the children to look at p.11 of Anthology 2 Book 2 and TTYP to find and read the lines where Jerome has a very short monologue:

  Jerome Nobody appreciates me… Why do I sit here, day after day, pretending to fish? There isn't even a pond…

- Tell the children that you have been thinking about how poor Jerome feels when he is put out on the stall at the car boot sale. Say that you can imagine him thinking out loud, and that Jerome should have a monologue in the new scene.
- Explain that they are going to be writing Jerome's monologue tomorrow, but they need to find out exactly how he feels as he sits on the stall at the car boot sale.
- Ask the children to look at the Build a script 2 activity on p.29 of their Pupils' Book.
- They are going to take turns to be Jerome in the hotseat and answer the questions their partner asks them.
- Walk around, listening in and noting ideas to feed back to the whole group.

Class log

understand, through being shown, the skills and processes essential to writing

Purpose: for children to share the process of keeping a class reading, writing and thinking log to record responses to texts and activities in a variety of forms

- Tell the children that you are going to write a monologue for Jerome in the Class log. TOL as you think about what to write. Let the children see your thinking and watch you write, cross out, change or add words. Draw them into the TOL, ask for suggestions and try them out.
- Use the example below as a basis for your writing or make up your own.

  Jerome Packed off to a car boot sale! How dare they? It's a bit lonely on this table. Strangers keep picking me up and putting me down again. One lad said I looked like Santa on a bad day. Oh, oh. Here comes another one who thinks I'm a toy. Oi! Put me down…

- Use MT/YT to say the lines, drawing attention to the fact that you have included question marks at the end of the questions. Say that this will help them to write their own monologues for Jerome tomorrow.

Curriculum link: participate in discussion and consider the opinions of others

Big Question (CD)

Purpose: for children to develop their skills of argument and discussion through a mini enquiry session based on a philosophical question relating to the work of the day

- Display today's Big Question on **CD (file 8.2):**

  Is being alone the same as being lonely?

- Follow the process as explained on Day 1.

develop stamina for writing by writing narratives about fictional experiences of others

Write a script 2 (CD) (PB)

Purpose: for children to develop their confidence and skill in script planning and development

- Before the lesson, print a copy of the writing frame from **CD (file 9.2)** for each child.
- Tell the children that they are going to write Jerome's important monologue, where he tells the audience his secret thoughts and feelings. Explain that they are going see some special moments in his life to help them to understand him.
- Display **CD (file 9.1)**. The audio will start automatically on each slide as you navigate through them.
- Ask the children to TTYP to share some words or phrases that show how Jerome is feeling. Collect responses and write them on the board or a flipchart.
- Say that you will play the presentation again, but will pause after certain slides so they can TTYP to share a sentence that Jerome might be saying at this point.
- Pause after three or four of the slides and make sure that the children's sentences are spoken in first person, to prepare them for writing their monologues.
- Tell the children they can look at the Build a script 2 activity again on p.29 of their Pupils' Book to remind them about the hotseat answers they gave yesterday.
- Give each child a copy of the writing frame from **CD (file 9.2).** Tell them that today they will just be focusing on the first section, writing the monologue. Guide them through the directions and ask them to write Jerome's monologue. Remind them to TTYP to share their ideas and say their sentences before writing in the spaces provided. Make sure they know that they are allowed to cross out and edit as they think and write.
- Ask the child to TTYP to read each other's writing. Choose a few children to read out their monologues.
- Explain that the new scene will be completed tomorrow.

role-play and other drama techniques to help pupils to explore characters

Build a script 3 (CD)

Purpose: for children to participate in the final stages of writing a script that will provide a stimulus and model for their own writing

- Tell the children that you are pleased that they have been building a new scene together and you want to show them your new scene so far. Display **CD (file 9.3)** to show how the script has progressed.
- Click 'Highlights' to show the original parts of the script. Click 'Highlights' again to show the new dialogue that has been added. Click 'TOL' to show the think bubbles to guide you as you talk through the script with the children.
- Navigate to the next slide to show Jerome's monologue. Click 'TOL' and ask the children to think of some appropriate stage directions for Jerome.
- Tell the children that you are going to display a flow chart showing the sequence of the next three events in the new scene. Navigate to the final slide to show the flow chart and read it aloud with the children chorally or use MT/YT.

- Explain that they are now going to work with their partners to create a short mime (no words) to show these three events. Tell the children to focus on playing Katie and Oliver. Give them time to discuss and rehearse their mimes, but do not allow them to become too long or elaborate.
- Tell the children that you will ask them to freeze at different points during their mimes. Choose a child to tap on the shoulder during a freeze-frame and ask what that character is thinking at this point.
- Tell the children that you have some speeches that will link to their mimes. Display **CD (file 9.4)** to show a picture of Oliver with an empty speech bubble. Draw the children into a TOL as you decide which speech you would give to Oliver, and why. Drag and drop the speeches into the speech bubble to try them out and check which is the best fit.
- Navigate to the next screens and repeat the process for Katie and Grandma.
- Display **CD (file 9.5)** to show the whole new scene and read it aloud to the children. Ask them to TTYP to share what they think of the new scene. Collect oral feedback and encourage further discussion and constructive criticism.

Curriculum link: participate in discussion and consider the opinions of others

Class log

Purpose: *for children to share the process of keeping a class reading, writing and thinking log to record responses to texts and activities in a variety of forms*

- Tell the children that you really like the title *Oh, Gnome!* but now that Jerome has been sent to the car boot sale, you have some other titles.
- TOL about play on words, rhyme and alliteration and their relevance to the new storyline, as you write these alternative titles in the Class log: *Gnome Alone, New Home for Jerome, Car Booted Out, Gnome for Sale, Jerome's Journey.*
- Use MT/YT to say each title. Ask the children to TTYP to discuss which title they would choose as an alternative to *Oh, Gnome!*
- Ask them to Popcorn their choices and then have a vote. Circle the winning title in the Class log.

DAY 10

understand, through being shown, the skills and processes essential to writing

Build a script 3 (continued) (CD)

Purpose: *for children to participate in the final stage of writing a script that will provide a stimulus and model for their own writing*

- Tell the children that you have written some notes about how to end the new scene. Display **CD (file 10.1)** to show the notes. Read them aloud to the children.
- Explain that you like this ending but it is not written in script form yet. Navigate to the next slide to show the notes written out as a script. Read it aloud using MT/YT, then talk through the changes and draw attention to the conventions of script form.
- Ask them to TTYP to share what they think about the ending and then choose two or three sets of partners to give feedback.

encapsulating what they want to say, sentence by sentence; re-reading to check that their writing makes sense

Write a script 3 (PB)

Purpose: *for children to choose a scenario and use prompts to write their own ending and complete a scene*

- Make sure the children have the Write a script 2 writing frames they were working with on Day 9.
- Ask the children to look at the Write a script 3 activity on pp.30–31 of their Pupils' Book. Ask them to TTYP to read the notes on p.30 together. Guide them to use the prompts to help them convert the notes into a script. Remind them to share ideas and sentences with their partner before writing them down. You may prefer them to write a first draft before they complete the rest of the printed sheet.

- As the children are writing, walk around, providing encouragement and support. Note good examples to share at the end of the writing session.
- Now ask the children to look at the idea for a different ending on p.31 of in their Pupils' Book. Tell the children to TTYP to talk about which ending they think Jerome would like best, and why.

Special effects

Purpose: for children to develop their understanding of sound and lighting effects and to identify where they could be used in their scripts

- Remind the children that they talked about using special effects in the *Oh, Gnome!* script last week. Ask them to TTYP and take turns to read each other's new scenes and decide where they would add sound, music or particular lighting, and why.
- You may want to model an example for them on the board, e.g.

  (A spotlight shines on Bluebell and romantic music begins to play.)

  Jerome (To himself) Bluebell! I thought I'd never see you again!
- Ask them to TTYP to share their ideas and then collect feedback from a few children to share with the whole class.

Curriculum link: evaluating their writing with the teacher and other pupils; make simple additions, revisions and corrections

Evaluate and edit (CD)

Purpose: for children to evaluate their own and their partner's work against specific criteria and then discuss how they could improve their work

- Display **CD (file 10.2)** to show the evaluation prompts and read them aloud using MT/YT.
- As a model, select an example of work where the writing has met the criteria, and share this with the other children, explaining why it works well.
- Tell the children to take turns to read their partner's writing in pairs and discuss together how well each piece of writing has met the criteria.
- Ask children to discuss at least two changes they could make to improve their work.

proofreading to check for errors in spelling, grammar and punctuation

Proofread

Purpose: for children to proofread their work and make changes to improve the accuracy of their grammar, punctuation and spelling

- Now ask the children to proofread their work. If you have noticed that several children need to improve on a particular aspect of spelling, grammar or punctuation, use this as a focus for the Proofread activity. Write an example which includes common errors from the children's writing and use this as a model.
- The children should always be checking for standard use of punctuation and correct spelling of common exception words.
- The following points would be relevant as the particular focus for this Unit:
  - checking spelling of multi-syllabic words
  - checking for correct use of punctuation, particularly exclamation marks, if appropriate, to show a command.

READING AND WRITING NON-FICTION

The Non-fiction week looks at persuasive texts in a variety of forms, including adverts, posters, leaflets and trailers.

See p.78 for the daily timetable for the Non-fiction week.

Non-fiction

Reading

Children will:

- identify persuasive words and phrases and recognise that these focus on the positive aspects of something
- notice how adverts persuade us by looking eye-catching and including information that is important and appealing to a certain audience
- experiment with features of leaflet layout, including pictures, boxes, headings and shapes.

Writing

Key writing purpose to be shared with the children:

To write and perform a voice-over for a persuasive trailer.

Writing evaluation to be shared with the children

My voice-over:

- uses words and phrases that will persuade the viewer to watch the play
- includes a slogan that catches the reader's attention.

Grammar:

- includes correct use of adjectives and nouns to make accurate and interesting descriptions.

See the Planning section of the Software ('Timetables' tab) for a printable version of the Writing purpose and evaluation.

DAY 11

Curriculum link: pupils should be guided to participate in discussion

Think and link

Purpose: for children to develop an interest in persuasive texts via one of the Big Questions they have explored

- Display the Big Question from Day 6 on **CD (file 6.5)**:

  How do people choose what to do?
- Ask the children to TTYP to recall some of the points they discussed when the question was introduced on Day 6 and take feedback.
- Point to the word *persuade* on the screen and remind them that the word *persuade* was useful when discussing what made people do things. For example, when Little Croc's friends tried to persuade him to keep the purse and money, or when Katie persuaded Oliver to tell the truth to Gran.
- Ask the children to TTYP to say what they have tried to persuade someone to do. Collect feedback and make sure you use the word *persuade* when you paraphrase their responses, e.g. '*So, you tried to* persuade *your mum to let you watch TV.*'
- Tell the children that you have found a poem that is about someone persuading someone to do something. Display **CD (file 11.1)** to show the poem 'How to Successfully Persuade Your Parents to Give You More Pocket Money' and read it aloud. (The children don't need to understand every word of the poem.)
- Ask the children to follow the text on the slide as you re-read it.
- Ask them to TTYP to say which part of the poem they enjoyed most. Use MT/YT to re-read some of the lines they pick out. Leave the poem on the screen for the next activity.

discussing their favourite words and phrases, new vocabulary

Word power

Purpose: for children to build on their knowledge of synonyms and familiarise themselves with some rarer vocabulary

cajole convince coax sway

- Explain that, as well as being a funny poem, 'How to Successfully Persuade Your Parents to Give You More Pocket Money' has some special words that mean the same as *persuade*.
- Using **CD (file 11.1),** navigate to the next slide to show the first two Power words and sentences. Use MT/YT to say the words and sentences.
- Navigate to the next slide to look again at the beginning of the poem. Ask the children to TTYP to find these special words in the poem.
- Explain that there are other words that mean the same as *persuade* that the poet could have used. Navigate to the final slide and use MT/YT to say the words and sentences.
- These words and other examples of persuasive words and phrases can be printed from printable **CD (file 11.2)** for display on your Persuasive writing wall.

Say it

Purpose: for children to become familiar with some persuasive words and phrases

- Display **CD (file 11.3)** to show some persuasive dialogue. Read it aloud to the children with appropriate intonation.
- Tell the children that there are lots of words and phrases we often use when we try to persuade someone. Ask: '*Who is using all the persuasive words and phrases?*'
- Click 'Highlights 1' to highlight some persuasive words and phrases. Use MT/YT to read the highlighted parts of the text and then remind the children that these persuasive words and phrases focus on the positive points.

- Now click 'Highlights 2' to show the counter arguments. Use MT/YT to read the highlighted parts of the text and then remind the children that these words and phrases focus on the negative points.

Curriculum link: role-play to help pupils to try out the language they have listened to

Role-play PB

Purpose: for children to develop their understanding of and ability to use persuasive language

- Tell the children that they are going to create a role-play using persuasive language, with two characters, Rosie and Adam. Rosie has not done her maths homework but Adam has done his. Ask them to role-play the situation where Rosie tries to persuade Adam to let her copy his homework.
- Ask the children to turn to p.32 in their Pupils' Book and look at the Role-play activity. Ask them to TTYP to create a mini role-play based on the situation. Say that Partner 1s will be Rosie and Partner 2s will be Adam. Tell them to use some of the persuasive words and phrases given as prompts but to try and come up with some of their own as well.
- Walk around as they are putting their role-plays together, noting good use of persuasive language. Ask one or two sets of partners to recreate their role-plays for the rest of the group.

being introduced to non-fiction texts that are structured in different ways

Class log

You will need to have collected a few examples of different kinds of adverts, e.g. leaflets, brochures, posters, magazine/comic/newspaper adverts before this part of the lesson.

Purpose: for children to share the process of keeping a class reading, writing and thinking log to record responses to texts and activities in a variety of forms

- Explain to the children that, as well as our friends, family and teachers, adverts also try to persuade us to do something or to buy something.
- Ask them to TTYP to think of different places where they have come across adverts. Take feedback and extend their understanding where necessary, e.g. referring to less obvious places where adverts can be found such as on the sides of buses, attached to lamp posts, etc. Write their answers in the Class log.
- Tell the children that you have brought some examples of adverts to show them. Talk through how you know they are adverts and pass them round for partners to look at.
- Explain that you are going to add an *Adverts* section to the Class log and paste in some of the examples you brought in into the Class log.
- Tell the children to find some adverts at home to paste into their Personal log.
- Make sure they understand that we are surrounded by adverts all the time and that they all use persuasive words and phrases.

DAY 12

Year 2 Grammar learning how to use expanded noun phrases to describe and specify

Grammar: adjectives and nouns CD PB HB

Purpose: for children to develop their awareness of expanded noun phrases for description and precision

- Remind the children that a noun is a word that names things, people or places. Point to objects in the classroom and name them. Ask the children to TTYP to give the noun for other objects in the room. Ask them to Popcorn their examples.
- Tell them that the general names for things, people or places, e.g. *schools, cats, countries* are called common nouns. Say that the special name of one particular thing, person or place, e.g. *Beecher Primary School, Sarah, Spain* is called a proper noun and always begins with a capital letter. Write these examples on the board or a flipchart under the headings *Common nouns* and *Proper nouns*. Add a few examples of your own.

- Explain that it is sometimes useful to give extra information about something by being more precise about what it looks or feels like, what it is doing or where it is.
- Tell the children that they are going to look at a situation where extra information is really necessary. Display **CD (file 12.1)** to show a picture square. Read the dialogue with appropriate intonation and tone. Navigate through the slides, reading the speech bubbles, until you reach the last picture square, on slide 4. Now ask the children to TTYP to say why the extra information was necessary or useful.
- Navigate to the final slide to show a sentence about a gnome. Ask children to TTYP to identity the common nouns in the sentence (*gnome, hat, spade*), and the adjectives (*cute, blue*). Click on the buttons to reveal them.
- Now ask the children to turn to p.32 in their Pupils' Book and look at the Grammar: adjectives and nouns activity. Ask them TTYP to read the first sentence and tell them that the noun and adjective have been underlined. Ask them to TTYP to read the other sentences and identify the nouns and adjectives. Challenge them to identify which sentence has a common noun and a proper noun.

Homework Book p.13 provides further practice on nouns and adjectives.

Curriculum link: being introduced to non-fiction texts that are structured in different ways

Adverts 1 (CD) (A)

Purpose: for children to be introduced to some of the persuasive techniques that advertisers use

- Remind them that Jerome the gnome was taken to a car boot sale. Explain that advertisers have to make their car boot sale sound more exciting than others.
- Say that they are going to see a poster, which is one kind of advert, for a car boot sale. Display **CD (file 12.2)** to show a very basic poster advertising a car boot sale. Ask the children to read the information on it aloud with you chorally.
- Point out the key information on the advert. TOL about the importance of this information. Ask the children to Popcorn marks out of three for the information on the poster.
- Remind them that, as well as giving this information, the advert needs to be interesting to persuade people to attend. Now click 'Prompts' to show three statements about the interest level of the advert.
- Ask the children to read them aloud chorally and then to TTYP to decide which statement they would choose to describe the advert. Ask the class for thumbs up/down for each of the statements.
- Click 'Prompts' again to hide the statements and ask the children to TTYP to say what could make the poster more interesting. Remind them to think about posters that they have seen before. Take feedback and write some ideas on the board or flipchart.
- Navigate to the next slide to show the advert with some additional features. Ask the children to TTYP to spot any of the additions. Take feedback and then click 'Changes' to show the changes and additions.
- Click 'Prompts' to show the three statements again. Ask the children to TTYP to decide which statement they would choose to describe the poster. Ask for thumbs up/down for each of the statements. Choose a couple of children to explain their choice.
- Repeat the process with the final version of the poster on the last slide.
- Tell the children to look at the poster on p.12 of Anthology 2 Book 2. Explain that you want them to TTYP to take turns reading different parts of the poster with as much enthusiasm as possible to persuade people to go to the car boot toy sale.

Curriculum link: writing for different purposes

Write 1

Purpose: for children to experiment with the language and layout used in adverts

- Before the lesson, print out copies of the poster template from **CD (file 12.3)** for as many children as you think will benefit from it.
- Tell the children to look at Write 1 on p.33 of their Pupils' Book. Explain that they are going to create a poster for their own table-top sale being held at school. Talk through the bullet points giving details of the sale.
- Ask the children to TTYP to re-read the details about the sale and to discuss information such as: what? where? when? and how much?
- Ask them to use the Word and Phrases banks to create a poster to persuade people to come to their table-top sale. Give children copies of the poster template from **CD (file 12.3)** as appropriate. Use the poster on p.12 of Anthology 2 book 2 to give them some ideas.
- When the children have completed their posters, ask them to TTYP to share what they have written. Ask them to tell each other two things they like about the other's poster and one thing that would make it even better.
- Choose two or three sets of partners to share and talk through their posters.
- Posters can be put into their Personal log or on your Persuasive writing wall.

explain the meaning of new words; writing down key words, including new vocabulary

Personal log

Purpose: for children to keep a personal reading, writing and thinking log in order to record thoughts and ideas for their own writing

- Explain that adverts are not allowed to tell lies, but they usually only tell us the good things and none of the bad things. They also often exaggerate how delicious or wholesome food is.
- Display the advert for some junk food on **CD (file 12.4)**. Click 'Highlights' to show all the words that tell us the good things about the food. Use MT/YT to say the words.
- Tell the children that lots of words have an *opposite, e.g. light* is the opposite of *dark; good* is the opposite of *bad*. Explain that swapping a word to its opposite can totally change the meaning of a piece of writing.
- Click 'Opposites' to replace the positive words in the junk food advert with their opposites. Click 'Highlights' again to see these words highlighted. Use MT/YT to say the words, then read the whole advert chorally with the children.
- Write these sentences from an advert on the board or flipchart: *Delicious, healthy cakes full of good things! Only the best, fresh ingredients used!*
- Underline the adjectives. If necessary, remind the children what an adjective is. TOL and include the children as you think of, ask for and write a list of a few opposites for each word, e.g. *delicious: disgusting, horrible, vile.*
- Try out some changes orally, e.g. '*Horrible, unhealthy cakes full of bad things! Only the worst, stale ingredients used!*'
- Ask the children to TTYP to try out their own versions using opposites from the lists. When they are happy with their sentences, ask them to write them down in their Personal log and underline the adjectives.

DAY 13

Curriculum link: understand, through being shown, the skills and processes essential to writing

Adverts 2

Purpose: for children to deepen their understanding of the language and layout features of leaflets

- Explain that there is another type of advert called a leaflet. Tell the children that leaflets usually contain more information than posters.
- Explain that the owners of a brand new Gnome Centre wrote to an advertising company asking them to create a leaflet advertising their grand opening.
- Display **CD (file 13.1)** to show the letter and ask the children to read it with you.
- Navigate to the next slide to show the advert writer's think bubbles. Use these and your own ideas to talk through the expert's process of planning the leaflet. You may want to navigate back to the letter to pick out certain points that might be useful.
- Now ask the children to look at the completed leaflet for the new Denton Gnome Centre on p.13 of Anthology 2 Book 2. Read it aloud to the children and then ask them to TTYP to re-read it together.
- Navigate to the next slide of **CD (file 13.1)** to show evaluation prompts. Use the prompts and TTYP to help the children to decide how well the advert company completed the task and to say whether they think it really is an 'amazing' advert.

writing for different purposes

Write 2

Purpose: for children to experiment with presentational devices for effect

- Before the lesson, print a copy of the leaflet features from **CD (file 13.3)** for each child or set of partners.
- Tell the children that because they are almost advert experts they have been asked to create a leaflet advertising the opening of a new children's bike shop.
- Ask them to look at Write 2 on p.34 of their Pupils' Book. Talk through the Top Tips.
- Now display **CD (file 13.2)** to show a presentation to model how text boxes, headings and pictures can be moved around to experiment with different layouts. Navigate through the slides to show a few different examples.
- Click in the text boxes to complete some of the information. You could model changing the name of the bike shop or completing slogans to make them rhyme.
- Give each child or each set of children the leaflet features **CD (file 13.3)**, a sheet of A4 paper, scissors and paste. Ask the children to use their paper to make a simple leaflet. Explain that they should cut out and experiment with pictures, boxes, headings and shapes to create their leaflet. Remind children to share ideas with their partner and look at the leaflet for the Denton Gnome Centre in the Anthology to help them.
- Ask them not to paste anything until they are sure they are happy with the layout. Tell the children to rehearse which words they are going to use before writing them down.

participate in discussion

Class log

Purpose: for children to share the process of keeping a class reading, writing and thinking log to record responses to texts and activities in a variety of forms

- Use the Class log time to share the leaflets the children have made. Ask the children to nominate two or three leaflets to be photocopied and added to the log.

DAY 14

Adverts 3

Purpose: for children to develop their awareness of film trailers as adverts

Curriculum link: listening to and expressing views about a wide range of non-fiction

- Ask the children if they have ever seen adverts for new films when watching a DVD or a film at the cinema. Tell them that these adverts are called trailers.
- Explain that they usually show the most exciting or funniest bits from a film to persuade you to want to see the rest. You may wish to find the trailer for the film *Gnomeo and Juliet* to show as an example.
- Say that you have a trailer for a film to show them. Display **CD (file 14.1)** and navigate through the slides to play the trailer.
- Ask the children to TTYP to discuss: what kind of film it is advertising, e.g. *animated film, cartoon;* who might want to go and see this film, e.g. *children, families.*
- Accept any answers as long as children can support their point of view. Say that you are going to play the trailer again with the sound muted. Ask children to TTYP to share what they could see. Take feedback and draw attention to the visual effects: colour/close-ups/bird's-eye view.
- Play the trailer again, but this time do not display it on the whiteboard. Ask the children to TTYP to share what they could hear.
- Take feedback and draw attention to:
  – tone of voice – *angry? excited? scared? spooky?*
  – words and phrases – *what is being said, and why?*
- Tell the children that the voice they heard is called a *voice-over* because you can hear it over the pictures but you cannot see whose voice it is.

Write 3

encapsulating what they want to say, sentence by sentence

Purpose: for children to choose and use appropriate words and phrases to create a piece of persuasive writing

- Before the lesson, print out a copy of **CD (file 14.2)** for each child.
- Remind the children what a voice-over is by using MT/YT to say the phrases below taken from the trailer. Make sure you use a suitably dramatic tone of voice: '*They don't know where he came from… They don't know why he's here… Is he on a secret mission to save the world from poisonous cheese?*'
- Tell the children that they are going to write a voice-over for another film trailer. Ask them to look at Write 3 on pp.34–35 of their Pupils' Book. Explain that the storyboard is showing bits of the play *Oh, Gnome!*, which is going to be made into a film.
- Ask them to TTYP to look at the storyboard and identify which parts of the play are being used for the film trailer. Collect feedback and tease out why they think these moments were chosen.
- Model how to use the first storyboard square and the voice-over lines to begin creating your voice-over script. Try out different phrases and TOL as you choose the best one. Use MT/YT to say the chosen line in a special voice-over voice and then write it on the board.
- Tell the children to TTYP to orally match each of the lines to the storyboard squares. Choose two or three sets of partners to share their answers. Check that they have the lines in the right order (1=C, 2=E, 3=A, 4=F, 5=D, 6=B).
- Draw attention to the adjectives (*quiet, new*) and nouns (*Jerome, love*) used in the voice-over, and encourage children to use adjectives and nouns in their own writing to make their voice-overs more interesting.
- Give each child a copy of printable **CD file (14.2)** and ask them to write their own voice-over lines for each image, except image 6, which they will write a slogan for later. Remind them to TTYP to say their lines aloud before writing them down. Monitor the children as they write.

Curriculum link: proofreading to check for errors in spelling, grammar and punctuation

Proofread

Purpose: for children to proofread their work, and make changes to improve the accuracy of their grammar, punctuation and spelling

- Now ask the children to proofread their work. If you have noticed that several children need to improve on a particular aspect of spelling, grammar or punctuation, use this as a focus for the Proofread activity. Write an example which includes common errors from the children's writing and use this as a model.
- The children should always be checking for standard use of punctuation and correct spelling of common exception words.
- The following points would be relevant as the particular focus for this Unit:
  - checking their spelling of more complex adjectives
  - checking capital letters have been used for proper nouns.

writing for different purposes

Class log

Purpose: for children to share the process of keeping a class reading, writing and thinking log to record responses to texts and activities in a variety of forms

- Remind the children that a slogan is a very special phrase that is used to advertise something. Give some examples of slogans from well-known TV adverts.
- Explain that slogans often rhyme or have words that begin with the same sounds – *alliteration* – to make sure we remember them.
- Say that you want some great slogans that people will remember for the trailer of the *Oh, Gnome!* film. Write these slogans in the Class log and use MT/YT to say them: '*You've never met a gnome quite like Jerome! Will Jerome the gnome find a new home? A little gnome with a BIG story!*'
- Ask the children to TTYP to think of a slogan. Give them time to discuss their ideas, then choose two or three partners to share their slogans with the group.
- Write some of their slogans on the board or a flipchart. Ask the children to choose a slogan. It might be one from the board or one of their own.
- Now ask the children to write their chosen slogan next to number 6 on their voice-over script.

DAY 15

read aloud what they have written with appropriate intonation to make the meaning clear

Dramatic reconstruction PB

Purpose: for children to work effectively in groups to present film trailers in dramatic form

- Join two sets of partners together to make groups of four. Say that they are going to work together to present their film trailers in dramatic form. Explain that that they need to decide whose voice-over script they want to use and then choose: a director to use the storyboard squares on p.35 of their Pupils' Book to direct the action, a narrator to read the voice-overs they have written, two actors to create freeze-frames of the storyboard.
- Remind the children that the narrator needs to use an appropriate, dramatic voice to persuade the audience to go and see the film.
- Allow plenty of time for children to plan and practise the trailers as the process and group work are as important as the actual presentations.
- Let groups perform their trailers in turn to the rest of the group. Try to create a cinema experience by setting the chairs in rows for the audience in the hall, with special lighting and a microphone for the narrator if possible.

Curriculum link: evaluating with the teacher and other pupils

Evaluate

Purpose: for children to evaluate another group's performance against specific criteria and think about how it could have been improved

- Display **CD (file 15.1)** to show the evaluation prompts and read them aloud using MT/YT.
- As a model, select an example of work where the group achieved the objective, and explain to the children why it worked well.
- Tell the children to think back to another group's performance and discuss how well they met the criteria and how it could have been improved further.

writing about real events

Personal log

Purpose: for children to keep a personal reading, writing and thinking log to record thoughts and ideas for their own writing

- Ask the children to record in their Personal log which role they had, e.g. director, actor, narrator. Tell the children to TTYP to say what they felt about the experience and their role.
- Ask them to write a few single words or a short sentence in their Personal log to describe the experience. Choose a few children to share what they wrote with the group.

Fiction: Traditional tales
Non-fiction: Instructions

Timetable

WEEK 1 **Reading fiction** Traditional tales *Beauty and the Beast*

Day 1	Day 2	Day 3	Day 4	Day 5
The story store 🖶	Special phrases 🖶	Word power 🖶	Grammar: conjunctions	Saying, feeling, thinking
Show me the story	Secret story 1	Read a story	What's most important?	Storyteller's voice
Think and link	Secret story 2	Multi-syllabic words	What if not…?	Carousel storytelling 🖶
Personal log	Secret story 3	Re-read a story	Personal log	Class log
Big Question	Class log 🖶	Characters 🖶	Big Question	Big Question
	Big Question	Personal log		
		Big Question		

WEEK 2 **Writing fiction** Traditional tales *Beauty and the Beast*

Day 6	Day 7	Day 8	Day 9	Day 10
Story makers	Build a story 1	Build a story 2	Build a story 3	Write a story 3 (continued)
Character fact file 🖶	Write a story 1 🖶	Write a story 2	Write a story 3 🖶	Dramatic storytelling
What if not…?	Personal log	Class log		Evaluate and edit
Class log	Big Question	Big Question		Proofread
Big Question				

WEEK 3 **Reading and writing non-fiction** Instructions

Day 11	Day 12	Day 13	Day 14	Day 15
Think and link	Grammar: adverbs 1	Instructions 2	Instructions 3	Follow instructions 🖶
Zoom in on instructions 🖶	Instructions 1 🖶	Write 2 🖶	Write 3 🖶	Evaluate and edit
How to turn your partner into a dinosaur	Write 1	Grammar: adverbs 2	Class log	Proofread
Instruction detectives	Class log	Personal log		
Class log				

🖶: shows that a file should be printed out from the Software

Overview of the Unit

This Unit uses a picture book, *Billy Monster's Daymare* by Alan Durant and Ross Collins, and a traditional version of *Beauty and the Beast* by Gill Howell to explore traditional (i.e. fairy) tales, looking at plot, setting, characters and the power of transformation and change.

The Non-fiction week, linked by the theme of transformation, looks at instruction texts. For more information about the Non-fiction week and the Non-fiction writing evaluation criteria, see p.126.

Where appropriate, the children will be encouraged to develop an awareness of audience and purpose in relation to the fiction and non-fiction texts they are reading and writing.

Teacher modelling is provided in the teaching notes and the Software, supporting the children's writing at every stage in the Fiction and Non-fiction weeks.

The Homework Book provides a homework activity related to the content of this Unit for each of the three weeks.

Fiction

Reading

Children will:

- explore the power of fairy tales by reading *Billy Monster's Daymare* and a traditional retelling of *Beauty and the Beast*
- recognise Special phrases used in fairy tales, e.g. *Once upon a time…, …happily ever after*
- identify the most important moments in the story
- explore how characters change.

Writing

Key writing purpose to be shared with the children:

To write a new fairy tale.

Writing evaluation to be shared with the children

My new fairy tale:

- has a beginning, a middle and an end
- includes traditional fairy tale phrases, e.g. *Once upon a time…, …happily ever after*
- uses adjectives to build effective descriptions of the characters and setting.

Grammar:

- includes conjunctions to link ideas.

See the Planning section of the Software ('Timetables' tab) for a printable version of the Writing purpose and evaluation.

READING FICTION

Resources
- PB Pupils' Book, pp.36–44
- A Anthology 2 Book 2, pp.14–24
- CD CD on interactive whiteboard, Unit 4
- GB Grammar Bank on CD
- HB Homework Book, pp.14–16

DAY 1

Curriculum link: participate in discussion about books, becoming familiar with a wide range of books

The story store

Purpose: for children to hear and enjoy a picture book story that introduces themes to be explored in the Anthology text

- Before the lesson, print out a copy of the TOL (Think out loud) points from **CD (file 1.2)**. In addition to this, make yourself a simple badge with a star to use as a Story star.
- Show the children your Story star. Explain that this means that they are going to hear a wonderful story.
- Display **CD (file 1.1)** to show the front cover of *Billy Monster's Daymare* by Alan Durant and Ross Collins.
- Ask the children to read the title and look at the picture and then TTYP (Turn to your partner) to share what they think the story might be about. Collect feedback and show how much you value their ideas.
- Navigate through the pages by clicking on the forward arrow or the corners of the pages. Read aloud to the children with great enthusiasm and obvious pleasure. Use TTYP to explore a few aspects of the story as they arise, emphasising the themes of being scared, being brave, monsters and humans.
- Tell the children that they are now going to help you to re-read the story.
- Navigate back to the beginning of the story. Use MT/YT (My turn/Your turn) to re-read the first page.
- As you re-read the story with the children, use the TOL points you printed from **CD (file 1.2)** and your own ideas and TTYP to explore the connections between the words and the pictures. Focus on the expressions on characters' faces and significant detail in the pictures. Draw attention to the effect of changes in font size and type on relevant pages.

Show me the story

Purpose: for children to show their understanding of the story through drama

- Explain to the children that you are going to read some pages from *Billy Monster's Daymare* but that they will not be able to see the pictures. Tell the children that you want them to work with their partners to 'be' the pictures.
- Refer to *Billy Monster's Daymare* on **CD (file 1.1)** without displaying it for the children to see on the board.
- Read the words on p.4 ('The bedroom door...') then model how you want them to create a dramatic mini-mime to illustrate that page.
- Ask the children to stand up as you read p.6 ('Daddy Monster tucked in...') to them with great enthusiasm and appropriate intonation. Stop to allow them to show you the story through their mini-mimes.
- Repeat for p.8 ('Daddy Monster crept away...'), p.11 ('Daddy Monster gave Billy Monster a cup of cold slime.'), p.13 ('AIIIIIEE!'), p.17 ('Daddy Monster looked...') and p.21 ('Daddy Monster gave Billy Monster a big monster kiss...'), reminding the children that they need to try to mime both actions and feelings.

Curriculum link: drawing on what they already know

Think and link

Purpose: for children to make connections between this story and other stories and their own experiences

- Display **CD (file 1.1)** to show the whole story again and use MT/YT to re-read the story. Pause on p.1 to discuss this TOL point with the children: '*Can you think of any other stories that have woods or forests in them?*'
- Use TOL and TTYP to encourage the children to also think about their own experiences.
- Continue to read the story and repeat the process for the following pages: p.10 ('Oh, Billy,'): '*Can anyone remember a time when they have woken up from a nightmare?*' p.15 ('There's no child...'): '*Is a light room spookier than a dark room?*' p.19 ('Once upon a time...'): '*What kind of stories often start with* Once upon a time…?'

writing about real events

Personal log

Purpose: for children to keep a personal reading, writing and thinking log in order to record thoughts and ideas for their own writing

- Tell the children that, just like Billy Monster, there are some things that you are scared of. Share two things that sometimes scare you. Try to use things that the children can relate to, e.g. the dark, noises when you are in bed.
- Tell them that you are going to record what you are scared of on the board and you are going to use the opening: *Sometimes I am scared of…* Say your first sentence using the opening and use MT/YT before writing it on the board.
- Repeat with a second sentence. Ask the children to TTYP to share one or two things they are sometimes scared of. Take feedback and say their sentences back to them using the opening: *Sometimes I am scared of…* Write a couple of their sentences on the board.
- Now ask them to write their own *Sometimes I am scared of…* sentences in their Personal log. Remind them to say their sentences aloud to their partners before writing them down.

participate in discussion and consider the opinions of others

Big Question

Purpose: for children to develop their skills of argument and discussion through a mini enquiry session based on a philosophical question relating to the work of the day

- Display today's Big Question on **CD (file 1.3)**:

  Is it ever good to be scared?

- Ask the children to TTYP to talk about this question. Collect feedback and write some responses on the board.
- Click 'Prompts' to show some statements that may help to encourage discussion.

DAY 2

recognising recurring literary language in stories

Special phrases

Purpose: for children to become familiar with some special phrases particular to fairy tales

Once upon a time… …happily ever after.

- Before the lesson, print out the Special phrases from **CD (file 2.1)**.
- Remind the children that Daddy Monster read Billy Monster's favourite story to help him get to sleep. Ask the children to TTYP to see if they can remember how Billy's bedtime story started. Collect feedback and make sure that they have recalled the phrase *Once upon a time there was a brave little monster…*

- Tell them that *Once upon a time...* is a Special phrase that is often used at the beginning of fairy tales. Write the phrase on card or print it out from **CD (file 2.1)** and display it on your Story wall for this Unit.
- Ask the children to TTYP to remember how Billy's bedtime story ended.
- Collect feedback and make sure that they have recalled the phrase ...*And the brave little monster lived happily ever after.*
- Tell them that ...*happily ever after* is a Special phrase that is often used at the end of fairy tales. Write the phrase on card or print it out from **CD (file 2.1)** and display it on your Story wall for this Unit.
- Ask the children to learn the two phrases off by heart. Remind them to listen out for the Special phrases because you might use them at any time!

Curriculum link: making inferences, answering and asking questions, predicting

Secret story 1 (CD)

Purpose: for children to be excited and motivated to 'unlock the secrets' of a new story. For children to make connections between the new story, the picture book story they read and other fairy tales they know well

- Tell the children that it is time for a Secret story. Wear or point to your Story star. Explain that you have found some clues about a Secret story and you need their help to find out more. Convey your own eagerness and enthusiasm and draw them into your excitement.
- Display **CD (file 2.2)** to show the Secret story basket. TOL as you show your curiosity and interest about the contents of the basket.
- Click 'Secret'. One picture, word or phrase will emerge from the basket. Click 'TOL' to show a think bubble. Use this and your own ideas and TTYP to speculate about the significance of the contents.
- Navigate through the slides, revealing different secrets until the basket closes.
- Make sure you do not reveal the title, any surprises or the ending of the story at this stage!

making inferences, answering and asking questions, predicting

Secret story 2 (CD)

Purpose: for children to hear more about the new story, to make links with their own experiences and make predictions. For the children to become more familiar with the story so far before they hear the full version

- Tell the children that there was one more item right at the bottom of the Secret story basket. Display **CD (file 2.3)**. Don't navigate past the first slide at this stage.
- Say that you are really excited about what might be written on the scroll as it could tell us more about the Secret story.
- Navigate to the next slide to show the unrolled scroll and then click 'Audio' to hear the contents read out by a narrator.
- On the next slide, click 'Audio' to hear the first section again. Ask the children to TTYP to discuss the question the narrator poses and then take feedback.
- Repeat the process for the next two sections.
- Navigate to the penultimate slide and click 'Audio' to hear the narrator's final message.
- Navigate to the final slide to show the scroll closing.

checking the text makes sense as they read, making inferences, discussing sequence of events

Secret story 3 (A) (teacher only) (PB)

Purpose: for children to hear and enjoy the full version of the story for the first time

- Tell the children that they are now going to hear the whole story for the very first time. TOL about which parts you can't wait to hear about.
- Tell the children to TTYP to share what they are looking forward to in the story.

- Say that you need to switch your Storyteller voice on. Make it a special moment as if you are getting ready for a performance. Remind the children to listen out for the Special phrases.
- Now turn to Anthology 2 Book 2 p.14 and read the full story to the children with great enthusiasm and appropriate intonation.
- At the end of the story, ask the children to look at the Secret story 3 activity on p.36 in their Pupils' Book and TTYP to read and discuss the questions. Encourage them to give their own ideas and opinions, as well as thinking about the events in the story. Remind them there are no right answers to these questions. Take feedback from a few sets of partners.

Curriculum link: participate in discussion and consider the opinions of others

Class log

Purpose: for children to share the process of keeping a class reading, writing and thinking log to record responses to texts and activities in a variety of forms

- Tell the children that today they are going to begin the section of their Class log for *Fairy tales*. Show them the new title page with just the heading on it.
- Display **CD (file 2.4)** to show the cover designs for *Beauty and the Beast*. Navigate through the slides to show each design.
- After the children have seen each design once, navigate back to the first design and ask them to TTYP to discuss what they like and dislike about the design. Use your own TOL to encourage them to think about the picture, the choice of font and whether the cover would make someone want to read the book.
- Navigate through the slides, repeating the process for each design.
- Now ask the children to TTYP to discuss which cover design they would choose if they were the publishers of the book, and why.
- Ask for feedback and then take a vote on the best cover. Before the next lesson, print their chosen cover from **CD (file 2.5)** and paste it onto the *Fairy tales* title page in the Class log.
- Ask the children to TTYP to see if they can remember the Special phrases. Write them into the Class log.
- Tell the children that they can bring in things to be pasted into the Class log, e.g. some material from Beauty's dress or from the clothes that her father brought back for her sister, or the petals from a rose, or a picture of a castle or a forest. Make sure you bring in anything that could be relevant as well.

participate in discussion and consider the opinions of others

Big Question

Purpose: for children to develop their skills of argument and discussion through a mini enquiry session based on a philosophical question relating to the work of the day

- Display today's Big Question on **CD (file 2.6)**:

  Can you tell what kind of person someone is from how they look?

- Follow the process as explained on Day 1.

DAY 3

discussing their favourite words and phrases, new vocabulary

Word power

Purpose: for children to learn the meaning of specific vocabulary used in the story and increase their knowledge of synonyms

magnificent cautiously lulled

- Tell the children that there were some words in the story they heard yesterday that the writer had chosen because they were powerful.

- Display **CD (file 3.1)** to show the Power words and their definitions. Look at the words with the children and then use MT/YT as you read the sentences to them.
- Explain that the writer could have chosen different words that mean the same thing. Navigate to the next screen and show the first sentence and a list of synonyms. Drag and drop different synonyms into the sentence and use MT/YT to read it aloud after each substitution.
- Ask the children to TTYP to share which word they think worked best.
- Navigate through the screens and repeat the process.
- These words and synonyms can be printed from **CD (file 3.2)** to display on your Story wall for this Unit. Let the children hear you using these words throughout the day, e.g. '*I saw the most* magnificent *autumn colours on my way to school today!*' Remember to praise them if they use one of the words.

Curriculum link: listening to a wide range of stories

Read a story

Purpose: for children to gain a deeper understanding of the story and to see the text for the first time

- Ask the children to turn to p.14 in Anthology 2 Book 2. Tell them that they can see the actual story for the first time. Explain that you are going to read the story and you would like them to follow it in the Anthology as you read. Say that you are going to emphasise the Power words (in bold) and that they may join in if they wish. Remind them to listen out for the Special phrases.
- Read the full version of the story aloud with great enthusiasm.

increase pupils' vocabulary

Multi-syllabic words

Purpose: for children to use their phonic knowledge to decode rarer multi-syllabic words taken from the text

- Tell the children that there are some long words in the story called *multi-syllabic* words. Write these words on the board: *business, magnificent, hospitality, cautiously.*
- Check they understand syllables and give a brief explanation if necessary.
- Say that before they read the whole story on their own, they are going to practise reading these words.
- You may need to complete a quick vocabulary check to make sure the children know the meaning of the words.
- Discuss any tricky graphemes in the words and use the *Read Write Inc.* Complex Speed Sounds chart on the CD to clarify or explain where they would be on the chart. The chart can be called up by opening the 'Complex Speed Sounds chart' from the top of the resources list for Day 3.

checking the text makes sense to them and correcting inaccurate reading

Re-read a story

Purpose: for children to read the text independently for the first time and increase their familiarity of the story

- Ask the children to turn to p.14 in Anthology 2 Book 2 and take turns to read alternate pages of the story with their partners with as much expression as they can. Explain that you will be listening in and hoping to hear some star storytellers.
- Give feedback to the whole class on good reading partners to model what skills and behaviour you expect. Choose partners who use lots of expression and are good listeners, remembering to provide examples of this when you praise them.

Characters

Purpose: for children to understand how our opinions about characters can change as a story develops

- Before the lesson, print a copy of the Word bank for each set of partners from **CD (file 3.3)**.
- Tell the children that fairy tales have kind characters and cruel characters. Explain that kind is the opposite of cruel.
- Ask the children to show you a mini-mime of *kind* and then *cruel*.
- Ask them to mime the opposites as you say them. Say: '*Show me big! Show me small! Show me happy! Show me sad!*'
- Explain that, just like in real life, most characters are a bit of a mixture and they can change at different points in a story.
- Tell the children that you think the Beast changes most often in the story. Remind them of when the Beast first appears in the story and ask them to TTYP to share what they think the Beast is like the first time we meet him. Make sure they know it is their own opinions that matter – there isn't a right answer and they may disagree with their partners.
- Take feedback and guide the children to think about how he behaves towards Beauty's father as well as his physical appearance.
- Choose some of the children's words and write them on the board next to the character's name, e.g. *terrifying, angry, spiteful, ugly, unkind.*
- Now give each set of partners a Word bank from **CD (file 3.3)**. Explain that they have pictures of two characters and a bank of words and opposites.
- Say that you want them to TTYP to choose at least three words from the Word bank to describe each of the characters. Remind them that the characters might change their behaviour or even their appearance during the story. They should write their chosen words in the space provided.
- Ask them to cut along the dotted lines so that each partner can have one character to paste in their Personal log.

Curriculum link: compose individual sentences orally and then write them down

Personal log

Purpose: for children to keep a personal reading, writing and thinking log in order to record thoughts and ideas for their own writing

- TOL about how you could orally build a sentence to describe Beauty, using one of the words from the Word bank.

  I think I would choose the word brave *to describe Beauty. Let me think… when was she really brave in the story? Oh, I know, the first time she went to the castle, she had to go all alone! Did she scream or try to run away? No! She was extremely brave and just quietly got on with her new life. I could make up a sentence, couldn't I? I could say:* Beauty was a brave girl.

- Use MT/YT to say the sentence and then model writing it on the board. Continue your TOL to develop the sentence by adding adjectives and synonyms, and changing punctuation. Use MT/YT after each addition or alteration as you build the sentence orally in your Storyteller voice, varying the intonation and adding emphasis for effect.
- Remind the children that *hideous* is a synonym for *ugly*. Use MT/YT to say the sentence: '*The Beast was hideous.*' Write it on the board or a flipchart.
- Now ask the children to write the sentence in their Personal log.
- Tell them to TTYP to take turns to build the sentence orally, using MT/YT just as you modelled with the sentence about Beauty's bravery.
- Give them time to try out different sentences and choose two or three sets of partners to share their final version with the class.

Curriculum link: participate in discussion and consider the opinions of others

Big Question

Purpose: for children to develop their skills of argument and discussion through a mini enquiry session based on a philosophical question relating to the work of the day

- Display today's Big Question on **CD (file 3.4)**:

  Should we always forgive someone if they do something bad?
- Follow the process as explained on Day 1.

DAY 4

Year 2 Grammar learning how to use co-ordination

Grammar: conjunctions

Purpose: for children to develop their awareness of conjunctions for co-ordination

- Remind the children that *and, or* and *but* are linking words. They link two ideas or pieces of information together in one sentence. Say that they are called *conjunctions*.
- Say that, during discussions about Beauty and the Beast, they will have used the conjunctions *but, and, or* to help them to explain their thoughts and ideas or give information about the characters and story.

But

- As an example, we could say that the Beast was a frightening creature. Use MT/YT to say: '*The Beast was a frightening creature.*' We could also say that he was kind to Beauty. Use MT/YT to say: '*He was usually kind to Beauty.*'
- Display **CD (file 4.1)** to show the sentences. Explain that we can make one sentence if we link them together. *But* is the best choice of conjunction because the second statement is not quite what we would expect to read. If the Beast is frightening, we might expect him to be unkind, *but* we are told he is usually kind to Beauty!
- Use MT/YT to say: '*The Beast was a frightening creature,* but *he was usually kind to Beauty.*'
- Click 'Reveal' to show the changes and read them out using MT/YT. Draw attention to how the punctuation has changed.

And

- Navigate to the next slide to show two more sentences and ask the children to TTYP to decide which conjunction they would use here to link them: *and* or *but?* Ask for a choral answer and choose a set of partners to explain their choice.
- Click 'TOL' to show a think bubble and use this to explain the most appropriate conjunction. Then click 'Reveal' to show the new sentence.
- Remind them that *or* is another conjunction that we can use to join ideas or information together, when there is a choice involved.

Or

- Navigate to the next slide. Use MT/YT to say the sentences. Click 'Reveal' to show them as one sentence linked by the conjunction *or*.
- Use MT/YT to say the new sentence, emphasising the word *or*. Ask the children to TTYP to say what else has changed in the new sentence.
- Take feedback and then click 'TOL' to show the changes. Use the think bubble to explain them.
- Now ask the children to turn to p.37 in their Pupils' Book and look at the Grammar: conjunctions activity. Ask them to TTYP to read through the sentences and discuss which conjunctions to use.

Homework Book p.14 provides further practice on conjunctions.

Curriculum link: making inferences on the basis of what is being said and done

What's most important? A

Purpose: for children to deepen their understanding of the story by increasing familiarity with the text and to think about pivotal moments in a story

- Explain to the children that there are important moments in every story. Ask them to TTYP to recall an important moment in *Beauty and the Beast*. Make sure they know there is not a right answer but that you are just looking for their opinions. Briefly collect some feedback.
- Explain that you want them to read *Beauty and the Beast* again really carefully and to decide which two moments in the story they think are the most important.
- Ask the children to turn to p.14 in Anthology 2 Book 2 and re-read the story either by themselves or with their partners.
- Now ask them to TTYP to share their ideas about the most important moments. Collect feedback and encourage the children to explain their choices.
- Write some of their choices onto pieces of card or paper and then number them to match the chronology of the story.
- Now ask the children to work with their partners to create a freeze-frame for the moment that happens first in the story. Allow enough time for them to think of an appropriate pose.
- Ask them to walk slowly around the room and then to create their freeze-frames when you say '*One... two... three... freeze.*' Walk around as they hold the poses and comment on what you see. If you wish, take photographs of a couple of freeze-frames.
- Repeat with each numbered key moment.
- If you took photographs, print them off at the end of the lesson and display them on your Story wall in chronological order.

making inferences on the basis of what is being said and done

What if not...? PB

Purpose: for children to imagine other directions that the story could take

- Ask the children to turn to p.37 in their Pupils' Book and look at the What if not...? questions. TOL to model how you think out loud about the first question, What if not *a rose*? What if Beauty had asked for *clothes like her sister*?

  Well, her father would not have picked the Beast's rose and Beauty wouldn't have to go and live with the Beast in his castle. Perhaps the Beast would never have been released from the evil fairy's spell!

- Now ask the children to TTYP and discuss the other What if not...? questions. Collect feedback and develop some of the answers.

think aloud as they collect ideas

Personal log

Purpose: for children to keep a personal reading, writing and thinking log in order to record thoughts and ideas for their own writing

- Ask the children to Popcorn (see Introduction p.17) all the characters in *Beauty and the Beast*. Write the names on the board or a flipchart. Make sure they include Beauty's sisters and the evil fairy. Ask the children to TTYP to discuss which character they would like to be.

- TOL to model choosing which character *you* would be if you were in the story.

  I don't think I would want to be the evil fairy, but I would like to have her powers! Would I want to be Beauty? I definitely wouldn't like to live with the Beast but she does get to marry the handsome prince in the end. It is so hard to decide, but I think I would be the Beast because, even though the evil fairy cast a spell on him, he knows might be a handsome prince again – and he lives in a magnificent castle!
- Collect feedback and encourage children to articulate reasons for their choices. Now ask them to TTYP to discuss whether they have changed their mind after hearing what others have said. Tell them to write the name of the character they would be in their Personal log and one or two sentences explaining their choice.
- Using the names on the board, tally how many children have chosen each character. TOL about the possible reasons for the most popular choice.

Curriculum link: participate in discussion and consider the opinions of others

Big Question (CD)

Purpose: for children to develop their skills of argument and discussion through a mini enquiry session based on a philosophical question relating to the work of the day

- Display today's Big Question on **CD (file 4.2)**:

  Can we change the way other people behave?
- Follow the process as explained on Day 1.

DAY 5

making inferences on the basis of what is being said and done

Saying, feeling, thinking (CD)

Purpose: for children to develop empathetic responses to characters and situations

- Display **CD (file 5.1)** to show a picture of the Beast with a speech bubble and an empty thought bubble. Use MT/YT to read the speech bubble. Ask the children to TTYP to identify which part of the story it is from. Tell them to think about what happened just before and just after, to put the dialogue in context.
- Explain that sometimes what we are saying doesn't match what we are really feeling and thinking, e.g. *'I said, "I'm not scared of the dark!" but I was really very scared and was thinking, 'Oh no! I'm petrified of the dark but I'll pretend to be brave!'*
- Use MT/YT to read the three thoughts that might be added to the thought bubbles. Ask the children to TTYP to decide which fits the best. Remind them that there isn't a right answer – you are just looking for their opinions.
- Collect feedback and talk through their answers to make sure they have made justifiable choices. Drag the thought that was chosen by the majority of the children to the blank thought bubble next to the character.
- Navigate to the next two screens and repeat the process.
- Navigate to the final screen to show a picture of Beauty with a speech bubble. Ask the children to TTYP to recall which part of the story it is from.
- Explain that you want them to TTYP to decide what that character might be feeling and thinking at that point.
- Collect feedback and write one of their answers into the empty thought bubble.

read accurately and fluently

Storyteller's voice (CD)

Purpose: for children to develop their awareness of dialogue and narrative and the need for storytellers to use different 'voices' to sustain the listeners' interest

- Display **CD (file 5.2)** to show a section from *Beauty and the Beast.* Click 'Highlights' to show the dialogue. Explain to the children that these are the parts where the characters are speaking and that it is called *dialogue*.
- Tell the children that the other parts of the text belong to the storyteller, who must use a special Storyteller voice.

- Demonstrate by using a dull, robotic voice for one short part of the narrative. Ask the children to use thumbs up or down to show what they think of the voice. Repeat the process, using your special Storyteller voice.
- Say that you are going to read all of the storyteller's parts and that you want the children to read the dialogue. Explain that you will use MT/YT to help the children to read the characters' dialogue (highlighted text). Tell them that when they read the dialogue you want them to imagine how the characters are feeling and what they might be thinking.
- Read your storyteller's parts with great expression and intonation.

Curriculum link: read accurately and fluently

Carousel storytelling

Purpose: *for children to practise being storytellers, using varied pace and intonation to sustain the listeners' interest*

- Before the lesson, print off a copy of the sections from the story for each set of partners from **CD (file 5.3)**.
- Tell the children that *they* are now going to practise using their Storyteller voice. Join two sets of partners to make groups of four. Make sure they can sit in a circle. Allocate a number from 1 to 4 to each child in the group.
- Give out two copies of the sections from the story from **CD (file 5.3)** to each group. Explain that they are going to take turns at being the storyteller by reading the sections marked with the number you allocated to them. Remind them that they must try to read with lots of expression to keep their listeners interested.
- Give them time to read through their own sections before they begin the Carousel storytelling session. Walk around, listening in and noting super storytelling to give feedback on when the activity has ended.

explain and discuss their understanding of stories

Class log

Purpose: *for children to share the process of keeping a class reading, writing and thinking log to record responses to texts and activities in a variety of forms*

- Tell the children that you have been wondering why the evil fairy turned the handsome prince into a beast. Say that it could be another story that happened before the one they have been reading.
- Say to the children: *'You are the evil fairy. Why did you turn the handsome prince into an ugly beast? What did he do to annoy you?'*
- Ask them to TTYP to share ideas. Choose two or three children to feed back their ideas. Record one simple idea in the Class log, e.g. *The Prince has a party for his 21st birthday.* ⟶ *Every good fairy in the kingdom is invited.* ⟶ *The evil fairy is not invited.* ⟶ *She is furious.* ⟶ *She turns up in disguise with a gift.* ⟶ *As soon as the Prince opens it, he turns into a beast.*

participate in discussion and consider the opinions of others

Big Question

Purpose: *for children to develop their skills of argument and discussion through a mini enquiry session based on a philosophical question relating to the work of the day*

- Display today's Big Question on **CD (file 5.4)**:

  Which is more important: what we say or how we say it?

- Follow the process as explained on Day 1.

WRITING FICTION

DAY 6

Curriculum link: discussing and expressing views about stories

Story makers

Purpose: for children to develop their understanding of how stories are created by writers and to learn that we can all become writers

- Show the children your Story star. Explain that it shows that this week we are going to find out more about how the stories we love are made. Tell them that, if we can all find the secrets to making great stories, we can all call ourselves Story makers.
- Ask the children to TTYP to share ideas about what makes a good story. Collect feedback and write notes on the board or a flipchart. Copy them onto card and display them on your Story wall for this Unit.

making inferences on the basis of what is being done

Character fact file

Purpose: for children to explore and record what they know about the characters in a fairy tale

- Before the lesson, print a copy of the fact file from **CD (file 6.2)** for each child.
- Tell the children that characters are an important part of a story. Explain that they are going to create a fact file for one of the characters in *Beauty and the Beast.* Ask them to turn to the page in their Personal log where they recorded words to describe some of the characters (Day 3) and look at the words they used to describe Beauty. Tell them to TTYP to share what they recorded.
- Say that you want them to create a freeze-frame to show one thing about the character of Beauty. Pick out some examples and ask the children to explain what they are showing.
- Display **CD (file 6.1)** to show the fact file and Word bank for Beauty. Choose one of the two statements and drag it under the *What we know Beauty does…* heading. TOL about what the statement shows us about Beauty and ask the children to TTYP to choose one of the words that matches the statement to describe Beauty's character. Drag and drop the best word into the *What we know Beauty is like…* area. Repeat with the second statement.
- Navigate through the screens, repeating the process.
- Tell the children that they are going to create their own fact file about the Beast. Ask them to look at the words they used to describe the Beast's character in their Personal log and TTYP to share what they know.
- Give each child a copy of the Beast's fact file from printable **CD (file 6.2)**. Explain how you want them to TTYP to use the statements, Word bank and the words in their Personal log to complete the grid and create a fact file for the Beast.
- Walk around as they work, supporting and guiding. Note good discussions and decisions to give feedback on when they have completed the task.

making inferences on the basis of what is being said and done

What if not…?

Purpose: for children to understand how a character affects other characters and events in a story

- Remind the children of one of the What if not…? questions they discussed in the reading week: What if not *a handsome prince?* What if the Beast had turned into *a frog when Beauty kissed him?*
- Tell the children that writers can choose which characters they want to put in their stories. For example, the writer might think, 'What if not a *Beast who was kind*? What if I made that character a *handsome prince who was cruel?*'

- TOL using any of the ideas below and your own ideas and TTYP to guide discussions about possible effects the changes would have on other characters and events:

  Beauty wouldn't have gifts and kind notes from a cruel prince, would she? Maybe he would make her work hard and treat her like a maid! She would be even lonelier than she was with the Beast. I don't think a cruel prince would give her a magic mirror or let her visit her father, so she might never see him again! Would she stay or try to run away? What if she did run away? Who would help her if she got lost? It could be another fairy tale character like a good fairy or a magical old woman. What if the handsome, cruel prince were transformed into a kind Beast? Would Beauty marry him if he asked her?
- Ask the children to TTYP to share ideas about other fairy tale characters the writer might have put in the story instead of the Beast, e.g. *a good fairy, a wicked wolf*. Remind them of characters in other fairy tales they have read. Collect feedback and write some of their ideas on the board.
- Make sure the children understand how the whole story would be different if just one character was changed.
- Ask them to TTYP to share which character from the ones on the board they might choose to use if they were writing a story and why. Collect feedback.

Curriculum link: explain and discuss their understanding of stories

Class log

Purpose: for children to share the process of keeping a class reading, writing and thinking log to record responses to texts and activities in a variety of forms

- Remind the children that they have been looking at characters, but that stories also have settings and that things happen in an order: they have a beginning, middle and an end.
- Use a flipchart or a piece of A3 paper. Explain that you want the children to help you to create a mind map for *Beauty and the Beast.*
- Have a branch each for *characters, settings, beginning, middle, end* and *Special phrases*. Explain that these are the main 'ingredients' of a fairy tale.
- Use TOL and TTYP to guide the children to recall all the characters in *Beauty and the Beast*. Record them using the minimum number of words and/or symbols.
- Repeat the process for the other branches.
- Once completed, fold the mind map and paste it into the Class log.

participate in discussion and consider the opinions of others

Big Question (CD)

Purpose: for children to develop their skills of argument and discussion through a mini enquiry session based on a philosophical question relating to the work of the day

- Display today's Big Question on **CD (file 6.3)**:

  What would you do if you had the power to transform someone into something else? *
- Follow the process as explained on Day 1.

  ** This Big Question will be revisited on Day 11 – the first day of the Non-fiction week.*

DAY 7

understand, through being shown, the skills and processes essential to writing

Build a story 1 (CD)

Purpose: for children to see a story grow through three stages of development and to see the first stage of a plan that will provide a model for their own planning

- Tell the children that, when a writer is building a story, they need to plan which characters will be in it, where the story will be set, what happens to the characters and how things end.
- Explain that they are going to help you to build a new fairy tale and you want to begin by creating two new characters using a Story maker game.

- Display **CD (file 7.1)** to show pictures of six fairy tale characters. Talk through them, using TTYP and feedback to share stories they can think of that the characters appear in, e.g. a wolf in *Little Red Riding Hood*, a giant in *Jack and the Beanstalk*.
- Explain that you cannot make up your mind which two characters to choose for your new fairy tale and so you are going to use the game to help you. Click 'Roll' and ask the children to tell you which character the number corresponds to. Click on the character to make a tick appear.
- Click 'Roll' again and repeat the process for a second character.
- Navigate to the next slide to display six fairy tale settings.
- Repeat the process. The first setting you tick will be used for the first character you ticked.
- Navigate to the final slide and click 'TOL'. Use the think bubbles and TTYP to explore and share ideas about what the characters and settings might be like and to predict how the story might develop. Explain that these are the first 'ingredients' of a new fairy story and they are going to go in your plan.
- Display **CD (file 7.2)** to show the Story maker grid and explain to the children that this grid will form the plan for your new story. Click 'Complete' to fill in the character and setting cells.
- Tell the children that they will be helping you to find more 'ingredients' to add to the plan tomorrow.

Curriculum link: planning or saying out loud what they are going to write about

Write a story 1

Purpose: for children to explore possibilities for a new fairy tale

- Before the lesson, print one copy of the Story maker grid for each child or set of partners from **CD (file 7.3)**.
- Tell the children to turn to the Write a story 1 activity on pp.38–39 of their Pupils' Book. Give each set of partners a dice. Ask them to play the Story maker game together, taking turns to shake the dice to select a character and then again to select a setting.
- Tell them to record the combinations in their Personal log after each turn, e.g. a *giant on a mountain, a frog in the woods, a wicked witch in a tower.*
- Allow them enough time to have a few turns each. The point of this activity is to encourage the children to picture different characters in different settings.
- Give each child a Story maker grid from printable **CD (file 7.3)**. Explain that you want them to choose one character and one setting from the ones given in their Pupils' Book. (It does not have to be one of the combinations they created when playing the game.)
- Ask them to record their character and setting in the *Who am I?* and *Where am I?* columns on their Story maker grid. Tell the children to TTYP to share their chosen character and setting and explain why they made these choices. Ask two or three sets of partners to share their choices and reasons with whole class.
- This is an important opportunity for you to TOL about what some their characters and settings might be like, e.g.

  You have a wolf! They are usually described as big and bad *in fairy tales, aren't they? Which fairy tales have a wolf in them? Perhaps your wolf is a small, kind wolf!*

  So, one of your settings is a mountain. I wonder whether it will be a freezing cold, snow-covered mountain or a rocky, grassy mountain with trickling streams?

  Perhaps it is a big, bad wolf that guards a rocky, snow-covered mountain… or maybe a small, kind wolf is lost on a freezing, snow-covered mountain!

- Build sentences and images as you TOL and use MT/YT to help the children to feel the rhythm and intonation of a descriptive sentence, e.g. '*A small wolf with a kind little face wandered, lost and lonely, on the freezing cold, snow-covered mountain.*'
- Use questions and TTYP to encourage the children to think of other adjectives or similies to describe characters and settings as you build up and edit the sentence orally.
- Tell the children they will add more 'ingredients' to their plan shortly.
- Thinking, sharing and exploring possibilities are the most important objectives of this activity.

Curriculum link: writing down ideas and key words, including new vocabulary

Personal log PB

Purpose: for children to keep a personal reading, writing and thinking log in order to record thoughts and ideas for their own writing

- Ask the children to turn to the Personal log activity on p.40 of their Pupils' Book. Explain that they have a Word bank showing adjectives and their opposites. Ask children if they can find the opposites of some of the words.
- Tell them to TTYP to read through the list of adjectives and to choose at least two words to describe their character. Next, ask them to choose at least two words to describe their setting. Now ask the children to record their words in the *What am I like?* and *Where am I?* columns on their Story maker grids. Explain that they will be able to change or add words later if they want to. (Children will complete their Story maker grids on Day 8.)
- Tell the children that you want them to use their Story maker grid to write a whole sentence in their Personal log about their character. Remind them that they will be building up a sentence so they need to include the character, what they are like and where they are. Model the process on the board using these examples: *The huge, lonely giant sat in his warm, cosy cottage. A small, happy frog hopped about in a magnificent, bright garden.*
- Make sure they know they must say their sentence to their partners before writing it down.
- Walk around, supporting and guiding as they write. Note examples to share with the whole class when they have completed the task.

participate in discussion and consider the opinions of others

Big Question CD

Purpose: for children to develop their skills of argument and discussion through a mini enquiry session based on a philosophical question relating to the work of the day

- Display today's Big Question on **CD (file 7.4)**:

  Should everyone be happy at the end of a story?

- Follow the process as explained on Day 1.

DAY 8

understand, through being shown, the skills and processes essential to writing

Build a story 2 CD

Purpose: for children to see a story grow through three stages of development and to see the second stage of a plan that will provide a model for their own planning

- Display **CD (file 8.1)** to show the Story maker grid that you were working on yesterday. Remind the children that this shows the characters and settings for your new fairy tale. Tell them that you have added some information about what the characters are like using the Word bank from yesterday.
- Explain that you want to add a bit more to the plan so you are going to use the question *What do I want?*. Use TOL and TTYP to encourage the children to think of ideas of what the princess might want. Collect feedback.

- Tell the children that you have a Fairy tales idea box. Click 'What do I want?' to show the first picture appearing from the box. Ask the children to identify it. Click 'What do I want' again to add *handsome prince* to the grid.
- Ask the children to TTYP to discuss how the princess might get what she wants. Take feedback and praise good ideas.
- Now click 'How do I get it?' to reveal how the the princess finds her prince.
- Navigate to the next slide and repeat the process for the wolf.

Curriculum link: writing down ideas and key words, including new vocabulary

Write a story 2 PB

Purpose: for children to develop the second stage of a plan for their own fairy tale

- Explain that the children need to find out what their character wants. Tell them to look at the prompts in the Write a story 2 activity on p.41 of their Pupils' Book.
- Ask them to TTYP to talk about what the character in their story might want. When they have decided, tell them to record it in the *What do I want?* column on their Story maker grid **(CD file 7.3)**.
- Now ask the children to look at their Personal log and find the sentence they wrote about their character yesterday.
- Guide them to the Special phrases in their Pupils' Book. Explain and model how they should choose one and use it to add what their character wants to the sentence in their Personal log, e.g. *The huge, lonely giant sat in his warm, cosy cottage. All he ever wanted was someone to love.* Or, *A small, happy frog hopped about in a magnificent, bright garden. Her heart's desire was to find something she had lost.*
- Now ask the children to TTYP to share what they have written.
- Choose two or three sets of partners to read what they have written to the rest of the class. Say that they have written the beginning of their story and now you want them to start thinking about how their character gets what they want.
- Ask the children to look at the *How do I get it?* questions on their Story maker grid. Read the first question chorally with the children. Give them time to think about it in relation to their own character and then ask them to TTYP to discuss their answer.
- Ask them to compose a sentence to answer the question and say it aloud to their partner before writing it in the *How do I get it?* section on their Story maker grid.
- Repeat the process with the other questions.
- Choose two or three sets of partners to share their answers. Explain that they have now developed their story.

recognising recurring literary language in stories

Class log

Purpose: for children to share the process of keeping a class reading, writing and thinking log to record responses to texts and activities in a variety of forms

- Remind the children of the Special phrases in fairy tales (Day 2). Point to the Special phrases on your Story wall.
- Remind them that there are other Special phrases that are often used to begin and end fairy tales. Say these other opening phrases using MT/YT: *In a land far, far away… In a time when wishes came true… Long, long ago in a far off land…*
- Explain that you are going to record these opening phrases in the Class log.
- Repeat the process for Special phrases used to end fairy tales, e.g. *…happily ever after, Everyone was happy from that day on, As far as anyone knows, they live there to this very day…*
- Record these Special phrases in the Class log.
- Tell the children that you will be using these phrases when you write your new fairy tale and that they can use them in their own fairy tale.

Curriculum link: participate in discussion and consider the opinions of others

Big Question (CD)

Purpose: for children to develop their skills of argument and discussion through a mini enquiry session based on a philosophical question relating to the work of the day

- Display today's Big Question on **CD (file 8.2)**:

  Why do we love hearing and telling stories?
- Follow the process as explained on Day 1.

DAY 9

understand, through being shown, the skills and processes essential to writing

Build a story 3 (CD)

Purpose: for children to see an example of a finished story that will provide a model for their own writing

- Display **CD (file 9.1)** to show the completed Story maker grid. Explain that now you have filled in your *How do I get it?* section, you can start to write or grow the new fairy tale from the plan. You are in role as the writer.
- Read through the grid to remind you and the children of the 'ingredients' for the new story. Click 'TOL' to show the first think bubble.
- After talking through the first think bubble, click 'Write' to reveal the beginning of the story. Any words in the text taken from the grid are in red. Draw attention to how you have used the conjunction 'but' to link two ideas in a sentence.
- Navigate through the slides and repeat the process until you reach the final two slides. Now read your story to the children.
- Click 'Highlights' to highlight the Special phrases you have added, and talk about how they improve the story.
- Display **CD (file 9.2)** to show the whole story again and ask the children to read it chorally to you.
- Click 'Evaluate' to show the evaluation questions. Use them and TTYP to help the children evaluate the story orally. Collect feedback and encourage further discussion and constructive criticism.
- You may wish to try out some of their suggestions on the board or flipchart.

encapsulating what they want to say before beginning

Write a story 3 (CD)

Purpose: for children to use their plans to write their own fairy tale

- Before the lesson, print out several copies of **CD (file 9.3a, b** or **c)**.
- Tell the children that they are going to begin to write their very own fairy tale using their Story maker grids **(CD file 7.3)** to help them.
- Remind them how you used your Story maker grid to write the new fairy tale and rehearsed your ideas for the beginning of your story by thinking out loud. If necessary, refer to the TOLs on the first two slides of **CD (file 9.1)**.
- Give each child a copy of the appropriate writing frame from **CD (file 9.3a, b** or **c)**: **a)** gives the least support and **c)** gives the most.
- Explain how they can use their Story maker grids and their writing frames to begin to write their own fairy tale. Remind them to think carefully about how to begin their story. Give them plenty of time to look at their grid and what they wrote in their Personal log.
- When they are ready, tell them to think of their opening sentence and to say it aloud to check it makes sense before they write onto their writing frames.
- As the children are writing their story openings, walk around, encouraging and supporting. You may like to read out good examples for inspiration.

DAY 10

Curriculum link: encapsulating what they want to say, sentence by sentence

Write a story 3 (continued)

Purpose: for children to have time to complete their work, so they can see that you value the act of writing

- Use the first half of the lesson to allow the children to complete the opening of their story.
- Ask the children to read through their story so far and then TTYP to share what they have written.
- Explain that you now want them to start working on the middle of their stories. Remind them to keep looking at their plans to check what they wrote for *How do I get it?*
- Remind them again how you used your plan to develop the new fairy tale and rehearsed your ideas for your story by thinking out loud. If necessary, refer to the TOLs on the third and fourth slides of **CD (file 9.1)**.
- For those children who are ready to work on the ending of their stories, you can use slides five and six on **CD (file 9.1)** as a reminder of your TOLs.
- Expect some children to only write the story in very simple sentences. Others should go on to develop their stories further with a clear beginning, middle and end and some use of storyteller's language. A few children should be able to develop the problem/resolution aspect more fully, write longer sentences and use appropriate punctuation for effect.

read aloud what they have written, with appropriate intonation to make the meaning clear

Dramatic storytelling

Purpose: for children to use their own stories to develop their own storytelling techniques and an awareness of the effects of their use of language in writing

- Remind the children that on Day 5 they practised telling a story using a special Storyteller's voice. Choose one of the children's stories (or you can use your new story – Build a story 3 **CD (file 9.2)**) and read it using your Storyteller voice. Use emphatic hand and body gestures and facial expressions as well as different intonation and character voices.
- Tell the children to practise reading their own story in this way. Give them time to rehearse, then ask them to TTYP to read their stories.
- Take photographs of the children's dramatic storytellings. Print some and add them to the Class log. You may also like to display a few on your Story wall.

evaluating their writing with the teacher and other pupils; make simple additions, revisions and corrections

Evaluate and edit

Purpose: for children to evaluate their own and their partner's work against specific criteria and then discuss how they could improve their work

- Display **CD (file 10.1)** to show the evaluation prompts and read them aloud using MT/YT.
- As a model, select an example of work where the writing has met the criteria, and share this with the other children, explaining why it works well.
- Tell the children to take turns to read their partner's writing in pairs and discuss together how well each piece of writing has met the criteria.
- Ask children to discuss at least two changes they could make to improve their work.

Curriculum link: proofreading to check for errors in spelling, grammar and punctuation

Proofread

Purpose: for children to proofread their work and make changes to improve the accuracy of their grammar, punctuation and spelling

- Now ask the children to proofread their work. If you have noticed that several children need to improve on a particular aspect of spelling, grammar or punctuation, use this as a focus for the Proofread activity. Write an example which includes common errors from the children's writing and use this as a model.
- The children should always be checking for standard use of punctuation and correct spelling of common exception words.
- The following points would be relevant as the particular focus for this Unit:
  - checking spelling of multi-syllabic words
  - checking their spelling of Special phrases such as *once upon a time…, …happily ever after.*

Further activity

- Publish: ask the children to type up their stories, making any changes from the Evaluate and edit, and Proofread activities, and make a class story booklet.

READING AND WRITING NON-FICTION

The Non-fiction week, linked by the theme of transformation, looks at how instruction texts present information so that it is clear for a reader to follow.

See p.106 for the daily timetable for the Non-fiction week.

Non-fiction

Reading

Children will:

- look at different forms of instructions, e.g. *written, spoken or pictorial* and think about why they are useful for different purposes
- notice how adverbs of time, e.g. *first, next, then* are used to sequence information and make it easy to follow
- follow simple instructions
- recognise how adverbs of manner are used in instruction texts to give more precise information.

Writing

Key writing purpose to be shared with the children:

To write a clear set of instructions for making a thaumatrope.

Writing evaluation to be shared with the children

My instructions for making a thaumatrope:

- give information about how to make a thaumatrope
- are in a clear order to make them easy for the reader to follow.

Grammar:

- includes clear and complete sentences that begin with adverbs of time
- uses adverbs of manner to clearly show the reader how to make a thaumatrope, e.g. *carefully, gently*.

See the Planning section of the Software ('Timetables' tab) for a printable version of the Writing purpose and evaluation.

DAY 11

Curriculum link: pupils should be guided to participate in discussion

Think and link

Purpose: for children to develop an interest in instruction texts via one of the Big Questions they have explored

- Display the Big Question from Day 6 on **CD (file 6.3)**:

  What would you do if you had the power to transform someone into something else?
- Ask the children to TTYP to recall some of the ideas they discussed when they looked at the question for the first time and take feedback.
- Tell the children that you have found a funny poem that gives instructions on how to turn a hamster into a dinosaur. Turn to p.24 in Anthology 2 Book 2 and read the poem 'How to Turn a Class Hamster into a Dinosaur' aloud to the children.
- Now ask the children to follow the text in the Anthology as you re-read it.
- Ask them to TTYP to say which part of the poem they enjoyed most. Use MT/YT to re-read some of the lines they pick out.

Zoom in on instructions

Purpose: for children to become familiar with some adverbs of time used in sets of instructions

how to… first… next… repeat…

- Explain that, as well as being a very funny poem, 'How to Turn a Class Hamster into a Dinosaur' has some special words hidden in the poem that show us that it is also an *instruction text.*
- Display **CD (file 11.1)** to show the words: *How to… First… Next… Repeat…* These words and other examples of words used in instruction texts can be printed from printable **CD (file 11.2)** for display on your Instructions wall.
- Tell the children that these words help us to understand what we are being instructed to do and the order or sequence we need to follow.
- Ask the children to look again at the poem on p.24 of Anthology 2 Book 2 and TTYP to find these special instruction words in the poem.
- Choose sets of partners to read out lines from the poem that begin with these words, e.g. *First, prepare your hamster; Next, motivate it.* Point to the words on **CD (file 11.1)** as the children say them.
- Ask them to TTYP to recap why these words are important in instructions. Take feedback and clarify where necessary.
- Tell the children that there is another word in the poem that is often found in sets of instructions: *diagrams.* Read these lines from the poem aloud: 'Give it lessons on how to scare teachers. (Diagrams may help.)' Ask the children to TTYP to explain what a diagram is and why one might be helpful.
- Collect feedback and point to any diagrams you have in books or on the classroom wall, e.g. a diagram of the building showing the fire exits.

How to turn your partner into a dinosaur (CD)

Purpose: for children to develop their ability to follow and give oral instructions

- Explain that instructions can be spoken and listened to, or written down and read.
- Ask the children to TTYP to think of some instructions that they have listened to already today e.g. *come and sit on the carpet, listen carefully, hang up your coats.* Collect responses, clarifying where necessary and give some examples of your own.
- Explain that spoken instructions need to be really clear and quite short.
- Say that you are going to practise saying and following spoken instructions by playing *How to turn your partner into a dinosaur!* Open **CD (file 11.3)** to show a animation of a Tyrannosaurus Rex.
- Explain that you want the children to look at the shape, expression and position of the dinosaur, as well as how it moves. Give them time to watch the animation carefully.
- Tell the children to stand up. Explain that Partner 1s are going to give Partner 2s instructions on how to stand, move and look like the Tyrannosaurus Rex, e.g. *bend your fingers like claws, shake your head, roar, look fierce, show your teeth, move quickly*.
- You may want to take some photographs to put in your Class log or for display on your Instructions wall.
- Now open **CD (file 11.4)** to show another animation of a Tyrannosaurus Rex. Explain that it is now Partner 2s' turn to instruct Partner Is in how to be a dinosaur. Ask the children to think about how the dinosaur moves in this animation and how it is different to the first animation.
- You may want to take some photographs to put in your Class log or for display.
- Make sure you walk around, listening to instructions. Once both partners have been instructors, feed back examples of clear, short instructions, good listening and good 'dinosaurs'!
- Explain that, even though it was good fun, listening to and giving instructions are part of our everyday life and they help us to do things properly and to keep safe.

Curriculum link: being introduced to non-fiction that is structured in different ways

Instruction detectives (PB)

Purpose: for children to be able to identify the purpose of a variety of written instructions

- Remind the children that instructions are not always spoken but are often written down. Read out sets of written instructions from the classroom, e.g. *fire drill, how to behave in school, instructions in the register.*
- Explain that there are different types of instructions for different purposes. Use TOL and TTYP to draw out the children's understanding of the purpose of the instructions that you read out, and suggestions of how they differ.
- Now ask the children to turn to the Instruction detectives activity on p.42 of their Pupils' Book.
- Tell them that they are Instruction detectives. Ask them to TTYP to read each set of instructions, decide what type of instruction they are and match them to the correct heading.

- Take feedback and clarify where necessary. TOL as you review their understanding of some key features of instruction texts and introduce them to the use of imperatives and adverbs of manner to describe actions, e.g. *sprinkle, place, pat, gently, carefully*.

Curriculum link: being introduced to non-fiction that is structured in different ways

Class log

Before the lesson, you will need to collect a few examples of different kinds of simple instructions, e.g. instructions from food packets, games, appliances.

Purpose: for children to share the process of keeping a class reading, writing and thinking log to record responses to texts and activities in a variety of forms

- Show your examples of written instructions to the children and talk through how you know they are instructions and what they are for. Pass them round for the children to look at.
- Explain that you are going to add an *Instructions* section to the Class log.
- Ask the children to Popcorn some of the special words used in instruction texts. Write their ideas in large writing in the Class log.
- Now paste some of the examples you brought in into the Class log.
- Tell the children to ask for help at home to find some examples of their own to bring in and paste into their Personal log.

DAY 12

Year 2 Grammar increase pupils' awareness of grammar

Grammar: adverbs 1 CD PB

Purpose: for children to be able to identify root words and endings. To develop children's awareness of adverbs in instruction texts

- Tell the children that there are lots of *verbs* and *adverbs* in instructions. Remind them that *verbs* tell us what to do and *adverbs* tell us how or when to do it.
- Tell the children that the words *Feed carefully* appeared in the poem they looked at yesterday. Ask them to TTYP to say which word is the verb and which one is an adverb of manner. Take feedback and clarify if necessary. Ask the children to join you in a mini-mime of *feed carefully*.
- Say that the adverb *finally* is an adverb of time that is often found in instructions and it tells us when to do something.
- Display **CD (file 12.1)** to show the adverb grid. Remind the children what a root word is. Click 'Root' to show the root word *final*. Click 'Ending' to show the ending *-ly*. Use MT/YT to say the root word and then the ending.
- Now click 'Adverb' to show the whole word *finally*. Use MT/YT to say the adverb.
- Repeat the process for the other words. Draw attention to the fact that, as 'gentle' ends in 'e', we have to remove the 'e' before adding 'ly'.
- Ask the children to turn to p.43 in their Pupils' Book and look at the Grammar: adverbs 1 activity. Guide them through the instructions and ask them to TTYP to complete the activity.
- Choose two or three sets of partners to share their ideas.

Instructions 1

Purpose: for children to be able to develop their awareness of non-verbal cues to aid understanding

- Before the lesson, print one copy of the instructions for making a cheese sandwich from **CD (file 12.2)**.
- Tell the children that you are going to use mime to show them the actions used to make something. Explain that it will be something very ordinary that you do quite often. Remind them to watch very carefully because they will need to work out what the task is.
- Perform a brief mime of making a grated cheese sandwich. Make sure that your mime clearly shows the different steps as detailed in printable **CD (file 12.2)**.
- Ask the children to TTYP to decide what the task was and identify the different steps. Repeat parts of the mime if necessary.
- Explain that you are going to add verbal instructions to make it clearer what you are doing. Repeat the whole mime, but this time explain what you are doing as you complete each step. Keep instructions short and clear but don't make it too polished.
- Ask the children to TTYP to discuss which was the easiest for them to understand: the mime without words or the mime with words.
- Collect feedback, drawing out reasons for their choices and guide discussion to include physical gestures, facial expression, who focused more on what they saw and who focused more on what they heard.

Curriculum link: opportunities for pupils to develop and order their ideas by playing roles

Write 1

Purpose: for children to think about the actions needed to perform a task and to demonstrate them through non-verbal communication

- Ask the children to turn to p.43 in their Pupils' Book and look at the Write 1 activity.
- Explain that the pictures show some activities they may have done at some point. Talk through the choices and ask the children to TTYP to decide which one they want to mime for everyone else. Remind them to keep their choice a secret from the rest of the group!
- Give the children time to plan their mime and then ask them to take turns performing it to the rest of the group.
- Ask the group to TTYP to decide what the task was and then to identify the different steps. Ask the performers to reveal what their mime was and explain any actions that were not clear.
- You may wish to take photographs to add to the Class log or for display on your Instructions wall.

discussing and expressing views about a wide range of non-fiction

Class log

Purpose: for children to share the process of keeping a class reading, writing and thinking log to record responses to texts and activities in a variety of forms

- Tell the children that you have some written instructions to go with your mime for making a cheese sandwich. Show them the instructions you printed from **CD (file 12.2)**.
- Ask the children to close their eyes as you read them out and to try to picture your mime.

- Draw attention to adverbs of time (e.g. *first, then, next, now, after that, finally*), imperatives (e.g. *place, spread, grate, sprinkle, cut*) and adverbs of manner (e.g. *thickly, gently, carefully*). Use MT/YT to say the words with appropriate intonation and expression to show understanding.
- Ask the children to TTYP to recall why verbs and adverbs are useful in instructions, e.g. *the verbs tell us what to do and the adverbs tell us when or how to do it.*
- Collect feedback and clarify where necessary.
- Point to the photos and labels. Explain why these are often added to written instructions.
- Paste the instructions and write the adverbs in the Class log.

DAY 13

Curriculum link: discussing the sequence of events; learn about cause and effect in non-fiction

Instructions 2 (CD)

Purpose: for children to understand why it is important to sequence written instructions in the correct order

- Tell the children that you have heard about a boy called Silly Sam who was asked to clean out his pet hamster, Harry. He had a set of instructions but they were all jumbled up.
- Display **CD (file 13.1)** to show the comic strip. Read the captions and speech bubbles aloud, then ask the children to read them aloud chorally.
- Ask the children to TTYP to see if they can spot any special words that we use when we write instructions, e.g. imperatives (*put, take, add*). Take feedback and clarify if necessary.
- Ask the children to TTYP to discuss what could be added to make the instructions clearer (e.g. adverbs of time).

discussing the sequence of events; learn about cause and effect in non-fiction

Write 2 (CD)

Purpose: for children to think about the logical order of commands in written instructions

- Before the lesson, print a copy of a grid and the instructions from **CD (file 13.2)** for each set of partners. Cut the instructions into strips, retaining the grids to give to the children.
- Ensure **CD file (13.1)** is not still on the screen and ask the children to TTYP to recount what happened to Harry the hamster and Silly Sam in the comic strip.
- Explain that you have copies of Sam's jumbled instructions. Give each set of partners a set of cut-out strips.
- Explain that you want the children to TTYP to put the instructions in the best order to help Silly Sam to do a better job next time. TOL as you model how you would work with a partner to sort out the sequence.
- Ask the children to place their instructions onto their grids in the correct order. Do not ask them to paste the strips as they may need to re-arrange them.
- Walk around as they work, noting good partner work, discussions and decision-making. When the children have completed the task, explain that they are now going to help you to put the instructions in order.
- Display **CD (file 13.3)** to show the jumbled instructions. TOL as you decide which instruction should come first. Don't make it sound too easy to decide. Drag your chosen instruction to the top of the list. Ask the children to TTYP to select the next instruction in the sequence, then drag it into place.

- Repeat with each instruction. Make sure the children re-arrange their own instructions if they are in the wrong order.
- When the children are happy with the order of their instructions, ask them to paste them onto their grids. They will need their grids in the next activity.

Curriculum link: Year 2 Grammar increase pupils' awareness of grammar

Grammar: adverbs 2

Purpose: for children to apply their knowledge of adverbs to build a set of instructions

- Remind the children of two adverbs of time for instructions they already know: *First...* and *Finally...* and point to them on your Instructions wall. Ask them to TTYP to decide where they would write these words on their instructions grid for how to clean out a hamster.
- Check their understanding through feedback and then ask them to write the words in the correct places in the first column of their grids.
- Now show or remind the children of two adverbs of manner you wrote in the Class log yesterday: *carefully* and *gently*. Write them on pieces of card or paper and add them to your Instructions wall.
- Ask them to TTYP to decide which sentence or sentences the adverb *carefully* could be added to, e.g. *Carefully put it somewhere safe to stop it running away.*
- Repeat with *gently*, e.g. *Gently put the hamster back in the cage.*
- Say the sentences each time using MT/YT and then ask the children to add the words to their grids.
- Now TOL about other adverbs of time you could use, e.g. *Next... Then... After that... Now...* Point to them on your Instructions wall. Tell the children to TTYP to complete their own grids by adding some of these words to the beginning of the remaining instructions.
- Ask the children to TTYP to read through their completed instructions and think of a title to add to them. Take feedback from a couple of sets of partners.
- Ask them to write their title in the space provided at the top of the grid and then paste the instructions into their Personal log.

planning or saying out loud what they are going to write about

Personal log

Purpose: for children to keep a personal log for recording and reflecting on their exploration of instruction texts

- Say to the children: '*You are Harry the hamster. Which three rules would you give to Silly Sam to make sure he looks after you properly?*'
- Ask them to TTYP to share their ideas and then write the rules in their Personal log. Remind them to give the rules a title and number them 1–3.

DAY 14

compose individual sentences orally and then write them down

Instructions 3 (CD)

Purpose: for children to participate in shared writing of a set of instructions

- Tell the children that you are going to show them some pictures of someone making a thaumatrope. Explain that this is an optical illusion toy that uses pictures and spinning to trick the eyes.
- Explain that they can use a thaumatrope to turn the Beast from *Beauty and the Beast* into a handsome prince.

- Display **CD (file 14.1)** to show still images of a TV presenter making a thaumatrope. Play the presentation all the way through.
- Navigate to the next slide to show the first slide again. TOL as you tell the children what you think the presenter might be saying to their audience in this picture: '*I think she will explain what she is going to make. Then I expect she will tell the audience what materials and equipment they will need.*'
- Model how you turn your spoken ideas into a written caption and type it into the box. Keep it short and clear, e.g. *I'm going to show you how to make a thaumatrope. You will need...* Use MT/YT to say the finished caption.
- Navigate to the next slide to show the second slide again and ask the children to TTYP to tell each other what they think the presenter is saying to the audience.
- Choose sets of partners to share their ideas and note useful words and phrases (not whole sentences) on a whiteboard or flipchart. Model how to turn their spoken ideas and the notes into a caption to write in the box. Make sure you use an adverb of time, *First...*, and some adverbs of manner. Use MT/YT to say the finished caption.
- Navigate to the next slide and repeat the process. Draw the children into modelling the writing by asking them to TTYP to think of some short sentences. Encourage them to use adverbs of time or manner, but support them if they find it too difficult.
- Repeat the process for each slide.
- Tell the children that, if the written instructions are really clear, they should make sense without the images.
- Navigate back to the first slide with a caption and click 'Hide' to hide the photo. Read the instructions aloud using MT/YT.
- Navigate through the slides and repeat for each caption.
- Ask the children to TTYP to evaluate how clear the written instructions are.
- Collect feedback and make a few changes based on the children's evaluations and your own ideas.

Curriculum link: develop stamina for writing by writing for different purposes

Write 3 CD PB

Purpose: for children to write a simple set of instructions independently

- Before the lesson, print an A3 copy of **CD (file 14.2b)**, and an A4 copy of either **CD (file 14.2a)** or **CD (file 14.2b)** for each child as appropriate: **a)** offers the least support and **b)** offers the most.
- Ask the children to look at the Write 3 activity on p.44 of their Pupils' Book. Say that the word *thaumatrope* comes from two Greek words for 'wonder' and 'turner' so a *thaumatrope* is a 'wonder turner'! A thaumatrope is quite easy to make as long as you have a clear set of instructions to follow.
- Explain that the pictures are the same ones they saw in the presentation. Ask them to TTYP to look at the pictures and talk about what is happening in each one.
- Now tell them that they are going to use the pictures and a writing frame to write their own set of instructions.

- Show the children a large photocopy of the writing frame printed from **CD (file 14.2b)** and model how to use it with the picture frames in their Pupils' Book to write a set of instructions for how to make a thaumatrope. You may like to add in some adverbs of manner, e.g. *carefully* cut..., *gently* put one circle...
- Give each child a copy of their own writing frame from either printable **CD (file 14.2a)** or **CD (file 14.2b)**.
- Guide the children through the process of writing their own set of instructions as independently as possible, but give support where necessary.

Class log

Purpose: for children to share the process of keeping a class reading, writing and thinking log to record responses to texts and activities in a variety of forms

- Explain that written instructions often include pictures or diagrams to help explain a process.
- On a large piece of paper, model how to draw and label one or two pictures or a simple diagram to go with the thaumatrope instructions. Paste them in the Class log.
- For homework, ask the children to draw a picture or simple diagram of a thaumatrope and to bring it to school to go with their written instructions in their Personal log.

DAY 15

Follow instructions

Purpose: for children to follow a set of instructions their partner has written

- Before the lesson, you will need to print off one template for each child of the Prince and the Beast from **CD (file 15.1)**.
- You may need to allow some time at the beginning of the lesson for the children to complete their written instructions from the Write 3 activity on Day 14.
- Put out the materials for each child to make their own thaumatrope: Prince/Beast templates **CD (file 15.1)**, sticky tape, straws, glue, scissors.
- Ask each child to give their set of instructions to their partner. Explain that they are going to use each other's instructions to make a thaumatrope that will magically transform a beast into a prince or a prince into a beast!
- Make sure they have time to read through their partner's instructions and make their thaumatropes.

Curriculum link: evaluating their writing with the teacher and other pupils; make simple additions, revisions and corrections

Evaluate and edit

Purpose: for children to evaluate their partner's work against specific criteria and then discuss how they could improve their work, in response to their partner's feedback

- Display **CD (file 15.2)** to show the evaluation prompts and read them aloud using MT/YT.
- As a model, select an example of work where the writing has met the criteria, and share this with the other children, explaining why it works well.
- Tell the children to take turns to read their partner's writing again and discuss how well they have met the criteria.
- Ask children to discuss at least two changes they could make to improve their work.

Curriculum link: proofreading to check for errors in spelling, grammar and punctuation

Proofread

Purpose: for children to proofread their work and make changes to improve the accuracy of their grammar, punctuation and spelling

- Now ask children to proofread their work. If you have noticed that several children need to improve on a particular aspect of spelling, grammar or punctuation, use this as a focus for the Proofread activity. Write an example which includes common errors from the children's writing and use this as a model.
- Children should always be checking for standard use of punctuation and correct spelling of common exception words.
- The following points would be relevant as the particular focus for this Unit:
  - checking their spelling of adverbs of time and manner, *first, next, carefully, gently* etc.
  - checking correct use of punctuation after adverbs of time and manner.

Fiction: Stories with a familiar setting
Non-fiction: Communication

Timetable

WEEK 1 Reading fiction Stories with a familiar setting *Chatterbox Ben*

Day 1	Day 2	Day 3	Day 4	Day 5
The story store 🖶	Tell me the story 🖶	Secret story 1	Word power 🖶	Find it or prove it
Show me the story	Think and link 2	Secret story 2	Re-read the story	Moods and feelings 🖶
Think and link 1	Personal log	Secret story 3	What if not…?	Class log 🖶
Personal log	Big Question	Class log 🖶	Personal log	Big Question
Big Question		Big Question	Big Question	

WEEK 2 Writing fiction Stories with a familiar setting *Chatterbox Ben*

Day 6	Day 7	Day 8	Day 9	Day 10
Story makers	Role on the wall 2 🖶	Write a story 1 🖶	Write a story 2 (continued)	Write a story 3
Similes	Build a story 1	Build a story 2	Build a story 3	Evaluate and edit
Role on the wall 1 🖶	Class log	Write a story 2	Dramatic reconstruction	Proofread
Character detectives	Big Question	Personal log	Class log	
Grammar: conjunctions		Big Question		
Personal log				
Big Question				

WEEK 3 Reading and writing non-fiction Communication

Day 11	Day 12	Day 13	Day 14	Day 15
Think and link	Communication language 🖶	Teamwork 1 🖶	Zoom in on style	Communication 3
Private writing	Communication 1	Teamwork 2 🖶	Communication 2	Grammar: apostrophes for contractions
Say it	Write 1 🖶	Teamwork 3	Write 2 🖶	Formal and informal vocabulary
Personal log	Class log	Personal log	Proofread	Write 3
			Class log	Evaluate

🖶: shows that a file should be printed out from the Software

Overview of the Unit

This Unit uses a poignant, engaging picture book, *The Night Shimmy* by Gwen Strauss and Anthony Browne, and a contemporary, humorous story, *Chatterbox Ben* by Adrian Bradbury to explore the themes of communication and relationships.

The Non-fiction week, linked by the theme of communication, looks at formal and informal language by exploring different forms of communication for specific purposes and audiences. For more information about the Non-fiction week and the Non-fiction writing evaluation criteria, see p.155.

Where appropriate, the children will be encouraged to develop an awareness of audience and purpose in relation to the fiction and non-fiction texts they are reading and writing.

Teacher modelling is provided in the teaching notes and the Software, supporting the children's writing at every stage in the Fiction and Non-fiction weeks.

The Homework Book provides a homework activity related to the content of this Unit for each of the three weeks.

Fiction

Reading

Children will:

- connect and explore the central themes of communication in *Chatterbox Ben* by drawing links between texts
- explore characters' motivations, thoughts and feelings through their speech and actions
- examine how personal writing, e.g. a *diary,* conveys a character's mood.

Writing

Key writing purpose to be shared with the children:

To develop a new character and to write a diary entry about something that happened to them.

Writing evaluation to be shared with the children

My diary entry:

- shows what my new character is like by what they do and say
- describes how Ben's invisible friend uses its powers to help Ben
- uses *showing* as well as *telling* sentences.

Grammar:

- includes correct use of first person, past tense
- uses conjunctions to link ideas.

See the Planning section of the Software ('Timetables' tab) for a printable version of the Writing purpose and evaluation.

READING FICTION

Resources

- PB Pupils' Book, pp.45–54
- A Anthology 2 Book 3, pp.2–13
- CD CD on interactive whiteboard, Unit 5
- GB Grammar Bank on CD
- HB Homework Book, pp.17–19

DAY 1

Curriculum link: participate in discussion about books, becoming familiar with a wide range of books

The story store

Purpose: for children to hear and enjoy a picture book story that introduces themes to be explored in the Anthology text

- Before the lesson, print out a copy of the TOL (Think out loud) points from **CD (file 1.2)**. In addition to this, make yourself a simple badge with a star to use as a Story star.
- Show the children your Story star. Tell the children that this means that they are going to hear a wonderful story.
- Display **CD (file 1.1)** to show the front cover of *The Night Shimmy* by Gwen Strauss and Anthony Browne.
- Ask the children to read the title and look at the picture and then TTYP (Turn to your partner) to share what they think the story might be about. Collect feedback and show how much you value their ideas.
- Navigate through the pages by clicking on the forward arrow or the corners of the pages. Read aloud to the children with great enthusiasm and obvious pleasure. Use TTYP to explore a few aspects of the story as they arise, emphasising the themes of being quiet, shy and misunderstood.
- Tell the children that they are going to help you to re-read the story.
- Navigate back to the beginning of the story. Use MT/YT (My turn/Your turn) to re-read the first page.
- As you re-read the story with the children, use the TOL points you printed from **CD (file 1.2)** and your own ideas and TTYP to explore the connections between the words and the pictures. Focus on the expressions on characters' faces and significant detail in the pictures, e.g. the painting on the wall on p.2, and how it has changed on p.3, and the lips and eyes that can be seen in the wallpaper patterns on p.7.

drama techniques to help pupils identify with and explore characters

Show me the story

Purpose: for children to show their understanding of emotions and feelings through drama

- Explain to the children that you are going to read some pages from *The Night Shimmy* but that they will not be able to see the pictures because you are not going to display it on the board.
- Tell the children that you want them to TTYP to create a freeze-frame of the picture that the words create in their minds.
- Without displaying it on the board, navigate to p.4 ('The Night Shimmy always chose…') of **CD (file 1.1)**. Then model how you want them to create a freeze-frame to illustrate the feelings or emotions which match the words. Explain what you are trying to show through your freeze-frame.
- Tell the children to stand up as you read p.7 ('The Night Shimmy could be invisible'...) with great enthusiasm and appropriate intonation. Stop to allow them to show you the story through their freeze-frames.
- Ask a few sets of partners to explain what image the words created in their heads and how they are showing this through their freeze-frame.
- Repeat for p.16 ('When he woke up…'), p.20 ('Marcia came to the…'), p.21 and p.23 ('All on his own…').

Curriculum link: drawing on what they already know

Think and link 1 (CD)

Purpose: for children to make connections between this story and other stories and their own experiences

- Display **CD (file 1.1)** to show the whole story again and use MT/YT to re-read it with the children. Pause on p.1 to discuss the TOL point: *'Do you ever feel like not talking to anyone?'*
- Use TOL and TTYP to activate the children's thoughts and recollections of other stories and their own experiences that could be linked to the picture book text.
- Continue to read the story and repeat the process for these pages: p.7 ('The Night Shimmy could be invisible...'): *'Have you ever made up a secret language or a secret signal to use with a friend?'* p.15 (the parrot looming over Eric's bed): *'Can you think of something that parrots can do that Eric won't do?'* p.24 ('They began to talk'): *'What other stories have you read about friendship?'*

participate in discussion and consider the opinions of others

Personal log

Purpose: for children to keep a personal reading, writing and thinking log in order to record thoughts and ideas for their own writing

- Explain that many young children have make-believe or invisible friends. Ask them to TTYP to think about what sort of invisible friend they would choose: *'What would they be called? What would they look like? What kind of things might they do?'*
- Choose two or three sets of partners to share what they have talked about with the whole group.
- Now tell them to write their invisible friend's name in their Personal log and write a sentence or two about it.

participate in discussion and consider the opinions of others

Big Question (CD)

Purpose: for children to develop their skills of argument and discussion through a mini enquiry session based on a philosophical question relating to the work of the day

- Display today's Big Question on **CD (file 1.3)**:

  Can an imaginary friend be better than a real friend?

- Ask the children to TTYP to talk about this question. Collect feedback and write some responses on the board.
- Click 'Prompts' to show some statements that may help to encourage discussion.

DAY 2

making inferences

Tell me the story (CD)

Purpose: for children to explore how characters' feelings are shown in illustrations, and to use synonyms to describe them

- Before the lesson, print out one copy of the feelings bubbles on **CD (file 2.1)** for each set of partners.
- Ask the children to TTYP to recall any feelings they think Eric felt at different moments during the story. Take feedback and write words or phrases on the board or a flipchart. Develop their vocabulary by paraphrasing or using more specific vocabulary, e.g. substituting *sad* with *miserable* or *glum*.
- Tell the children that Anthony Browne created the illustrations for *The Night Shimmy*. Ask them to TTYP to say whether they think the *words* or the *pictures* showed them the most about Eric's feelings. Make sure they know that there isn't a right answer and that you are just looking for their own opinions. Collect feedback, encouraging them to give reasons for their answers.

- Display **CD (file 1.1)** to show *The Night Shimmy* again. Look at the first page and ask the children how they think Eric might be feeling in this picture.
- Give each set of partners a copy of the feelings bubbles you printed from **CD (file 2.1)**. Read through the words using MT/YT and check that the children know the meaning of all of the words.
- TOL about the different emotions that we can 'read' from the picture on p.1 and ask the children to TTYP to discuss which words in the feelings bubbles they would use to describe how Eric is feeling in this picture.
- Navigate to p.9 (Eric watching Marcia fly her kite) in the story and ask the children to TTYP to select which feelings bubbles they would use to describe how Eric is feeling now.
- Repeat the process for p.17 (Eric looking under his bed) and p.19 (Eric standing amongst his broken toys).
- Finally, navigate to p.25 (Eric and Marcia talking) and ask the children to TTYP to share how this picture makes them feel, without referring to the feelings bubbles. Now ask them to Popcorn (see Introduction p.17) words they have come up with.
- Ask the children to paste some of the feelings bubbles into their Personal log.

Curriculum link: listening to and expressing views about a wide range of stories

Think and link 2 (CD)

Purpose: for children to develop their lateral thinking skills to explore the text

- Tell the children that sometimes writers and artists use things as symbols, e.g. a cloud could represent sadness, a rose with a thorn could represent beauty that has a hidden danger, a lion could represent bravery.
- Display **CD (file 2.2)** to show a picture of some kites. Click 'TOL' and use the think bubble to discuss the image. Click 'TOL' again and talk about how the image could be linked to *The Night Shimmy*.
- Navigate to the next two slides and repeat the process, drawing the children into the TOL using TTYP and feedback.
- Navigate to the next slide to show a photograph. Ask the children to look at the photograph and to TTYP to say how it could be linked to the story. Remind the children that there isn't a right answer, you are just looking for their own ideas and opinions. Take feedback and show how much you value their ideas.
- Navigate to the next slide and repeat for the last photograph.

participate in discussion and consider the opinions of others

Personal log

Purpose: for children to keep a personal reading, writing and thinking log in order to record thoughts and ideas for their own writing

- Remind the children that the Night Shimmy disappeared very suddenly. Ask them to TTYP to share their thoughts about where the Night Shimmy might have gone. Provide them with some prompts if necessary, e.g.
  - *'Has the Night Shimmy gone to be the voice of another child who doesn't speak?'*
  - *'Has he really disappeared or is he just hiding and keeping an eye on Eric until he is sure he is OK?'*
  - *'Did the Night Shimmy only exist while Eric needed him?'*
- Choose two or three sets of partners to feed back to the class. Model how to write some of their answers on the board or a flipchart as full sentences.
- Ask the children to tell their partner where they think the Night Shimmy went and then to write it down in their Personal log using a full sentence.
- Choose two or three children to share what they have written.

Curriculum link: participate in discussion and consider the opinions of others

Big Question

Purpose: for children to develop their skills of argument and discussion through a mini enquiry session based on a philosophical question relating to the work of the day

- Display today's Big Question on **CD (file 2.3)**:
  Should you always search for something you have lost?
- Follow the process as explained on Day 1.

DAY 3

making inferences, answering and asking questions, predicting

Secret story 1

Purpose: for children to be motivated to 'unlock the secrets' of a new story

- Tell the children that it is time for a Secret story. Wear or point to your Story star. Explain that you have found some clues about a Secret story and you need their help to find out more about them. Convey your own eagerness and enthusiasm and draw them into your excitement.
- Display **CD (file 3.1)** to show the Secret story box. TOL as you show your curiosity and interest about the contents of the box.
- Click 'Secret'. One picture, word or phrase will emerge from the box. Click 'TOL' to show a think bubble. Use this and your own ideas and TTYP to speculate about the significance of the contents.
- Navigate through the slides, revealing a different secret on each one until the box closes.
- Make sure you do not reveal the title, any surprises or the ending of the story at this stage!

making inferences, answering and asking questions, predicting

Secret story 2

Purpose: for children to hear more about the new story, to make links with their own experiences and make predictions. For children to become more familiar with the story so far before they hear the full version

- Tell the children that there was one more item right at the bottom of the Secret story box. Display **CD (file 3.2)**. Don't navigate past the first slide at this stage.
- Say that you are really excited about what might be written on the scroll as it could tell us more about the Secret story.
- Navigate to the next slide to show the unrolled scroll and then click 'Audio' to hear the contents read out by a narrator.
- On the next slide, click 'Audio' to hear the first section again. Ask the children to TTYP to discuss the question the narrator poses and then take feedback.
- Repeat the process for the next two sections.
- Navigate to the penultimate slide and click 'Audio' to hear the narrator's final message.
- Navigate to the final slide to see the scroll closing.

checking the text makes sense as they read, making inferences, discussing sequence of events

Secret story 3 A (teacher only) PB

Purpose: for children to hear and enjoy the full version of the story for the first time

- Tell the children that they are now going to hear the whole story for the very first time. TOL about which parts you can't wait to hear about.
- Ask the children to TTYP to share what they are looking forward to in the story.
- Say that you need to switch your Storyteller voice on. Make it a special moment, as if you are getting ready for a performance.
- Now turn to Anthology 2 Book 3 p.2 and read the full story to the children with great enthusiasm and appropriate intonation.

- At the end of the story, ask the children to look at the Secret story 3 activity on p.45 of their Pupils' Book and TTYP to read and discuss the questions. Remind them there are no right answers – you are just looking for their own ideas and opinions. Take feedback from a few sets of partners.

Curriculum link: making inferences on the basis of what is being said and done

Class log

Purpose: for children to share the process of keeping a class reading, writing and thinking log to record responses to texts and activities in a variety of forms

- Before the lesson, print a copy of the cover design for *Chatterbox Ben* from **CD (file 3.3)**.
- Tell the children that today they are going to begin the section of their Class log for this story. Show them the new title page with the heading *Chatterbox Ben* and paste the cover that you printed from **CD (file 3.3)** onto it.
- Ask the children to TTYP to recall the names of as many characters as they can. Ask them to Popcorn their answers and then record the names in the Class log.
- Explain to the children that there are key or really important moments in every story where something happens, or someone says or does something that affects the rest of the story. Ask them to TTYP to recall one important moment in *Chatterbox Ben*. Make sure they know there is not a right answer – you are just looking for their own opinions.
- Take a class vote on which two moments are the most important.
- Use MT/YT to say the first most important moment and write it in the Class log.
- Repeat for the second most important moment.
- Tell the children that they can bring things in from home to be pasted into the Class log, e.g. souvenirs from a football match, stories set in school, examples of sponsor forms. Make sure you bring in anything that could be relevant as well.

participate in discussion and consider the opinions of others

Big Question

Purpose: for children to develop their skills of argument and discussion through a mini enquiry session based on a philosophical question relating to the work of the day

- Display today's Big Question on **CD (file 3.4)**:

  Can you say something without talking?*

- Follow the process as explained on Day 1.

  ** This Big Question will be revisited on Day 11 – the first day of the Non-fiction week.*

DAY 4

discussing their favourite words and phrases, new vocabulary

Word power

Purpose: for children to learn the meaning of specific vocabulary used in the story and increase their knowledge of synonyms

peering hunched glowered swivelled

- Tell the children that there were some words in the story they heard yesterday that are unusual.
- Display **CD (file 4.1)** to show the Power words and their definitions. Use MT/YT to read the words and their definitions, then the sentences.
- Explain that the writer could have chosen different words that mean the same thing. Navigate to the next screen to show the first sentence and some synonyms.
- Use drag and drop to substitute synonymous words into the first sentence and use MT/YT to read it aloud after each substitution.
- Ask the children to TTYP to share which word they liked best.

- Navigate through the screens to repeat the process for the other words.
- Model how you could show the word *hunched* with your body. Say to the children: '*Show me* peered! *Show me* glowered! *Show me* swivelled!'
- These words and synonyms can be printed from **CD (file 4.2)** to display on your Story wall for this Unit. Let the children hear you using these words throughout the day, e.g. '*Let's not sit* hunched *in our seats!*'
- Praise them if they use one of the words in their conversation.

Curriculum link: checking the text makes sense to them and correcting inaccurate reading

Re-read the story A

Purpose: for children to gain a deeper understanding of the story and to see the text for the first time

- Ask the children to turn to p.2 in Anthology 2 Book 3 and to follow the text as you re-read the full version of the story aloud with great enthusiasm. Put special emphasis upon the Power words (*peering, hunched, glowered, swivelled*).
- Now ask the children to read alternate sections of the story with their partners with as much expression as they can. Explain that you will be listening in and hoping to hear some star storytellers.
- Give feedback on good storytelling to the whole class to model what skills and behaviour you expect.
- Now give each set of partners two sticky notes. Tell them to TTYP to discuss and choose their favourite part of the story and their favourite character. Ask them to write their answers on the sticky notes and stick them in the Class log.
- Pick out a few sticky notes and ask the children to explain their choices.

making inferences on the basis of what is being said and done

What if not...? PB

Purpose: for children to consider how character and plot affect each other

- Remind the children that characters, actions, and consequences are all connected in stories. Say that if a writer changes one thing, it can change the whole story.
- Ask the children to turn to p.46 in their Pupils' Book and look at the What if not...? questions. Model how you TOL about the first question: What if not *a Sponsored Silence?* What if Class 2J did *a Sponsored Talk?*

  Well, Ben would be absolutely thrilled, wouldn't he, because he can talk for ages! Miss Johnson would be really worried that Ben might be away because she would rely on him to keep talking. Ben would be the class hero! It would be a disaster for Ben if he lost his voice when the class were doing a Sponsored Talk. Everyone would be very frustrated!

- Now use your own TOL to guide the children to TTYP to discuss the next What if not...? question. Remind the children that there isn't a right answer, you are just looking for their own opinions. Collect feedback and develop their responses. Repeat for the final What if not...? question.

discussing their favourite words and phrases

Personal log

Purpose: for children to keep a personal reading, writing and thinking log in order to record thoughts and ideas for their own writing

- Remind the children of the words they looked at in the Word power activity on Day 3 (*peered, hunched, glowered, swivelled*). Write them on the board or a flipchart, or point to them on your Story wall and ask the children to copy them into their Personal log.
- Explain that Partner 1 should choose their favourite Power word from the list and say it to Partner 2.
- Now ask both partners to TTYP to create a short sentence using Partner 1's word. When they are happy with the sentence and are sure it makes sense, they should say it aloud before writing it in their Personal log.

- Repeat the process with Partner 2 choosing their favourite Power word.
- Choose two or three sets of partners to share their chosen words and sentences.
- Write a few examples in the Class log.

Curriculum link: participate in discussion and consider the opinions of others

Big Question (CD)

Purpose: for children to develop their skills of argument and discussion through a mini enquiry session based on a philosophical question relating to the work of the day

- Display today's Big Question on **CD (file 4.3)**:

  Are we the same person in a group as we are when we are alone?

- Follow the process as explained on Day 1.

DAY 5

answering questions, making inferences

Find it or prove it (CD) (PB) (A)

Purpose: for children to develop their literal and inferential thinking skills

- Remind the children that the words in a story tell us lots of things, but they don't always tell us everything. Explain that often we need to search for clues that might tell us more about what characters are thinking, feeling or doing, or even what the setting is like. Sometimes we have to use our imagination to find out more.
- Display **CD (file 5.1)** to show a *find it* question. Click 'Find it' to show a think bubble and use it to TOL about how you would find the answer. Click 'Find it' again to show an extract from *Chatterbox Ben* and model how you found the extract that answers the question.
- Model how to compose your answer orally before writing it down on the board or a flipchart. Make sure the children hear you rehearsing not just what you are going to say but how you are going to say it before you write it down, e.g.

  It tells me that Ben says, "I was only spelling the word out loud." So my answer is: 'Ben was spelling the word out loud'. Or I could say: 'Ben talked during the spelling test because he was spelling the word out loud'.

- Navigate to the next slide to show a *prove it* question. Remind them that this means the answer is trickier. Click 'Prove it' to show a think bubble and use it to TOL about how you would find the answer. Click 'Prove it' again to show an extract from *Chatterbox Ben* and model how you look for clues to help you form an opinion or an answer.
- Model how to compose your answer orally before writing it down on the board or a flipchart. Make sure the children hear you rehearsing not just what you are going to say but how you are going to say it before you write it down, e.g.

  Well it doesn't say that Class 2J don't trust Ben, but it shows us through their actions, doesn't it? It says, 'Twenty-nine heads swivelled round towards Ben, and sixty eyes glared at him.' So my answer is: 'No, because the whole class glared at Ben as if to give him a warning not to talk'. Or I could say: 'No, we know the children in Class 2J do not trust Ben to stay silent because they all glared at him as a warning not to talk'.

- Now ask the children to turn to p.46 in their Pupils' Book and look at the Find it or prove it activity. Make sure they refer to Anthology 2 Book 3 pp.2–11 to find the answers. Say that, for each question, they need to decide whether it is a *find it* or a *prove it* question.
- Remind them that there isn't always a right answer to the questions, sometimes it is just asking for their own opinion.
- Ask the children to TTYP to read and discuss the first question. Choose two or three partners to feed back and repeat the process for each question.

Curriculum link: making inferences on the basis of what is being said and done

Moods and feelings

Purpose: for children to be able to identify different moods and feelings conveyed in a story

- Before the lesson, print a copy of **CD (file 5.2)** for each pair of children and cut out the adjectives.
- Tell the children that we all experience different moods and feelings through the day. Describe your mood when you first woke up this morning. Now ask the children to TTYP to share what their mood was when they woke up this morning. Choose two or three sets of partners to feed back.
- Say that your mood changed after a while. Tell them how it changed, and why. Now ask them to TTYP to share at what point their mood changed and what made it change.
- Remind them that, in *Chatterbox Ben*, the writer tells us and shows us lots of different moods and feelings.
- Display **CD (file 5.3)** to show some adjectives that describe moods and feelings. Use MT/YT to say the words and their definitions.
- Click 'Adjectives' to show the words without their definitions. Hand out a set of adjectives to each pair and ask them to spread the words out on their table so that they can see them clearly.
- Say that you are going to read sections from *Chatterbox Ben* and they are going TTYP to identify which part of the story it is from and then choose a word that describes the mood or feeling at that point in the story. Make sure the children understand that there aren't any right answers, you are just looking for their own opinions and ideas.
- Without displaying it on the screen, navigate to the next slide and read the extract with appropriate intonation and expression to convey meaning and impact.
- Ask the children to TTYP to identify the point of the story it comes from. Ask them to choose an appropriate mood/feeling word and to TTYP to explain how the writer has told or shown them this feeling. Ask them to hold up their adjective. Choose two or three sets of partners to explain their choice.
- Reveal the extract on the board. Pick out which parts show or tell us about the mood or feeling of this part of the story.
- Repeat the process for the following two slides.

listening to, discussing and expressing views; consider the opinions of others

Class log

Purpose: for children to share the process of keeping a class reading, writing and thinking log to record responses to texts and activities in a variety of forms

- Remind the children that storybooks usually have a *blurb* on the back cover and ask them to TTYP to recall what its purpose is. Choose two sets of partners to feed back, and clarify if necessary.
- Explain that you want their help to choose a blurb for the back cover of *Chatterbox Ben*. Display **CD (file 5.4)** to show the first sample blurb for the story. Read it through chorally with the children and TOL about how effective it is.
- Navigate to the next slide to show another sample and repeat the process. Draw the children into your TOL and use TTYP to encourage the children to share opinions and notice differences between the two.
- Navigate to the next slide to show the final sample and repeat the process. Now ask the children to TTYP to discuss which one they would choose if they were the publishers of the story, and why. Ask for feedback and then take a class vote for the best blurb. Print the most popular blurb from **CD (file 5.5)** and paste it into the Class log.

Curriculum link: participate in discussion and consider the opinions of others

Big Question (CD)

Purpose: for children to develop their skills of argument and discussion through a mini enquiry session based on a philosophical question relating to the work of the day

- Display today's Big Question on **CD (file 5.6)**:

  Should we change our behaviour if someone wants us to?
- Follow the process as explained on Day 1.

WRITING FICTION

DAY 6

listening to, discussing and expressing views about a wide range of stories

Story makers

Purpose: for children to develop their understanding that stories are created by writers and that we can all become writers

- Show the children your Story star. Explain it shows that this week they are going to find out more about what makes a good story, with a special focus on characters.
- Tell them that if we can all find the secret to making great stories and creating great characters, we can all call ourselves Story makers.
- Explain that writers enjoy creating characters for their stories and they use descriptions to help us understand what characters look like and how they behave.
- Ask the children to TTYP to think of a favourite character from a story they know well. Collect responses and ask them to share what they like about the character they have chosen.
- Say that they are going to have a closer look at some of the characters from *The Night Shimmy* and *Chatterbox Ben*.

discussing their favourite words and phrases

Similes (CD)

Purpose: for children to increase their awareness of similes

- Remind the children that on Day 2 (in Think and link 2) they looked at symbols that were used to represent things in *The Night Shimmy*. Say that a *simile* is a bit like symbol. It compares someone or something to something else and can be useful when talking or writing about characters.
- Display **CD (file 1.1)** to show *The Night Shimmy* and navigate to p.10 ('Marcia and Eric climbed...'). Use MT/YT to read the text. Point to the line ...*swung around like monkeys* and tell the children that this is a simile. Then show them the illustration on p.11 and TOL to demonstrate how this links to the simile on the previous page.
- Say that you want some similes to show what Eric is like at different points in the story. Display **CD (file 6.1)** to show a stem sentence about Eric and a selection of similes that could be used to complete the sentence. Drag and drop any of the similes into the box and use MT/YT to say it aloud. Repeat using the other similes.
- Now ask the children to TTYP to say which simile they would choose. Gather feedback from two or three sets of partners and encourage them to give reasons.
- Navigate to the next screen and repeat the process.

Role on the wall 1

Purpose: for children to think more deeply about a character they are familiar with

- Before the lesson, print the body outline from **CD (file 6.2)** onto A3 paper.
- Display **CD (file 1.1)** to show *The Night Shimmy*. Ask the children to read the text aloud chorally to remind them about Eric.
- Attach the body outline from **CD (file 6.2)** to a wall. Ask the children to use the headings to TTYP to describe Eric. Navigate through the story on **CD (file 1.1)** to help the children with their descriptions. Choose sets of partners to feed back. Write some of their responses under the headings around the body.

Curriculum link: answering questions; participate in discussion and consider the opinions of others

Character detectives

Purpose: for children to build up a description of a character they are familiar with

- Tell the children that they are going to focus on the character of Marcia. Ask them to TTYP to say one thing they recall about Marcia. Choose two or three sets of partners to share their answers.
- Explain that they are going to have a look at parts of the story where Marcia appears. Display **CD (file 1.1)** and navigate to p.8 ('…or the crack of a kite…'). Read pp.8–13 aloud, then skip to p.20 (Marcia came to the front door.') and read to the end of the book.
- Now ask the children to turn to p.47 in their Pupils' Book and look at the Character detectives activity. Ask them to TTYP to discuss the first question. Make it clear that there isn't a right answer to these questions, you are just looking for their own opinions. Collect feedback.
- Repeat the process for the next two questions. TOL to agree or offer your own ideas, showing that you value opinions and ideas that differ from your own.
- Ask the children to TTYP to discuss which character they would prefer as a friend, Eric or Marcia. Ask some partners to feed back and give their reasons.

Year 2 Grammar learning how to use subordination

Grammar: conjunctions

Purpose: for children to develop their awareness of conjunctions for subordination

- Remind the children that *when, if, that* and *because* are linking words. They help us to link parts of a sentence together. Say that they are called *conjunctions*.
- Explain that, during discussions about *The Night Shimmy* and *Chatterbox Ben*, they will have used the conjunctions *when, if, that* and *because* to help them explain their thoughts and ideas or give information about the characters and stories.
- Use MT/YT to say this sentence, giving exaggerated emphasis to the conjunction *because*: '*The Night Shimmy is a mysterious being* because *he is invisible.*'
- Display **CD (file 6.3)** and use MT/YT to say the sentence. Click 'TOL' to show think bubbles which identify the two parts of the sentence and the conjunction.
- Navigate to the next slide and repeat the process. Take feedback and clarify if necessary.
- Ask the children to repeat the process for the last two sentences. Say them using MT/YT, then ask the children to TTYP to identify the two parts of the sentence and the conjunction.
- Now ask the children to turn to p.47 in their Pupils' Book and look at the Grammar: conjunctions activity. Tell them to TTYP to discuss which conjunction they would use in each sentence.

Homework Book p.18 provides further practice on conjunctions.

Curriculum link: planning or saying out loud what they are going to write about

Personal log

Purpose: for children to keep a personal reading, writing and thinking log in order to record thoughts and ideas for their own writing

- Explain to the children that they are going to write at least two sentences about Marcia. Remind them to use the questions they have already discussed in the Character detectives activity on p.47 of their Pupils' Book to help them.
- Write a few stem sentences on the board or a flipchart and point out the conjunctions that can be used to link different parts of their full sentences, e.g. *I felt sorry for Marcia* when… *I would like Marcia as a friend* because… *I would not like Marcia as a friend* if… *Marcia doesn't seem to mind* that *Eric*…
- Remind them to rehearse each sentence aloud to their partner before writing them down in their Personal log.
- Ask some children to share what they have written with the group.

participate in discussion and consider the opinions of others

Big Question

Purpose: for children to develop their skills of argument and discussion through a mini enquiry session based on a philosophical question relating to the work of the day

- Display today's Big Question on **CD (file 6.4)**:

  Is the best kind of friend someone who is like us or different to us?

- Follow the process as explained on Day 1.

DAY 7

making inferences on the basis of what is being said and done

Role on the wall 2

Purpose: for children to think more deeply about a character they are familiar with

- Before the lesson, print out a copy of the body outline from **CD (file 7.2)** for each child or set of partners.
- Tell the children that they are going to be thinking about the character of Ben from *Chatterbox Ben*. Ask them to find the story on pp.2–11 of Anthology 2 Book 3. Tell them to TTYP to take turns to read alternate sections of the story.
- Display **CD (file 7.1)** to show a role on the wall outline for Ben. Read the headings using MT/YT. Explain the heading *Personality*. Define the word in simple terms, e.g. '*Personality means the kind of person you are.*'
- Ask the children to TTYP to share information or ideas about Ben that they have gathered from reading the story. Remind them that all readers create their own pictures in their heads as they read stories so they might have different ideas.
- Choose sets of partners to feed back and tease out whether they are giving an opinion or have evidence in the story to support their ideas.
- Give each child or set of partners a copy of printable **CD (file 7.2)** and explain that you want them to write their ideas about Ben under the different headings. Select a few to share with the class.

understand, through being shown, the skills and processes essential to writing

Build a story 1

Purpose: for children to see a character in a story grow through three stages of development that will provide a model and stimulus for their own writing

- Remind the children that when they looked at the What if not…? questions on Day 4, they talked about the question: What if not *a chatterbox?* What if *Ben was like Eric in the Night Shimmy and didn't like to talk?* and What if not *Ben talking?* What if *he had an invisible friend who spoke for him?*

- Say that you are going to change the story so that Ben doesn't like talking and create a brand new character – Ben's invisible friend. Explain that you have made some changes to the opening of the story based on Ben having an invisible friend who speaks for him. Display **CD (file 7.3)** to show your new version of the story opening (over two slides) and read it aloud to the children.
- Say that you are going to create a mind map about Ben's invisible friend. Display **CD (file 7.4)**. Use the think bubble to TOL about what you imagine Ben's imaginary friend to look like. Click 'Image' to show what you imagined the character to look like. Now click 'Notes' to show your notes and use MT/YT to read them aloud. Remind the children that these are notes, not full sentences.
- Repeat the process for the rest of the slides.
- Say that in the next lesson, they will get the chance to create a mind map to explore the character of Ben's invisible friend for themselves. Explain that they will have lots of choices to make as writers.

Class log

You will need a small amount of lemon juice and a cotton wool bud for this activity.

Purpose: *for children to share the process of keeping a class reading, writing and thinking log to record responses to texts and activities in a variety of forms*

- Tell the children that you were thinking about Eric's invisible friend, the Night Shimmy, and Ben's new invisible friend and you wondered if they would use invisible ink to write messages. Tell the children that there is such a thing as invisible writing and you are going to show them how to do it.
- Dip your cotton bud into the lemon juice and use the tip to write a message from Ben's new friend on a piece of plain paper, e.g. *I always know what's going on/ Inside my friend Ben's head./ My special powers should help him out,/ But things go wrong instead*… Do not tell the children what the message is!
- Hold it up to show the children that they can barely see the writing. Tell them that when it dries it will disappear completely. Put the sheet of paper in a dry place away from direct sunlight or heat and leave it to dry. Tell the children that you will reveal the message in tomorrow's lesson (Personal log activity).
- When the lemon juice is dry, slip the paper into the Class log.

Curriculum link: participate in discussion and consider the opinions of others

Big Question (CD)

Purpose: *for children to develop their skills of argument and discussion through a mini enquiry session based on a philosophical question relating to the work of the day*

- Display today's Big Question on **CD (file 7.5)**:

  If you tell someone a secret, is it still a secret?

- Follow the process as explained on Day 1.

DAY 8

writing down key ideas and/or words, including new vocabulary

Write a story 1 (CD)

Purpose: *for children to complete the first stage of developing a character*

- Before the lesson, print a copy of the mind map from **CD (file 8.1)** for each child.
- Give each child a copy of the mind map from **CD (file 8.1)** and explain that they are going to be creating their own mind map for Ben's invisible friend. Display **CD (file 8.2)** to show your mind map. Tell them that, as writers, they can make the character of Ben's invisible friend quite different from yours, or borrow ideas from your notes.

- Explain that you want them to make their own choices about the appearance, personality and special powers that Ben's invisible friend will have and write them as notes in the space provided. Model one example for them if necessary.
- Remind them to share ideas with their partners before writing them down.
- Walk around as they are working, supporting and praising where appropriate. When they are finished, choose two or three sets of partners to share their choices.

Curriculum link: understand, through being shown, the skills and processes essential to writing

Build a story 2 (CD)

Purpose: for children to see a character grow through three stages of development that will provide a model and stimulus for their own writing

- Display **CD (file 8.3)** to show your mind map again. Tell the children that you used the notes to create a more detailed description of the new character.
- Navigate to the next slide to show the notes you made on *appearance*. Click 'Description' to display your more detailed description. Read it aloud to the children.
- Click 'Highlights' to show the words you used from the notes to create the description. Explain that these are *telling* sentences. They *tell* us information about what the character looks like.
- Navigate to the next slide to show the notes you made on *personality*. Click 'TOL' to display a think bubble. Use this to discuss why it is sometimes better to *show* and not *tell* readers something.
- Now click 'Writing' to display more sentences about Ben's invisible friend. Read them aloud to the children. Ask them to TTYP to decide which parts *show* us that he is funny and which parts *show* us that he is unpredictable. Take feedback and clarify if necessary.

encapsulating what they want to say, sentence by sentence

Write a story 2 (CD)

Purpose: for children to begin the second stage of developing a character

- Tell the children that they are going to use the notes on their own mind map to write some *telling* and some *showing* sentences to describe their character.
- Ask them to read their notes about their new character's appearance.
- Tell them to TTYP to describe what their new character looks like.
- Now ask the children to write their sentences down in their Personal log. Remind them to keep their *telling* sentences quite short and that they must say each sentence aloud to their partner or to themselves before writing them down.
- Walk around, supporting, praising and noting good sentences and discussion.
- Explain that they are now going to write some *showing* sentences. Show **CD (file 8.3)** again and remind them of how you thought about something the character had done that would *show* us that he is funny and something to *show* us that he is unpredictable.
- Ask the children to TTYP to look at their mind map and to share the words they used to describe their character's personality.
- Ask them to think about what their character could do to *show* their partner what they are like. This is a more challenging activity for the children and some may need more support from you as they work.
- Now ask them to write their sentences down. Remind them to keep their examples simple and to share them with their partner before writing them down.
- You will probably need the first part of the next session to allow the children to complete this activity.

Personal log

Each child will need a small amount of lemon juice and a cotton wool bud for this activity.

Purpose: for children to keep a personal reading, writing and thinking log in order to record thoughts and ideas for their own writing

- Remind the children that you still need to reveal the secret message written in invisible ink.
- Hold the paper with the message on it over a heat source until the message begins to appear in a brownish colour.
- Show it to the children and read the message aloud. '*I always know what's going on/ Inside my friend Ben's head./ My special powers should help him out,/ But things go wrong instead…*'
- Ask the children to TTYP to share their thoughts about what clues or ideas the message gives them about Ben's invisible friend. Ask: '*Do you think he is going to be a big help or cause big trouble for Ben?*' Choose two or three sets of partners to give feedback.
- Paste the message into the Class log.
- Explain that they are now going to have a go at writing their own message in invisible ink. Place one small pot of lemon juice and a cotton wool bud per child on each table.
- Now ask them to use the lemon juice to write their own name and then a name they have chosen for Ben's invisible friend in their Personal log.
- During another session, put them near a heat source to make the writing appear and share some of the names the children have chosen with the whole class.

Curriculum link: participate in discussion and consider the opinions of others

Big Question (CD)

Purpose: for children to develop their skills of argument and discussion through a mini enquiry session based on a philosophical question relating to the work of the day

- Display today's Big Question on **CD (file 8.4)**:

  Are names important?

- Follow the process as explained on Day 1.

DAY 9

develop stamina for writing by writing narratives

Write a story 2 (continued)

Purpose: for children to complete the second stage of developing a character

- Tell the children that you are going to give them some time to finish writing their character descriptions. Ask them to TTYP to share what they have written so far. Choose two or three children to share a sentence with the class.
- Now tell them to continue working on their descriptions until they are happy with them.
- Ask them to TTYP to share their completed descriptions. Ask a few children to share their descriptions with the rest of the class.

understand, through being shown, the skills and processes essential to writing

Build a story 3 (CD)

Purpose: for children to see a character grow through three stages of development that will provide a model and stimulus for their own writing

Thinking

- Explain that you have added your descriptions of Ben's invisible friend to the opening for the new story. Display **CD (file 9.1)** to show the last section of the new opening with your description added. Read it aloud to the children.

- Remind the children that, just like the Night Shimmy, you gave Ben's invisible friend some special powers. Navigate to the next slide to show the section from your mind map showing the special powers.
- Ask the children to TTYP to share some ideas about how Ben's invisible friend might use his powers to help Ben or make him laugh. Remind them it is their ideas and opinions you are looking as there are no right answers. Encourage them to be imaginative and willing to explore ideas. Collect feedback.
- Say that you have been thinking about how Ben's invisible friend might use his special powers and you have created a storyboard to show them how you pictured it in your head.
- Navigate to the next slide to show the first story square and talk the children through the action using the caption and picture. Ask them to TTYP to predict what might happen next. Collect feedback.
- Repeat the process for the rest of the story squares, ending on slide 6.

Saying

- Navigate to the next slide to show the image from the first story square again. Explain that Partner 1s are going to provide Partner 2s with a summary of what happens in it.
- Navigate to the next slide to show the second story square again and ask Partner 2s to provide Partner 1s with a summary of what happens in this part of the story.
- Repeat the process with Partners 1s and 2s taking turns to summarise the action in the next two story squares.

Writing

- Remind the children that, in *Chatterbox Ben*, Ben keeps a diary. Display **CD (file 9.2)** to show a diary entry from *Chatterbox Ben*. Ask the children to read it chorally with you.
- Explain that, in the new story, you want Ben to write in his diary about how his invisible friend used his special powers when Miss Johnson was reading the story.
- Navigate to the next slide and use the TOL to talk through how you began to write the diary entry. Navigate to the next slide and point out that, although diaries usually record events, they often include characters' thoughts and feelings. Use the TOL to help you to explain how Ben is feeling here. Navigate through the rest of the slides to model how you built up the new diary entry.

Curriculum link: drama techniques to help pupils identify with and explore characters

Dramatic reconstruction CD PB

Purpose: for children to develop empathetic responses to characters and situations, and to become familiar with a scenario to be used in their writing

- Tell the children that you are going to show them another storyboard about Ben and his invisible friend. Display **CD (file 9.3)** to show the first story square and talk the children through the action. Remind them that Ben's invisible friend has special powers to help Ben, and ask them to TTYP to predict what might happen next. Collect feedback.
- Repeat the process for the second, third and fourth squares.
- Explain that you want the children to TTYP to plan and practise a role-play for each story square. Ask them to turn to p.48 in their Pupils' Book and look at the Dramatic reconstruction activity. Partner 1s will be Ben and Partner 2s will be Ben's invisible friend. Guide them through the prompts and ask them to TTYP to discuss them.
- Allow time for the children to plan and practise their role-plays. Ask the whole group to perform their role-plays at the same time. You might want to freeze the action of any one set of partners at certain points and ask them to explain their actions and feelings at the point you stopped them.

- Walk around as they perform, noting empathetic responses, effective dialogue and good partner work to use as the basis for your feedback after the performances. You may wish to take photographs to paste in the Class log or to display on your Story wall for this Unit.
- Give feedback. Ask the children to TTYP to choose two or three words to describe the feelings of the character they played and to write them in their Personal log.

Class log A

Curriculum link: explain the meaning of new words; increase pupils' vocabulary

Purpose: for children to share the process of keeping a class reading, writing and thinking log to record responses to texts and activities in a variety of forms

- Tell the children to look at p.9 of Anthology 2 Book 3 and to find Ben's second diary entry. Ask them to TTYP to read it together.
- Ask for a choral response to the question: '*Which word has Ben made up himself?*' Clarify if necessary that the word *fantabulous* is not a real word.
- Write the word on the board or a flipchart. Explain that this word has been made up by taking parts of two real words to make one new or made up word. Write these words in different colours on the board or flipchart, e.g. *fantastic* (red), *fabulous* (green). Now re-write the word *fantabulous* using the same two colours to indicate which part of each word Ben has used, e.g. *fant* (red), *abulous* (green).
- Say that this made-up word makes Ben's writing sound more interesting.
- Ask the children to Popcorn ideas about which words have been used to form each of these words: *brunch (breakfast + lunch), smog (smoke + fog), blog (web + log).*
- Tell the children that Lewis Carroll wrote *Alice in Wonderland* and also a famous poem called *Jabberwocky*. Say that he used lots of made-up words in his writing (decide whether you want to explain that these are called *portmanteau words* or just leave it as *made-up words*).
- Read this section of the poem *Jabberwocky* to the children (do not spend time explaining the meaning of the verse, the point is to let the children hear and enjoy the sound of the made up words):

  "And has thou slain the Jabberwock?
  Come to my arms, my beamish boy!
  O frabjous day! Callooh! Callay!"
  He chortled in his joy.

- Explain that Lewis Carroll made up the word *chortle* from the words *chuckle* and *snort* and now it is in the dictionary and used by millions of people!
- Use the coloured pens again to add *chuckle, snort* and *chortle* to the Class log, e.g. *chuckle* (green), *snort* (red), *ch* (green), *ort* (red), *le* (green).
- Ask the children to TTYP to make up a new word from these pairs of words: *skate + bike* (*skike* or *skake*), *pen + brush* (*prush* or *pesh*), *chip + fish* (*chish* or *fip*).
- Now tell them to Popcorn their answers as you run through one pair of words at a time. Write some examples in the Class log.

DAY 10

develop stamina for writing by writing fictional experiences of others

Write a story 3 CD PB

Purpose: for children to complete the third stage of developing a character based on their role-plays

- Remind the children of the diary entry you modelled on the board based on Ben's experiences during the story about Naughty Natalie. You may wish to display **CD (file 9.2)** again to remind them of it. Draw attention to how you used the conjunction *and* to link ideas on slide 4.

- Tell the children that they are going to write Ben's diary entry describing the events in the story squares that they acted out in their role-play.
- Display **CD (file 9.3)** again and ask the children to TTYP to summarise what is happening in each story square as you navigate through them.
- Now ask them to turn to p.49 in their Pupils' Book and look at the Write a story 3 activity. Ask them to read the instructions and choose an adjective to describe what kind of day it has been. Now ask them to TTYP to read the prompts. If necessary, clarify what it means to write in the first person and past tense and write some examples on the board or flipchart, e.g. ***I*** *never* ***thought*** *that…* ***My*** *invisible friend was…* ***I was*** *the only one who could stop the ball.* ***I felt*** *so small in that huge goal.* ***I was*** *scared.*
- Remind the children that their versions of Ben's invisible friend might be different to yours, so they should try to show what their invisible friend is like through its actions and dialogue.
- Remind the children to rehearse what they are going to write by saying it aloud to themselves or their partner before writing it down. Walk around as they talk and write, offering support and praise where appropriate.

Curriculum link: evaluating their writing with the teacher and other pupils; make simple additions, revisions and corrections

Evaluate and edit (CD)

Purpose: *for children to evaluate their own and their partner's work against specific criteria and then discuss how they could improve their work*

- Display **CD (file 10.1)** to show the evaluation points and read them aloud using MT/YT.
- As a model, select an example of work where the writing has met the criteria, and share this with the other children, explaining why it works well.
- Tell the children to take turns to read their partner's writing in pairs and discuss together how well each piece of writing has met the criteria.
- Ask children to discuss at least two changes they could make to improve their work.

proofreading to check for errors in spelling, grammar and punctuation

Proofread

Purpose: *for children to proofread their work and make changes to improve the accuracy of their grammar, punctuation and spelling*

- Now ask the children to proofread their work. If you have noticed that several children need to improve on a particular aspect of spelling, grammar or punctuation, use this as a focus for the Proofread activity. Write an example which includes common errors from the children's writing and use this as a model.
- The children should always be checking for standard use of punctuation and correct spelling of common exception words.
- The following points would be relevant as the particular focus for this Unit:
  - using past tense correctly and consistently
  - using first person correctly and consistently.

Further activities

- Publish: ask the children to use their diary entry to create and type up a new story of their own.
- Allow the children to write, type up and print out a blurb for the new story.

READING AND WRITING NON-FICTION

The Non-fiction week, linked by the theme of communication, looks at formal and informal language by exploring different forms of communication for specific purposes and audiences.

See p.136 for the daily timetable for the Non-fiction week.

Non-fiction

Reading

Children will:

- explore how different forms of communication, e.g. *email, letter, invitation* are appropriate for different situations
- recognise formal and informal language and understand that the level of formality is dependent on the context.

Writing

Key writing purpose to be shared with the children:

To use formal or informal language for different forms of communication, e.g. email, an invitation, role-play.

Writing evaluation to be shared with the children

My email:

- includes key information about the date, time and location of the class fair
- asks for help on the day, donations for prizes and suggestions for ideas.

My invitation:

- includes key information about the date, time and location of the class fair
- is written in informal language, as it is for children.

My role-play:

- includes Mr Hartley's complaints and Mrs Sharp's responses to them
- is presented in formal language, as it is a complaint.

Grammar:

- includes contractions if the writing or the role-play is informal.

See the Planning section of the Software ('Timetables' tab) for a printable version of the Writing purpose and evaluation.

DAY 11

Curriculum link: pupils should be guided to participate in discussion

Think and link

Purpose: for children to develop an interest in communication texts via one of the Big Questions they have explored

- Display the Big Question from Day 3 on the **CD (file 3.4)**:

  Can you say something without talking?
- Ask the children to TTYP to recall some of the ideas they discussed when they looked at the question for the first time and take feedback.
- Point to the second bullet point on the slide and say that in a diary we sometimes write things that we would like to say aloud but can't. Remind them that diaries can be a record of events, memories and experiences.
- Tell the children you have found a funny poem that is written in the style of a diary entry. Display **CD (file 11.1)** to show the poem 'Football Training'. Ask the children to try to picture what is being described as you read it aloud. (You may need to explain that a *reserve* is an extra player in a team and can also be called a *substitute*.)
- Now click 'Highlights'. Say that you will read the highlighted parts and that the children should read the non-highlighted parts chorally (either with or without you).
- Ask the children to TTYP to say which part of the poem they enjoyed most and why. Choose two or three sets of partners to share their choices and reasons. Use MT/YT to re-read some of the lines they pick out.

develop positive attitudes towards writing for different purposes

Private writing

Purpose: for children to develop their understanding of the purpose of diaries

- Explain that diaries can be used to remind us of things we need to do. Display **CD (file 11.2)** to show a page from a diary. Read it aloud to the children.
- Say that diaries can also be used to record our personal thoughts and feelings about things that haven't happened yet. Navigate to the next slide to show another diary entry. Read it aloud and then ask the children to TTYP to share ideas about why the writer might have written her feelings down.
- Remind the children that in the poem 'Football Training', the boy or girl was using his or her diary to write about things that had already happened.
- Navigate to the next slide to show another diary entry and read it out aloud. Point out the use of past tense in this entry.
- Ask the children to TTYP to share ideas about who a diary is written for: '*Who is the reader going to be?*' Choose two sets of partners to feed back and use their ideas to guide the discussion around the audience and purpose of diaries.
- Tell them that this is *private writing* written from one person's point of view for that person to read themselves.

making inferences on the basis of what is being said

Say it

Purpose: for children to develop their ability to adopt a role and use talk to express feelings

- Ask the children to turn to pp.50–51 in their Pupils' Book and look at the Say it activity. Explain that this is an entry from Miss Dixon's diary. Tell them that Miss Dixon is a teacher from an imaginary school called Denton Dale Primary.
- Read the diary entry aloud and then ask the children to join in with you to read it again chorally. Check that they understand all the vocabulary used in the entry. Guide them to use the prompts as they TTYP to talk about how they think Miss Dixon might be feeling about the class fair.
- Ask a few sets of partners to share their ideas with the rest of the group.

Curriculum link: develop stamina for writing by writing for different purposes

Personal log

Purpose: for children to keep a personal reading, writing and thinking log to record thoughts and ideas for their own writing

- Tell the children that they are now in role as a pupil in Miss Dixon's class. Explain that: '*Each class has been asked to help to raise money for new outdoor play equipment for Denton Dale School. Miss Dixon has decided that Class 2D will organise a class fair with lots of stalls, games and prizes. It will be held in the school hall and will be open in the afternoon for other classes to visit and after school for parents and carers to visit.*'
- Ask them to TTYP in role as pupils at the school, to discuss how they are feeling about the class fair. Choose two sets of partners to share their ideas and model how to write them as diary entries on the board or a flipchart, starting with *Dear Diary…* Remind the children that this will be a child's personal point of view so they should use the personal pronoun 'I'.
- Explain that they are going to write a diary entry in their Personal log in role as a pupil in Miss Dixon's class, showing their thoughts and feelings about the class fair.
- Remind them to rehearse their opening sentence before writing it down.

DAY 12

increase pupils' vocabulary

Communication language

Purpose: for children to increase their awareness of specific vocabulary

communicate private public

- Tell the children that a diary is one way we can *communicate* with ourselves and is a form of *private* writing. Explain that there are lots of times when we need to communicate with other people and this could be called *public* writing.
- Display **CD (file 12.1)** to show some words. Read each word, then click 'Definition' show its definition. Use MT/YT to read the word again and its definition. Repeat for each word.
- Tell the children that you will be using these words a lot during the week and they should listen out for them and try to use them in their own talk and writing.
- Print out the words and definitions from **CD (file 12.2)** and display them on your Communication wall for this Unit.

think aloud as they collect ideas

Communication 1

Purpose: for children to develop their awareness of different forms of communication

- Tell the children that one of the reminders that Miss Dixon wrote down in her diary was to choose a date for the class fair. Ask them to TTYP to try to recall what she had to check before choosing a date (*when the school hall is free*). Ask them to give their answers chorally, and clarify if necessary.
- Now explain that, to find out when the hall is free, Miss Dixon needs to write to everyone who works at Denton Dale Primary School. Ask them which word they have learnt that means to share information (*communicate*). Clarify if necessary and point to the word on the Communication wall.
- Say that Miss Dixon decided that an email would be the easiest and quickest way to communicate with everyone.
- You are now in the role of the writer. Display **CD (file 12.3)** to show Miss Dixon's mail box. Click on 'TOL' to show the think bubbles. Use them and your own ideas to talk about what you want to say in your email and how you will begin.
- Type in the beginning of your email in the editable text box.

- Click 'TOL' again and use the next think bubble to talk about what you need to write next. Type the sentence in the editable text box.
- Repeat for the final TOL.
- Use MT/YT to read the sentences and encourage the children to make suggestions to improve them. Model how you edit the sentences until you and the children are happy with them.
- Ask the children to read the whole email aloud chorally to check it makes sense.

Curriculum link: develop stamina for writing by writing for different purposes

Write 1

Purpose: for children to develop their ability to write with clarity when communicating with others

- Before the lesson, print out a copy of the email template from **CD (file 12.4)** for each child. Give each child a copy of the template from **CD (file 12.4)**. Tell them that Miss Dixon has now chosen a date for the class fair and is sending another email to all the staff to let them know. She also wants to ask for help, suggestions or donations to make sure the fair is successful.
- Tell the children to turn to p.52 in their Pupils' Book and look at the Write 1 activity. Explain that they are going to write Miss Dixon's email for her and they must think carefully about what they need to communicate. Say that they need to make sure the information is clear so that others understand their message.
- Ask the children to TTYP to read the diary notes and to use them to help them to decide what to write. Allow plenty of time for discussion and remind them to say their opening sentence to their partner before writing it down. Make sure they know that they can cross out, add to and edit their writing as they would be able to if they were typing an email.
- When the children have completed their emails, ask them to TTYP to share what they have written and to tell each other one thing they liked about the other's email and one thing that could make it even better.
- Choose two or three children to read out their emails to the class. The emails can be pasted into their Personal log. A few could be copied for the Communication wall or the Class log.

Class log

Purpose: for children to share the process of keeping a class reading, writing and thinking log to record responses to texts and activities in a variety of forms

- Tell the children that you are going to start a *Communication* section in the Class log. Write *Communication* as a heading at the top of the page.
- Remind the children that Miss Dixon communicated by email with other members of staff. Ask the children to TTYP to think of other ways humans communicate with each other, e.g. *letter, text message, telephone.*
- Ask them to Popcorn their answers. Write answers underneath the heading in the Class log.
- Remind the children of less obvious ways of communicating, e.g. facial expressions, body language, sign language, braille.
- You could find examples of a couple of simple Makaton or British Sign Language symbols to teach the children and then paste them into the Class log.

DAY 13

Teamwork 1

Purpose: for children to develop their understanding of different kinds of communication and its importance in teamwork

Curriculum link: listening to, discussing and expressing views about a wide range of non-fiction; consider the opinions of others

- Before the lesson, print a copy of 'Rules for Top Teamwork!' from **CD (file 13.2)** for each child or set of partners and a copy for yourself.
- Tell the children that you have a record of how Class 2D communicated with each other to plan the fair. Display **CD (file 13.1)** and navigate through the slides, reading the speech bubbles aloud and talking through the pictures.
- Ask the children to TTYP to talk about the different ways that Class 2D communicated with each other, e.g. talking, making notes, using the Communication Board. Collect feedback and write their answers on the board or a flipchart.
- Say that you really liked Miss Dixon's idea of creating a Communication Board to record their ideas, plan tasks and share roles. Ask the children to TTYP to say why they think this is a good way to communicate. Choose two or three sets of partners to share their answers.
- Remind them that Miss Dixon divided the class into small teams. Now tell them to TTYP to think of two reasons why team members need to communicate effectively with each other. Choose two sets of partners to feed back.
- Say that working in small teams was one of the ways that Class 2D made their fair a success. Give each child or set of partners a copy of 'Rules for Top Teamwork!' from **CD (file 13.2).**
- Explain that Partner 1s should read the rules and Partner 2s should read the tips. Ask them to talk about which rule and which tip they consider to be the most important or useful. Choose two or three sets of partners to share their ideas with the whole class and encourage them to give reasons for their answers.

Teamwork 2

Purpose: for children to develop their communication skills to work effectively as a team

listening to, discussing and expressing views about a wide range of non-fiction; consider the opinions of others

- Before the lesson, print off copies of each of the Team Challenge templates from **CD (files 13.4a–e)**. Each group will need two copies of the same template. (It doesn't matter if two groups have the same template.)
- Tell the children that you are going to be in role as Miss Dixon and that they are going to be in role as the children in Class 2D.
- Display **CD (file 13.3)** to show your teamwork challenge. Explain that this is an example of the template that each group will be given. They are going to work in teams of four to organise one stall or activity for Class 2D's fair.
- Explain how you want each team to communicate with each other and work together to check the team's talents, to list and allocate tasks, to make lists of equipment, etc.
- Organise the class into groups of four by joining two sets of partners together. Remind them that one of the rules in the 'Rules for Top Teamwork!' text was to choose a leader. Ask them to TTYP to recall what the tip was about choosing a leader.
- Give each team two copies of one of the templates from printable **CD (files 13.4a–e)**. Each version has a different stall or activity circled to show what the team has to plan and organise. Explain that the group leader must make sure that the team discusses and records each part of the process, using the headings as a guide.

- Walk around as the children work. Have the 'Rules for Top Teamwork!' text with you and intervene if the team is struggling to follow any of the rules, e.g. *Give everyone a chance to share their ideas.*
- Note examples of top teamwork and good communication to refer to when you feed back on how well they worked together. Remember that the point of the activity is to develop their communication and teamwork skills, not to make the most spectacular contribution to the fair!

Curriculum link: read aloud what they have written with appropriate intonation to make the meaning clear

Teamwork 3 (CD)

Purpose: for children to develop their team presentation skills to communicate effectively to a large group

- Still in role as Miss Dixon, say that you are keen to hear what each team is going to contribute to the fair. Explain that you would like them to present their plans to the rest of the group. Give them some time to decide how to present them.
- Display **CD (file 13.5)** and say that you want them to take turns to explain one of the points listed on the first slide. Use MT/YT to read each point.
- Navigate to the next slide to show some prompts to remind them how to communicate well. Use MT/YT to read each prompt.
- Navigate back to the first slide and leave the points on display to help the children as they plan and prepare their presentations.
- When they have had some time to prepare, allow each team to give a short presentation, either to the whole class or to two or three groups on a rotation basis.

increase pupils' vocabulary; writing down new vocabulary

Personal log

Purpose: for children to keep a personal reading, writing and thinking log to record thoughts and ideas for their own writing

- Remind the children that many people use mobile phones to communicate with each other, and that they can be used to communicate by speaking or writing (texting).
- Explain that, because some words can take a long time to type on a mobile phone, people invented ways of shortening words when sending text messages.
- Explain that people shortened words long before mobile phones and text messages were invented. Write these common abbreviations on the board or a flipchart and ask the children to TTYP to discuss what each abbreviation is short for. Ask them to Popcorn their answers.

  Dr PC Mr TV PE

- Clarify where necessary and write the full word/s next to the abbreviation. (The abbreviation PC can stand for *police constable* or *personal computer*.)
- Now ask the children to write the abbreviations and words in full in their Personal log.

DAY 14

Zoom in on style (CD)

Purpose: for children to develop their awareness of writing styles and the audience or reader

- Tell the children that writing looks and sounds different depending on how well we know the person we are writing to and what we want to communicate to them.
- Explain that if we write or communicate to a friend, we might write in a chatty *informal* style. If we are writing to someone we don't know very well or a person much older than ourselves, we might write in a more serious *formal* style.
- Tell the children that styles of writing are a bit like the style of clothes we choose to wear! If we are going to a wedding or an important event, we might have to wear formal clothes.

- Display **CD (file 14.1)** to show the word *Formal* and a picture. Say that if we are messing about with our friends at the park, we wear our casual, informal clothes. Click on 'Next' to show the word *Informal* and a picture.
- Ask the children to stand up to show you a mini-mime for *formal*. Now ask them to change their mini-mime to show you *informal*.
- Click 'Next' again to show a piece of text matched to the formal picture. Read it aloud to the children, exaggerating the formality of the tone.
- Repeat the process for the informal picture, exaggerating the casualness of the tone.
- Tell the children that you are going to take away the pictures. Click 'Hide' to remove the pictures. Ask the children to TTYP to share ideas about how we can tell that one piece of writing is formal and one is informal.
- Choose two or three sets of partners to share their answers. Paraphrase and clarify as necessary, guiding them to see the difference in some of the vocabulary and use of contractions and colloquialisms.

Curriculum link: think aloud as they collect ideas; discussing and expressing views about a wide range of non-fiction

Communication 2 (CD)

Purpose: for children to explore different forms of invitations as a model for their own writing

- Tell the children that, as well as letters and emails, another way of communicating with other people is by sending them an invitation. Ask them to Popcorn answers to the question: '*What kind of events do we send or receive invitations for?*' Write answers on the board or a flipchart.
- Explain that invitations can be created in lots of different ways. Display **CD (file 14.2)** and read the first invitation to the children.
- Now ask the children to read the invitation chorally with you.
- Click 'TOL' and use the think bubbles to help you to talk through the language and format of the example.
- Ask the children to TTYP to share ideas about whether they think the invitation would be sent to an adult or a child. Collect feedback and encourage them to explain their answers.
- Remind the children that invitations can look and sound very different. Navigate to the next slide to show another style of invitation. Read it aloud to the children.
- Now ask the children to read the invitation chorally with you.
- Click 'TOL' and use the think bubbles to help you to talk through the similarities and differences in the language and format.

develop stamina for writing by writing for different purposes

Write 2 (CD) PB

Purpose: for children to use information to create an informal invitation for a specific audience

- Before the lesson, print a copy of the invitation template on **CD (file 14.4)** for each child. You might also find it useful to print a copy of slide 1 of **CD (file 14.3)** for you to refer to later.
- Explain that they are going to help you to write an invitation to a new children's section at a local museum featuring a 3D, interactive dinosaur gallery! Tell them that, as the invitation is aimed at children, they should use informal language to write it.
- Display **CD (file 14.3)** to show an information box. Explain that this will help you to give the correct information to people about the event and to persuade them to visit the new gallery.
- Navigate to the next slide to show an invitation template. Use the TOLs and your own ideas as you model writing the invitation in the editable text boxes. Draw the children into the writing process.

- When you have filled in all of the boxes, ask the children to read it through chorally with you. Ask them to TTYP to say what they thought was the most important and the least important part of the invitation. Give them some forced alternatives, e.g. *'Was it the time and place of the opening? Was it the information about the celebrity?'* Collect feedback and encourage them to give reasons for their choices.
- Now tell the children to turn to p.53 in their Pupils' Book and look at the Write 2 activity. Explain that they are going to create an invitation for the class fair. Ask them to TTYP to read the information in the table and the prompts.
- Give each child a copy of the invitation template from **CD (file 14.4)** and remind them to think about the audience and purpose. Explain that, as the style is *informal* and *chatty*, they can use contracted words like *don't* (Don't miss it!) or *it'll* (It'll be great!)
- Remind them to tell their partner what they are going to write before they create their own invitation. Tell them to use the grid and the prompts in their Pupils' Book and the words and phrases in the bank to help them.
- Monitor the children as they write.

Curriculum link: proofreading to check for errors in spelling, grammar and punctuation

Proofread

Purpose: for children to proofread their work and make changes to improve the accuracy of their grammar, punctuation and spelling

- Now ask the children to proofread their work. If you have noticed that several children need to improve on a particular aspect of spelling, grammar or punctuation, use this as a focus for the Proofread activity. Write an example which includes common errors from the children's writing and use this as a model.
- Children should always be checking for standard use of punctuation and correct spelling of common exception words.
- The following point would be relevant as the particular focus for this Unit:
  - checking that apostrophes are used correctly in contractions.

discussing and expressing views about a wide range of non-fiction

Class log

You will need to have collected a few examples of different kinds of invitations, including formal, informal and at least one with the abbreviation RSVP.

Purpose: for children to share the process of keeping a class reading, writing and thinking log to record responses to texts and activities in a variety of forms

- Show the children some examples of different invitations that you have collected. Read out some of the wording on them and ask the children to identify different features, e.g. formal/polite or informal/chatty, audience and purpose.
- Point out the abbreviation RSVP on one of the invitations and then write it in large letters in the Class log. Explain that this is short for a French phrase that means *please reply*. Tell them the phrase is *répondez s'il vous plaît* and then write it in the Class log. Have fun using MT/YT and TTYP to say the phrase in French.
- Ask the children to TTYP to say why it is important to reply to invitations if they ask you to. Choose two or three sets of partners to feed back and record some of their responses in the Class log.

DAY 15

Curriculum link: read accurately and fluently; participate in discussion and consider the opinions of others

Communication 3

Purpose: for children to develop their awareness of writing for a specific purpose and audience

- Tell the children that Miss Dixon and the head teacher decided to reward Class 2D for working so hard by taking them to a local theme park called Thrill City.
- Explain that things didn't work out as well as they had expected. Display **CD (file 15.1)** and navigate through the slides to show photographs from the theme park. Ask the children to TTYP to discuss what the pictures communicate to us about the theme park experience. Collect feedback.
- Say that one of the children emailed her friend to tell her about the trip and the head teacher wrote a letter of complaint to the manager of Thrill City.
- Ask the children to look at p.12 of Anthology 2 Book 3 and follow the text as you read the email that one of the children sent to her friend telling her about the trip. Ask the children to TTYP to take turns to read sections of the email.
- Now ask them to turn to p.13 in the Anthology to look at the letter. Read the text aloud.
- Now ask the children to TTYP to say which text they would describe as chatty and informal and which one as serious and formal. Ask them to share ideas and tell each other what clues they found to help them.
- Choose two sets of partners to feed back. Clarify if necessary and encourage the children to explain their decision in their own words. The point of this activity is to encourage the children to hear the differences in style rather than be technically proficient at identifying the differences.

Year 2 Grammar learning how to use punctuation correctly, including apostrophes for contracted forms

Grammar: apostrophes for contractions

Purpose: for children to develop their awareness of apostrophes to mark contractions, and their understanding of how contracted forms of words can indicate informality in written texts

- Remind the children of the email and the letter that they read in the previous activity. Say that one of the differences in the two texts is the way words like *could not* and *do not* are written.
- Display **CD (file 15.2)** to show a section from the formal letter. Click 'Highlights' to highlight words in the text. Use MT/YT to say the sentences and emphasise the highlighted words.
- Navigate to the next slide to show a section from the informal email. Click 'Highlights' to highlight the contracted forms of the same words. Use MT/YT to say the sentences and emphasise the highlighted words.
- Explain that we usually use the shortened (contracted) words when we are talking to a friend and when we write a chatty letter or email to someone we know.
- Remind the children that the apostrophe takes the place of the missing letters. Navigate to the next slide to show a selection of words e.g. *it is, did not, is not, I am, was not*. Click 'Contraction' to show the contracted form, e.g. *it's, didn't, isn't, I'm, wasn't*.
- Now ask the children to turn to p.54 in their Pupils' Book and look at the Grammar: apostrophes for contractions activity. Tell them to TTYP to read the sentences and decide which ones they would use in a formal piece of writing and which ones they would use in an informal chat with a friend.

Homework Book p.19 provides further practice on apostrophes for contractions.

Curriculum link: increase pupils' vocabulary; draw on and use new vocabulary

Formal and informal vocabulary (CD)

Purpose: for children to develop their awareness of formal and informal language

- Say that another difference between the formal letter and informal email is the words the writers have chosen.
- Display **CD file (15.3)**. Click 'Highlights' to highlight words in the text. Use MT/YT to say the sentences and emphasise the highlighted words.
- Explain that there are different words which have the same meaning in the informal email. Navigate to the next slide to show another section from the email and ask the children to TTYP to spot the words.
- Choose two sets of partners to share their answers and clarify if necessary. Remind them that these are called *synonyms*.
- Click 'Highlights' to highlight these words in the text.
- Now say that you want them to TTYP to think of synonymous words or phrases for this phrase from one of the texts: *broke down*.
- Ask them to Popcorn their answers. Repeat the process with some or all of these words from the texts: *terrified, extremely, shoved.*

drama techniques to help pupils identify with and explore characters

Write 3 A PB

Purpose: for children to use role-play to explore ways of communicating effectively using speech and body language

- Ask the children to turn to p.13 in Anthology 2 Book 3 and look at the formal complaint letter again. Read the letter aloud to the children.
- Explain that the manager of Thrill City was rather upset to receive the letter and invited the head teacher to a meeting to discuss the complaints.
- Now ask them to turn to p.54 of their Pupils' Book and look at the Write 3 activity. Explain that they are going to create a role-play of the meeting between the head teacher and the manager of Thrill City. Say that Partner 1s are going to be the head teacher, Mr Hartley, and Partner 2s are going to be the manager of Thrill City, Mrs Sharp. Remind the children that, as this is a formal situation, you would expect them to use formal language.
- Guide them through the prompts that will help them to plan and practise their role-play of the meeting. Emphasise the different ways they can communicate their feelings to each other when in role.
- Allow plenty of time for the children to plan and practise their role-plays and then ask them to perform them. Walk around, noting good examples of body stance, facial expression, vocabulary, tone, etc. to feed back on at the end of the activity.
- Choose two or three sets of partners to perform their role-plays again to the class and ask the rest of the class to TTYP to share what they thought was the most effective part of the role-plays and why.

Curriculum link: evaluating with the teacher and other pupils

Evaluate (CD)

Purpose: for children to evaluate their partner's performance against specific criteria and think about how it could have been improved

- Display **CD (file 15.4)** to show the evaluation prompts and read them aloud using MT/YT.
- As a model, select an example of work where the children achieved the objective, and explain to the children why it worked well.
- Tell the children to think back to their partner's performance and discuss with them how well they met the criteria and how it could have been improved further.
- Tell them to TTYP to discuss what they felt about the experience and the role they took on.
- Now ask them to write a few single words or a short sentence to describe the experience in their Personal log.

Fiction: Fantasy worlds
Non-fiction – Information texts

Timetable

WEEK 1 Reading fiction Fantasy worlds *Chocolate Planet*

Day 1	Day 2	Day 3	Day 4	Day 5
The story store 🖶	Secret story 1	Word power 🖶	Moods and feelings	Step into the setting
Show me the story	Secret story 2	Read the story	Fantasy settings	Soundscape 🖶
Think and link	Secret story 3	Find it or prove it	What if not…?	Grammar: verb tenses
Personal log	Class log 🖶	Personal log	Class log	Personal log
Big Question	Big Question	Big Question	Big Question	Big Question

WEEK 2 Writing fiction Fantasy worlds *Chocolate Planet*

Day 6	Day 7	Day 8	Day 9	Day 10
Multi-syllabic words	What if not…?	Build a story 2	Build a story 3	Write a story 3 🖶
Story makers	Build a story 1	Grammar: tenses in texts	Story talk	Evaluate and edit
Build a setting 🖶	Write a story 1 🖶	Write a story 2	Dramatic reconstruction	Proofread
Personal log	Class log	Personal log		
Big Question	Big Question	Big Question		

WEEK 3 Reading and writing non-fiction Information texts

Day 11	Day 12	Day 13	Day 14	Day 15
Think and link	Information words 🖶	Glossaries	Information 3	Presentations 1
Alphabetical texts	Information 1	Information 2	Write 3	Presentations 2 🖶
Presenting information	Write 1 🖶	Write 2 🖶	Personal log	Proofread
Class log	Personal log	Class log		Exhibition
				Evaluate

🖶: shows that a file should be printed out from the Software

Overview of the Unit

This Unit use a picture book, *G.E.M.* by Jane Clarke and Garry Parsons and a contemporary, humorous fantasy adventure story, *Chocolate Planet* by Jon Blake, to explore settings and ideas used in fantasy stories.

The Non-fiction week, linked by the theme of chocolate, looks at information texts. For more information about the Non-fiction week and the Non-fiction writing evaluation criteria, see p.185.

Where appropriate, the children will be encouraged to develop an awareness of audience and purpose in relation to the fiction and non-fiction texts they are reading and writing.

Teacher modelling is provided in the teaching notes and the Software, supporting the children's writing at every stage in the Fiction and Non-fiction weeks.

The Homework Book provides a homework activity related to the content of this Unit for each of the three weeks.

Fiction

Reading

Children will:

- connect and explore the central themes of envy and courage in *Chocolate Planet* by drawing links between texts
- explore features of different fantasy settings
- use drama to explore the motivations behind characters' actions and behaviour.

Writing

Key writing purpose to be shared with the children:

To write a fantasy story set in space.

Writing evaluation to be shared with the children

My fantasy story:

- includes a quest, a problem and a resolution
- includes sights, smells, tastes, sounds or feelings to create atmosphere
- shows a problem the characters face and how they overcome it.

Grammar:

- includes correct use of past or present tense.

See the Planning section of the Software ('Timetables' tab) for a printable version of the Writing purpose and evaluation.

Resources

PB Pupils' Book, pp.55–64
A Anthology 2 Book 3, pp.14–24
CD CD on interactive whiteboard, Unit 6
GB Grammar Bank on CD
HB Homework Book, pp.20–23

READING FICTION

DAY 1

Curriculum link: participate in discussion about books, becoming familiar with a wide range of books

The story store

Purpose: for children to hear and enjoy a picture book story that introduces themes to be explored in the Anthology text

- Before the lesson, print out a copy of the TOL (Think out loud) points from **CD (file 1.2)**. In addition to this, make yourself a simple badge with a star to use as a Story star.
- Show the children your Story star. Explain that this means that they are going to hear a wonderful story.
- Use the **CD (file 1.1)** to show the front cover of *G.E.M.* by Jane Clarke and Garry Parsons.
- Ask the children to read the title and look at the picture and then TTYP (Turn to your partner) to share what they think the story might be about. Collect feedback and show how much you value their ideas.
- Navigate through the pages by clicking on the forward arrow or the corners of the pages. Read aloud to the children with great enthusiasm and obvious pleasure. Use TTYP to explore a few aspects of the story as they arise, emphasising the themes of envy, jealousy, desires and the fantasy world setting.
- Tell the children that they are now going to help you to re-read the story.
- Navigate back to the beginning of the story. Use MT/YT (My turn/Your turn) to re-read the first page.
- As you re-read the story with the children, use the TOL points you printed from **CD (file 1.2)** and your own ideas and TTYP to explore the connections between the words and the pictures. Focus on the expressions on characters' faces and significant detail in the pictures. Draw attention to the effect of changes in font size and type on relevant pages.

drama techniques to help pupils identify with and explore characters

Show me the story

Purpose: for children to show their understanding of the story through drama

- Explain to the children that you are going to read some pages from *G.E.M.* but they will not be able to see the pictures because you are not going to display the story on the board. You want them to work with their partners to 'be' the pictures. They can use facial expressions and their bodies to help them.
- Look at *G.E.M.* on **CD (file 1.1)**. Navigate to p.3 ("Gark's birthday party begins..."). Read the text at the bottom of the page, then model how you want the children to create a dramatic mini-mime to illustrate that page.
- Ask them to stand up as you read p.6 ("Heel!" Royd ordered...) aloud with great enthusiasm and appropriate intonation. Pause to allow them to show you the story through their mini-mimes.
- Repeat for p.9 ('At 3 pips past 33…'), p.13 (SPOOOSH! Royd's G.E.M. grew...') and p.23 ("Great party!"), reminding the children they need to try to mime both actions and feelings.

Curriculum link: drawing on what they already know

Think and link (CD)

Purpose: for children to make connections between this story and other stories and their own experiences

- Display **CD (file 1.1)** to show the whole story again and use MT/YT to re-read the story with the children.
- Pause on p.4 ('SPOOOSH! Royd was so jealous...') to discuss this TOL point with the children: '*Can you think of any other stories where a character gets jealous? I remember the stepsisters getting jealous of Cinderella and the wicked stepmother was jealous of Snow White.*'
- Use TOL and TTYP to encourage the children to think about other stories and their own experiences that could be linked to the picture book text.
- Continue to read the story using MT/YT and repeat the process for the following pages: p.8 ("Wow!"): '*Have you ever felt jealous of someone?*' p.20 ("Things aren't always fair,"): '*Have you ever felt that something wasn't fair?*' p.25 ("I'd rather have someone..."): '*What would you prefer to have: lots of toys to play with or a good friend to play with?*'

drawing on what they already know

Personal log

Purpose: for children to keep a personal reading, writing and thinking log in order to record thoughts and ideas for their own writing

- Tell the children that, just like Royd, you felt jealous of a friend because you wished you had something they had. Use this TOL point and your own ideas to share something you wished you could have, and why, e.g. '*When I was younger I really wanted a bike the same as my friend's. Theirs was really shiny and mine was a rusty, old bike.*'
- Explain that you are going to write down a sentence using the opening *I really wish I could have...*
- Say your first sentence using MT/YT before writing it on the board or a flipchart. Ask the children to TTYP to share one or two things they wish they could have and why. Take feedback and say their sentences back to them using the opening '*I really wish I could have...*' Write a couple of their sentences on the board or flipchart.
- Now ask them to write their sentences in their Personal log. Remind them to say their sentences aloud to their partners before writing them down.

participate in discussion and consider the opinions of others

Big Question (CD)

Purpose: for children to develop their skills of argument and discussion through a mini enquiry session based on a philosophical question relating to the work of the day

- Display today's Big Question on **CD (file 1.3)**:

  Is wanting something the same as needing something?

- Ask the children to TTYP to talk about this question. Collect feedback and write some responses on the board.
- Click 'Prompts' to show some statements that may help to encourage discussion.

DAY 2

making inferences, answering and asking questions, predicting

Secret story 1 (CD)

Purpose: for children to be motivated to 'unlock the secrets' of a new story. For children to make connections between the new story, the picture book story they read and other fantasy stories they know well

- Tell the children that it is time for a Secret story. Wear or point to your Story star. Explain that you have found some clues about a Secret story and you need their help to find out more. Convey your own eagerness and enthusiasm and draw them into your excitement.

- Display **CD (file 2.1)** to show the Secret story box. TOL as you show your curiosity and interest about the contents of the box.
- Click 'Secret'. One picture, word or phrase will emerge from the box. Click 'TOL' to show a think bubble. Use this and your own ideas and TTYP to speculate about the significance of the contents.
- Navigate through the slides, revealing a different secret on each slide, until the box closes. Make sure you do not reveal the title, any surprises or the ending of the story at this stage!

Curriculum link: making inferences, answering and asking questions, predicting

Secret story 2 (CD)

Purpose: for children to hear more about the new story, to make links with their own experiences and to make predictions. For the children to become more familiar with the story so far before they hear the full version

- Tell the children that there was one more item right at the bottom of the Secret story box. Display **CD (file 2.2)**. Don't navigate past the first slide at this stage. Say that you are really excited about what might be written on the scroll as it could tell us more about the Secret story.
- Navigate to the next slide to show the unrolled scroll and then click 'Audio' to hear the contents read out by a narrator.
- Navigate to the next slide and click 'Audio' to hear the narrator's first section again. Ask the children to TTYP to discuss the question the narrator poses and then take feedback. Repeat the process for the next two sections.
- Navigate to the penultimate slide and click 'Audio' to hear the narrator's final message.
- Navigate to the final slide to show the scroll closing.

checking the text makes sense as they read, making inferences, discussing sequence of events

Secret story 3 (A) (teacher only) (PB)

Purpose: for children to hear and enjoy the full version of the story for the first time

- Tell the children that they are now going to hear the whole story for the very first time. TOL about which parts you can't wait to hear about.
- Ask the children to TTYP to share what they are looking forward to in the story.
- Say that you need to switch your Storyteller voice on. Make it a special moment, as if you are getting ready for a performance.
- Now turn to Anthology 2 Book 3 p.14 and read the full story to the children with great enjoyment, enthusiasm and appropriate intonation.
- At the end of the story, ask the children to look at the Secret story 3 activity on p.55 in their Pupils' Book and to TTYP to read and discuss the questions. Encourage the children to give their own ideas and opinions, as well as thinking about the events in the story. Remind them there are no right answers to these questions. Take feedback from a few sets of partners.

participate in discussion and consider the opinions of others

Class log (CD)

Purpose: for children to share the process of keeping a class reading, writing and thinking log to record responses to texts and activities in a variety of forms

- Tell the children that today they are going to begin the section of their Class log for *Fantasy worlds*. Show them the new title page with just the heading on it.
- Explain that you want their help to choose a great book cover. Display **CD (file 2.3)** to show a cover design for *Chocolate Planet*. TOL about the features of the design, e.g. *illustration, font style, layout, colour.*

- Repeat the process for the next two slides and draw the children into your TOL. Ask them to TTYP to share opinions and notice differences between the designs.
- Now ask the children to TTYP to discuss which design they would choose if they were the publishers of the book, and why.
- Request feedback, then ask the children to vote for their favourite cover. Before the next lesson, print their chosen cover from **CD (file 2.4)** and paste it onto the *Fantasy worlds* title page in the Class log.
- Tell the children that they can offer things to be pasted into the Class log, e.g. pictures of the moondog or maps of Planet Um or Wob, or chocolate bar wrappers. Make sure you bring in anything that could be relevant as well.

Curriculum link: participate in discussion and consider the opinions of others

Big Question

Purpose: *for children to develop their skills of argument and discussion through a mini enquiry session based on a philosophical question relating to the work of the day*

- Display today's Big Question on **CD (file 2.5)**:

  Do you have to face danger to be scared?

- Follow the process as explained on Day 1.

DAY 3

discussing their favourite words and phrases, new vocabulary

Word power

Purpose: *for children to learn the meaning of specific vocabulary used in the story and increase their knowledge of synonyms*

aroma *cowered* *scrumptious* *menacing*

- Tell the children that there were some words in the story they heard yesterday that the writer of the story had chosen because they were powerful.
- Display the Power words and their definitions on **CD (file 3.1)**. Look at the words and their definitions with the children and then use MT/YT as you read the sentences to them.
- Explain that the writer could have chosen different words that mean the same thing. Navigate to the next screen to show the first sentence and a list of synonyms.
- Drag and drop different synonyms into the sentence and use MT/YT to read it aloud after each substitution.
- Ask the children to TTYP to share which word they think worked best.
- Navigate through the screens and repeat the process for the other sentences.
- These words and synonyms can be printed from **CD (file 3.2)** to display on your Story wall for this Unit. Let the children hear you using these words throughout the day in an exaggerated fashion, e.g. '*There is the most* scrumptious *aroma coming from the school kitchen today!*'
- Use MT/YT to model how you could *show* the word *aroma*, e.g. by pretending to smell a flower that you are holding in your hand.
- Say to the children: '*Show me* scrumptious! *Show me* cowering! *Show me* menacing!' You may need to suggest some ideas if they are struggling.
- Praise them if they use one of the words in their conversation.

read accurately and fluently; discussing and expressing views about stories

Read the story

Purpose: *for children to gain a deeper understanding of the story and to see the text for the first time*

- Ask the children to turn to p.14 in Anthology 2 Book 3 and follow the story as you re-read it aloud with great enthusiasm. Put special emphasis on the Power words (in bold).

- Now ask the children to read alternate sections of the story with their partners, using lots of expression. Explain that you will be listening in and hoping to hear some star storytellers.
- Give each set of partners two sticky notes. Tell them to TTYP to choose their favourite part of the story and their favourite character. Ask them to write their responses on their sticky notes and come up to the front to stick them in the Class log. Pick out a few sticky notes and ask the children to explain their choices.

Curriculum link: answering questions; making inferences on the basis of what is being said and done

Find it or prove it CD PB A

Purpose: for children to develop their literal and inferential thinking skills

- Tell the children that the words on the page in a story tell us lots of things, but don't always tell us everything. We often need to search for *clues* that might tell us a bit more about what characters are thinking, feeling or doing, or even what the setting is like. Say that we sometimes have to use our imagination to find out more information.
- Display **CD (file 3.3)** to show a *find it* question. Click 'Find it' and use the think bubble to model how you find the part of the text that gives the answer.
- Navigate to the next slide to show a *prove it* question. Remind them that this means the answer is trickier. Click 'Prove it' and use the think bubble to model how you might answer the question. Click 'Prove it' again to show another think bubble and an example from the text to support it.
- Repeat the process by clicking 'Prove it' once more.
- Now ask the children to turn to p.56 in their Pupils' Book and look at the Find it or prove it activity. Make sure they refer to Anthology 2 Book 3 pp.14–21 to find the answers. Say that, for each question, they need to decide whether it is a *find it* or a *prove it* question.
- Remind them that you are looking for their own opinions, supported by evidence from the text, not something they have found in the artwork.
- Ask the children to TTYP to read and talk about the first question. Choose two or three partners to feed back and repeat the process for each question.

listening to, discussing and expressing views; consider the opinions of others

Personal log CD

Purpose: for children to keep a personal reading, writing and thinking log in order to record thoughts and ideas for their own writing

- Remind the children that books usually have a *blurb* on the back cover and ask them to TTYP to recall what its purpose is. Choose two set of partners to feed back, and clarify if necessary.
- Select a few books from different genres and read out some examples of blurbs. Explain that you want them to choose a blurb for the back cover of *Chocolate Planet.*
- Display **CD (file 3.4)** to show an example of a blurb. Read the blurb aloud to the children. Click on 'TOL' and use the think bubbles and your own ideas to talk about what you like about the blurb.
- Ask the children to TTYP to discuss what they like about the blurb. Remind them that you are looking for their opinions as there are no right answers. Take feedback from two or three sets of partners.
- Navigate to the next slide and repeat the process.
- Navigate to the next slide and read the final blurb to the children. This time, ask them to TTYP to discuss what they like about the blurb before you add your ideas. Take feedback and add some of your own thoughts if necessary.
- Ask the children to TTYP to discuss which blurb they think would be best for the back cover of *Chocolate Planet* and why. Remind them to think about the purpose of a blurb. Collect responses and encourage them to give reasons.

- Say that you want them to write a blurb for *Chocolate Planet* to go with the front cover they voted for and pasted in the Class log. Model saying your own opening sentence aloud, writing it down, then changing one thing to improve it. Now ask them to TTYP to share their ideas about their opening sentence.
- Choose two or three children to share their opening sentence. Write their ideas on the board or a flipchart and model how to improve their sentence.
- Make sure they rehearse what they want to say before they write anything down in their Personal log. Repeat the process for a second and third sentence.
- Over the next couple of days, choose and photocopy a few blurbs to paste in the Class log and to display on your Story wall for this Unit.

Curriculum link: participate in discussion and consider the opinions of others

Big Question (CD)

Purpose: for children to develop their skills of argument and discussion through a mini enquiry session based on a philosophical question relating to the work of the day

- Display today's Big Question on **CD (file 3.5)**:

  Does all the food grown around the world belong to everyone?

- Follow the process as explained on Day 1.

DAY 4

drama techniques to help pupils identify with and explore characters

Moods and feelings (A)

Purpose: for children to develop an empathetic response to characters and situations

- Tell the children that, just like in real life, characters' feelings and behaviour can change at different points in a story. Remind them that, in *G.E.M.*, Royd started off feeling jealous of Gark, then his feelings changed towards the end of the story.
- Ask them to think back to the story they have just read, *Chocolate Planet*. Tell them to TTYP to answer the question: '*Who says she is not scared of anything?*'
- Take feedback and direct the children to the evidence in the text on p.21 of Anthology 2 Book 3 if necessary. Ask the children to show you a mini-mime for *scared*. Say that Gala might not be afraid of anything because she is very *brave* or *courageous*. Now ask the children to show you a mini-mime for *brave*.
- Ask the children to TTYP to recall a moment in the story when Gala is afraid and a moment when she shows bravery and courage.
- Now read the description of the moondog to the children: 'A moondog as big as a space yak! With two heads! Two heads with blood-red eyes and teeth like tombstones!' Tell the children to TTYP and work together to create a still-image for the moondog (make sure they know what yaks and tombstones are).
- Remind the children that the writer told us what the moondog looks like, but the text doesn't tell us about the moondog's feelings. Ask the children to TTYP to share ideas about what mood the moondog is in and how it feels when it sees Frag and Gala.
- Collect responses and encourage them to support their ideas with evidence from the text.

listening to, discussing and expressing views about a wide range of stories

Fantasy settings (CD)

Purpose: for children to be able to identify features of a fantasy story set in space

- Tell the children that there are lots of clues in the story that show us that it is a fantasy story set in space.
- Display **CD (file 4.1)** to show a section of *Chocolate Planet*. Click 'Audio' to hear this section read by a narrator.
- Tell the children that they are going to hear the section again and this time they should listen for any words that tell us that the story is set in space.

- Play the narration again, then ask the children to TTYP to recall relevant words. Collect feedback and then click 'Highlights' to see some examples.
- Navigate to the next slide to show another section of *Chocolate Planet*. Explain that this time you want the children to listen out for any words or phrases that tell us that the story is a fantasy story. Ask them to think about what things happen in the story that would not happen in real life.
- Click 'Audio' to hear the narration and repeat the process.

Curriculum link: making inferences on the basis of what is being said and done

What if not...? PB

Purpose: for children to consider how character, setting and plot affect each other

- Ask the children to turn to p.57 in their Pupils' Book and look at the What if not...? questions. Use TOL to model how you might think about the first question: What if not *dull?* What if Planet Wob were *exciting and full of scrumptious things to eat?*

  Well, Gala and Frag would not have wanted to leave and visit Planet Um to search for the chocolate mines. The two-headed moondog might have travelled to Wob though! Perhaps it would have taken hundreds of moondogs with it and taken over the planet!

- Now TOL using your own ideas to guide the children to TTYP to discuss the next What if not...? questions. Remind them that there isn't a right answer, you are just looking for their own ideas and opinions. Collect feedback and develop their responses.

making inferences on the basis of what is being said and done

Class log

Purpose: for children to share the process of keeping a class reading, writing and thinking log to record responses to texts and activities in a variety of forms

- Explain to the children that there are key moments in every story. Ask them to TTYP to recall one important moment in *Chocolate Planet* and to plan and practise a freeze-frame to represent the moment.
- Ask two or three sets of partners at a time to show their freeze-frames to the rest of the group. Ask the rest of the group to say which moment they think is being shown in each freeze-frame.
- Allow time for partners to explain their freeze-frames and the reason for their choice. Repeat until all sets of partners have performed their freeze-frames.
- Write the important moments that the children chose in the Class log.

participate in discussion and consider the opinions of others

Big Question CD

Purpose: for children to develop their skills of argument and discussion through a mini enquiry session based on a philosophical question relating to the work of the day

- Display today's Big Question on **CD (file 4.2)**:

  How do we know if something is real life or fantasy?

- Follow the process as explained on Day 1.

DAY 5

Step into the setting A CD

Purpose: for children to use their imagination to explore the story setting

- Ask the children to TTYP to recall any descriptions of Planet Um that they read in the story. Collect feedback and then ask them to check if they have all the information given in the story. Tell them to look at p.14 in Anthology 2 Book 3 and TTYP to find the description of Planet Um 'hanging in the streaky sky'. Ask them to read the description: 'The Planet Um was glowing a silky, milky brown.'
- Write the lines on the board or a flipchart under the heading *Setting*.

- Now ask the children to TTYP to find the description of Planet Um as Frag and Gala set off across it. Ask them to read the description: 'down wobbly paths of jelly stones, over winking streams of lemon water, till they saw a wall of galactic rock. The smell of chocolate was overpowering.' (on p.17.)
- Write the lines on the board or a flipchart under the heading *Setting*.
- Tell the children that you have found an astronaut called Captain Slog who has agreed to take them on a virtual tour of Planet Um. Explain that that they must prepare for take-off and must do exactly as the Captain tells them.
- Display **CD (file 5.1)** to show the instructions from Captain Slog. (Make sure the children mime putting their virtual goggles on when the captain tells them to!) Click 'Audio' to start the audio.
- On the following slide, click 'Audio' again to take them on a guided fantasy tour of Planet Um.
- Navigate to the final slide and ask the children to use the questions to TTYP to share what they were imagining during the exercise.

Soundscape

Purpose: for children to explore the story setting through a soundscape and to develop an awareness of how sound creates atmosphere

- Before the lesson, print five copies of Captain Slog's narrative from **CD (file 5.2)** (one each for four groups and one for yourself).
- Tell the children that they are going to use their voices and bodies (e.g. clapping, stamping) to create a *soundscape* for Planet Um. Explain that a soundscape is a way of recreating a setting through sound to help them imagine the planet more clearly.
- Divide the class into four groups and give each group a number from 1 to 4. These numbers will match a section of Captain Slog's narrative on the printed sheet.
- Explain that they must read their section of the narrative and decide which sounds to use to represent what is happening or being described. Allow time for the groups to plan and practise their sounds.
- Bring the children back together, but keep them sitting in their small groups. Ask for complete silence and show them the start and stop signals you will be using as the conductor.
- Try out different ways of using the sounds to create different moods, e.g. Ask some or all of the groups to get louder, quieter, faster, slower, etc. or start different groups off at different times, with the groups repeating their sounds to create a crescendo.
- Tell the children that they are now going to add their soundscape to Captain Slog's virtual tour. Explain that they must listen really carefully to know when to make their sounds. In the role of conductor, help them by indicating when it is their turn. Play audio **CD (file 5.3)** to listen to the tour again. Conduct the soundscape orchestra to support the narration.

Curriculum link:
Year 2 Grammar
verbs to indicate time are used correctly and consistently

Grammar: verb tenses

Purpose: for children to develop their understanding of what 'tense' means and their awareness of how it is indicated through verb endings

- Tell the children that the word *tense* comes from an old French word, *tens*, that means *time*. Write the two words on the board or a flipchart.
- Explain that, when we are talking or writing, verbs describe not just an action, but also the *time* of the action. Say that you are talking to them *now* and we call *now* the *present*. Use MT/YT to say: '*I am talking now.*'
- Display **CD (file 5.4)** and use it to re-state the explanation of the present tense.

- Tell the children that you also talked to them earlier – *before now* – and we call *before now* the past. Click 'Reveal' to show this and use it to re-state the explanation of the past tense.
- Tell the children that, as you listened to Captain Slog's virtual tour, you made some notes to help you to remember the journey. Navigate to the next slide and read your notes aloud using MT/YT. Ask the children to TTYP to decide whether your notes are written in the past or present tense. Remind them that they will need to give a reason for their answer. Tell them to give their answer chorally when you give a signal.
- Clarify that there are lots of verbs that end in *-ing* and they tell us that things are happening now, in the present: they are *present tense verbs*. Click 'Highlights' to highlight these verbs.
- Say that you want to use your notes to write a recount of your experience of Captain Slog's virtual tour. You will need to write it in the past tense. Explain that verbs that end in *-ed* tell us when things have happened before now, in the past: they are *past tense verbs*.
- Navigate to the next slide to show your recount written in the past tense with the verbs highlighted. Read it to the children, pointing out the past tense verbs.
- Ask the children to turn to p.57 in their Pupils' Book and look at the Grammar: verb tenses activity. Ask them to TTYP to look at the table as you talk them through it. Say that you want them to think of two different sentences using the words in the table: one using a present tense verb and one using a past tense verb.
- Choose two or three sets of partners to share their sentences. If necessary, clarify which ones use the past tense and which ones use the present tense.
- Now ask the children to write their two sentences in their Personal log.

Homework Book pp.20–21 provides further practice of verb tenses.

Curriculum link: encapsulating what they want to say before beginning

Personal log

Purpose: for children to keep a personal reading, writing and thinking log in order to record thoughts and ideas for their own writing

- Tell the children that Captain Slog is making a leaflet to accompany travellers on his fantasy tour and wants to give them advice before they visit Planet Um.
- Ask them to TTYP to think of three pieces of advice they would give to someone who was thinking of travelling to Planet Um. Remind them that they might want to point out good things to see and do, as well as advice about preparing for dangers.
- Collect feedback and build on some of their suggestions. Model how to write two or three pieces of advice in the Class log.
- Now tell them to TTYP and tell them their first piece of advice using a full sentence, before they record it in their Personal log.
- Guide them to repeat the process for their next two pieces of advice.

participate in discussion and consider the opinions of others

Big Question (CD)

Purpose: for children to develop their skills of argument and discussion through a mini enquiry session based on a philosophical question relating to the work of the day

- Display today's Big Question on **CD (file 5.5)**:

  Is there such a thing as a perfect place?

- Follow the process as explained on Day 1.

WRITING FICTION

DAY 6

Curriculum link: increase pupils' vocabulary

Multi-syllabic words

Purpose: for children to use their phonic knowledge to spell multi-syllabic words they have encountered in the text

- Tell the children that some of the words in the story have more than one syllable. Ask them if they can remember what a syllable is and clarify if necessary. Remind the children that we call words that have more than one syllable *multi-syllabic* words.
- Display **CD (file 6.1)** to show the multi-syllabic words: *ferocious, precious, scrumptious, imagination*. Read them aloud using MT/YT. Explain that all these words end in *-cious, -tious* or *-tion*.
- Point to *ti* or *ci* in each word and use the *Read Write Inc.* Complex Speed Sounds chart to clarify the sound these graphemes make. The chart can be called up by opening the 'Complex Speed Sounds chart' from the top of the resources list for Day 6.
- Now ask the children to turn to p.58 in their Pupils' Book and look at the Multi-syllabic words activity. Tell them to TTYP to read the words and synonyms. Ask them to choose at least two words each and to build a short sentence around each one.
- Remind them to say each sentence aloud to their partner before writing it into their Personal log. Collect examples from a few sets of partners.

listening to, discussing and expressing views about a wide range of stories

Story makers

Purpose: for children to develop their understanding of how stories are created by writers and to learn that we can all become writers

- Show the children your Story star. It shows that this week they are going to find out more about writing stories with fantasy settings. If we find the secret to making great stories, we can all call ourselves Story makers.
- Explain that many stories contain similar ideas, events or settings. Ask the children to TTYP to share ideas about how *G.E.M.* and *Chocolate Planet* are similar.
- Collect feedback and draw out the fantasy settings and similar events in the two stories, e.g. *the space transport; Royd, Gark, Gala and Frag all wanting something they haven't got; the creatures.*
- Say that we can all borrow ideas from stories we know well and make changes to create our own stories.

think aloud as they collect ideas; compose individual sentences orally and then write them down

Build a setting

Purpose: for children to see and participate in the creation of a fantasy setting

- Before the lesson, print out one copy of the TOLs on **CD (file 6.3)**.
- Ask the children to look at *Chocolate Planet* on pp.14–21 of Anthology 2 Book 3. Tell them to TTYP to read the story again with lots of expression. They should try to picture the setting as they travel to and explore Planet Um with Frag and Gala.
- Say that you have had an idea for developing the description of Planet Um. Display **CD (file 6.2)** to show some extracts from the story that describe the setting.
- Use MT/YT to read the extracts. Ask the children to TTYP to say which parts of the description they like best, and why. Collect feedback.
- TOL, using your own ideas, as you use the questions on the next slide to encourage the children to imagine the tastes, smells and sounds on Planet Um.

- Draw the children into your TOL and ask them to TTYP to share their ideas. Take feedback and write some of the words and phrases they come up with on the board or flipchart.
- Tell the children that a space probe, sent to explore new planets, has sent some photos back to Earth of a hidden, unexplored part of Planet Um called West Um.
- Navigate to the next slide to show the first photo from West Um. Use the TOL points on printable **CD (file 6.3)** and your own ideas to model how you could describe this setting. Make sure you model trying out different words and phrases orally and then rehearsing the whole sentence before writing it down. (Deliberate use of adjectives, metaphors and similes is needed to stimulate the children to use their imagination and interesting vocabulary.)
- Ask the children to TTYP to describe the scene orally in their own words. Collect responses and write some of the words and phrases they come up with on the board or a flipchart.
- Now navigate to the next slide to show another photo and repeat the activity. Use the TOL points on printable **CD (file 6.3)** and your own ideas to begin to model the process again.
- Navigate to the next slide to show the two photos side by side. Remind the children of the virtual journey they went on with Captain Slog. Explain that you want them to 'step inside' the photos to explore West Um. Ask them to shut their eyes, then click 'Audio' to play atmospheric music.
- Ask the children to suggest any words or phrases that popped into their minds when they were exploring West Um. Take feedback and write some of their ideas on the board or a flipchart.

Curriculum link: discussing and expressing views about stories

Personal log (CD)

Purpose: for children to keep a personal reading, writing and thinking log in order to record thoughts and ideas for their own writing

- Leave the photos of West Um on **CD (file 6.2)** displayed on the board. Ask the children to look again at the new setting and try to imagine they are there.
- Explain that when writers describe their story settings, they use the senses to help them create interesting descriptions. Ask the children if they know what the five senses are. Collect feedback and clarify if necessary.
- Ask children to TTYP to share ideas about what they can *see*. Ask them to think of a sentence to describe what they can see. Tell them to say their sentence aloud to their partner and then write it into their Personal log.
- Repeat the process, asking them to write sentences in their Personal log to describe what they can *hear*, *smell*, *taste* and *feel*.
- Choose two or three partners to share what they have written with the group.

participate in discussion and consider the opinions of others

Big Question (CD)

Purpose: for children to develop their skills of argument and discussion through a mini enquiry session based on a philosophical question relating to the work of the day

- Display today's Big Question on **CD (file 6.4)**:

  Does changing where you live change who you are?

- Follow the process as explained on Day 1.

DAY 7

Curriculum link: making inferences on the basis of what is being said and done

What if not…? PB

Purpose: for children to consider how setting can affect the characters and action in a story

- Remind the children that when they looked at the What if not…? questions in Week 1, they talked about how the story would be different if the characters or setting were changed. Explain that you want to write a new adventure for Gala and Frag, and using What if not…? is going to help you to explore ideas.
- Say to the children that you want to explore the question: What if not the *Chocolate Planet?* What if *Gala and Frag decided to visit a different planet?*
- Ask the children to turn to pp.58–59 in their Pupils' Book and look at the What if not…? activity. Tell them that the first picture on p.59 shows another planet that Gala and Frag could visit. Ask them to look at the picture and to TTYP to describe what is special or different about the planet. Collect feedback.
- Use the TOL below and your own ideas to share your impression of the planet, and opinions on why Gala and Frag might want to go there:

  This looks like a very sparkly and shiny place. It might not be very comfortable though – everything looks so hard. Look! Even the stepping stones are made from diamonds! I wonder what there is to eat? Perhaps no one can live here because there is no food or water! Why do you think Gala and Frag would visit this planet? It could be that they like shiny things or perhaps they just want to explore. I wonder if there are any dangers on Planet Precious. What do you think?

- Draw children's attention to the second picture, showing another planet that Gala and Frag could visit. Ask the children to look at the picture and TTYP to describe what is special and unusual about this planet. Encourage them to think about what it might smell, taste or feel like, as well as what it looks like.
- Collect feedback and write words and phrases under the heading *Planet Party* on the board or a flipchart.
- Ask them to TTYP to share ideas and TOL about why Gala and Frag might want to visit Planet Party, what they would see and any possible dangers.
- Collect ideas and add them to the notes on the board or flipchart.
- Explain to the children that they might find these ideas useful when they write their own fantasy story. Ask them to choose one idea to write into their Personal log.

understand, through being shown, the skills and processes essential to writing

Build a story 1 CD

Purpose: for children to see a story grow through three stages of development that will provide a model and stimulus for their own writing

- Say that you have chosen one of the new planets as the setting for your new story and *borrowed* some ideas from *Chocolate Planet* to begin your new fantasy adventure.
- You are in role as the writer for this part. It is important that you use your own ideas as well as the think bubbles provided to show how you plan and develop your story.
- Display **CD (file 7.1)**. Read the think bubble and ask the children what they can remember about Planet Precious.
- Click 'Story square' to display your first story square and another think bubble. Read the story square aloud to the children and ask them which bits they think you have used from *Chocolate Planet*. Take feedback.
- Click 'Highlights' to highlight the ideas that you borrowed from *Chocolate Planet* and point out any that the children hadn't identified. Click 'Highlights' again to remove them. Then click 'Story square' again to hide the story square and ask the children to TTYP to summarise what they have just read.
- Choose two sets of partners to share their summaries. Then click 'Story square' to show the text again to allow them to check their answers.

Curriculum link: planning or saying out loud what they are going to write about; encapsulating what they want to say, sentence by sentence

Write a story 1

Purpose: for children to develop the first stage of a story

- Before the lesson, print a copy of the appropriate story squares for each child from **CD (file 7.2a, b** or **c)**: **a)** gives the least support and **c)** gives the most.
- Give each child a copy of the story squares from **CD (file 7.2a, b** or **c)** and say that they will help them to write their own fantasy story where Gala and Frag visit Planet Party.
- Explain that you have some questions which will help them to think of ideas for their story. Write these questions on the board or a flipchart: *Why do Gala and Frag want to visit this place? What will they be searching for? How do they feel about the trip? Does Gala feel the same as Frag?*
- Ask the children to turn to p.59 in their Pupils' Book and look at the picture of Planet Party. Ask them to TTYP to discuss ideas for their story using the questions as a guide. Choose two or three sets of partners to share their ideas.
- Remind the children that you used a story square to write your story opening. Display **CD (file 7.3)** to show your completed story square again. Leave it up as a model and explain how they should use Story square A (on their print out) to write the beginning of their story. They will complete the rest of the story squares later.
- When they have had time to think about and plan their opening sentence, remind the children to say it aloud to their partners before they write it in their story square.

listening to, discussing and expressing views about a wide range of stories

Class log

Purpose: for children to share the process of keeping a class reading, writing and thinking log to record responses to texts and activities in a variety of forms

- Ask the children to TTYP to share ideas for a title for your new Gala and Frag fantasy story. Remind them that the title must give a clue about what the story is about and also make someone want to read the story. Collect ideas and write your favourites in the Class log.

participate in discussion and consider the opinions of others

Big Question

Purpose: for children to develop their skills of argument and discussion through a mini enquiry session based on a philosophical question relating to the work of the day

- Display today's Big Question on **CD (file 7.4)**:

  Should everyone have an adventure?
- Follow the process as explained on Day 1.

DAY 8

understand, through being shown, the skills and processes essential to writing

Build a story 2

Purpose: for children to see a story grow through three stages of development that will provide a model and stimulus for their own writing

- Tell the children that you are adding the next part of your new Gala and Frag fantasy story today. Ask them to TTYP to recall: '*What planet were Gala and Frag travelling to? What were they searching for? Why did they want it?'* Remind the children that they are answering these questions about your story, not theirs.
- Explain that you want to focus on Gala and Frag's arrival on the new planet and that you have looked at *Chocolate Planet* to help you.
- Ask the children to look at p.16 of Anthology 2 Book 3. Tell them to read together from 'At last the spaceship landed…' to "It's sure to lead us to the chocolate mines."'

- Say that you used these lines to help you to write the next part of your story. Display **CD (file 8.1)** and read the first think bubble. Then click 'Story square' to show your next story square.
- Use MT/YT to read the text. Tell the children that the ideas you *borrowed* from *Chocolate Planet* are in red.
- Ask them to TTYP to share how they think Gala and Frag felt when they landed on Planet Precious.
- Navigate to the next slide to display the think bubble. Explain that you want to add a really interesting description of Planet Precious.
- Ask the children to look at p.17 of Anthology 2 Book 3. Tell them to read together from 'The two friends set off…' to '…wall of galactic rock.'
- Say that these lines helped you to write your description of Planet Precious. Click 'Story square' to show your next story square. Use MT/YT to read the text. Ask the children what else they think Gala and Frag might find on Planet Precious.

Curriculum link: Year 2 Grammar
verbs to indicate time are used correctly and consistently

Grammar: tenses in texts CD PB HB

Purpose: for children to become aware of the need for the consistent use of tense in texts

- Remind the children that the word *tense* is useful when we are explaining whether something is happening now or whether it has already happened.
- Explain that when we write a story, we decide which tense it will be in and we have to make sure we don't accidentally change the tense as we write.
- Say that you made a few tense errors when you were writing your first draft of your story square and you could hear the errors when you read it aloud.
- Display **CD (file 8.2)** and tell the children that this was your first draft and it was meant to be written in the past tense. Ask the children to read it aloud chorally.
- Click 'TOL' to show a think bubble. Use this and your own ideas to explain the tense inconsistency. Click 'TOL' again to repeat the process.
- Navigate to the next slide to show the draft with errors and the corrected text. Ask the children to read them out chorally so they can hear the differences.
- Ask the children to turn to p.60 in their Pupils' Book and look at the Grammar: tenses in texts activity. Tell them to take turns to read the sentences and then discuss which is written in the past tense and which is written in the present.

Homework Book p.22 provides further practice on tenses in texts.

planning or saying out loud what they are going to write about; encapsulating what they want to say, sentence by sentence

Write a story 2 PB CD

Purpose: for children to develop the second stage of a story

- Make sure the children have their story squares from Day 7 **CD (file 7.2a, b** or **c).** Tell the children to look at the picture of Planet Party again on p.59 of their Pupils' Book. Ask the children to TTYP to discuss what things they might include in their description of Planet Party. Take feedback.
- Now display **CD (file 8.3)** to show your completed story square as a model for how they should use Story square B to write the next part of their story. Draw attention to how you have included sights like the golden river, and sounds like the crunching of diamond stones beneath Frag and Gala's feet, and encourage children to include sights and sounds in their own writing.
- When they have had time to think and plan, remind them to say their sentences aloud to their partners before starting to write. Choose two or three sets of partners to share their writing.

- Navigate to the next slide to show your next story square as a model for how they should use Story square C to write the next part of their story. When they have had time to think and plan, remind them to say their sentences before they write them down. Walk around as they write, giving support and praise.

Personal log

Purpose: for children to keep a personal reading, writing and thinking log in order to record thoughts and ideas for their own writing

- Ask the children to TTYP to share ideas for a title for their own fantasy adventure story. Remind them that the title must give a clue about what the story is about and also make someone want to read the story. Collect and discuss ideas orally, scribing a few on the board or a flipchart. Tell the children to write their title in their Personal log.

Curriculum link: participate in discussion and consider the opinions of others

Big Question (CD)

Purpose: for children to develop their skills of argument and discussion through a mini enquiry session based on a philosophical question relating to the work of the day

- Display today's Big Question on **CD (file 8.4)**:

  Should you always search for something you want? *

- Follow the process as explained on Day 1.

  ** This Big Question will be revisited on Day 11 – the first day of the Non-fiction week.*

DAY 9

understand, through being shown, the skills and processes essential to writing

Build a story 3 (A) (CD)

Purpose: for children to see a story grow through three stages of development that will provide a model and stimulus for their own writing

- Tell the children that today you are going to add another part to your new Gala and Frag fantasy story.
- Remind the children that in *Chocolate Planet*, Gala and Frag had a big problem when they reached the chocolate mines. Ask the children to look at pp.18–19 of Anthology 2 Book 3. Tell them to read together from 'A moondog! A moondog as big as a space yak…' to '…it would torment her for the rest of her life.' Say that you used these lines to help you to write the next part of your story.
- Display **CD (file 9.1)** and read the first think bubble. Then click 'Story square' to show your next story square. Use MT/YT to read the text. Tell the children that the ideas that you borrowed from *Chocolate Planet* are in red.
- Ask the children to TTYP to share what they think could happen next. Remind them that you are looking for their ideas and opinions as there are no right answers. Take feedback.
- Ask the children to TTYP to say how Gala and Frag solved their problem of the giant moondog. Collect feedback and then ask them to check their answers by looking at pp.20–21 of Anthology 2 Book 3. Tell them to read together from the top of p.20 to 'They carried two tonnes of chocolate back to their spaceship and prepared to set off home.'
- Say that these lines helped you to write the final parts of your new story. Navigate to the next slide. Read the bubble and then click 'Story square' to show your final story square.
- Use MT/YT to read the text. Ask the children to TTYP to share what they thought of your story ending. Take feedback.

Curriculum link: answering questions; participate in discussion and consider the opinions of others

Story talk PB

Purpose: for children to develop orally the third and final stage of a story

- Tell the children that they are going to share ideas about the final parts of their new fantasy adventure for Gala and Frag.
- Ask them to turn to p.60 in their Pupils' Book and look at the Story talk activity.
- Guide the children through the first set of questions to help them to think of a problem Gala and Frag could encounter during their quest. TOL to help stimulate ideas and to model keeping their ideas simple and manageable.
- Choose two or three sets of partners to feed back some of their ideas to the rest of the group.
- Ask the children to read the prompts about how Gala and Frag overcome the problem and TTYP to discuss them. Relate the prompts back to *Chocolate Planet* and your new fantasy story.
- TOL to help stimulate ideas and to model keeping their ideas simple and manageable. Encourage the children to make links between things they would find on Planet Party and the solution to the problem that Gala and Frag face.

drama and role-play for pupils to develop their ideas by improvising scenes

Dramatic reconstruction

Purpose: for children to create freeze-frames to consolidate ideas for the final part of their own writing

- Tell the children that they are each going to create a freeze-frame to represent the final part of their new fantasy story for Gala and Frag. Each set of partners will be creating two freeze-frames. Partner 1s can direct Partner 2s to help them to create a freeze-frame based on their story and vice versa.
- Allow time for the children to plan and practise their freeze-frames. Decide whether you want each set of partners to perform for the rest of the class individually or have all the Partner 1s' freeze-frames happening simultaneously and then all the Partner 2s'.
- You may wish to take photographs to add to your Story wall for this Unit or to paste into the Class log.
- Give feedback on what you have seen and encourage the children to explain in detail exactly what was happening in the moment they decided to freeze-frame.

DAY 10

develop stamina for writing by writing narratives

Write a story 3 CD

Purpose: for children to write the third and final stage of a story

- Before the lesson, print each child a copy of the story squares from **CD (file 10.1a** or **b)**: **a)** gives the least support and **b)** gives the most.
- Give each child a copy of the story squares from **CD (file 10.1a** or **b)**. Explain to the children that they are going to use the story squares to write the final stages of their stories.
- Ask the children to TTYP to recall the *problem* Gala and Frag encountered in your new story. Collect feedback.
- Display **CD (file 10.2)** to show your completed story square. Leave it up as a model for how they should use Story square D to write the next part of their story. Point out how you described that Gala felt scared of the giant bird, and encourage children to include their character's feelings in their own writing.
- Remind the children of their discussions about the final parts of their own stories and of the freeze-frames they created. If you have some photographs to show, use these to remind the children of some of their ideas.

- Allow the children time to think about and plan how to describe the problem Gala and Frag encounter. Remind them to say their opening sentence aloud to their partners before starting to write.
- Now ask the children to TTYP to recall how Gala and Frag *resolved* the problem in your new story. Collect feedback.
- Navigate to the next slide to show your final story square, E. Leave it up as a model for how they should use the final square on their sheets to write the resolution for their story.
- Tell the children that they now need to think about how to explain how Gala and Frag overcame the problem in their own stories. Allow plenty of time for them to think and to TTYP to discuss their resolution.
- When they have had time to think and plan, remind them to say their opening sentence aloud to their partners before starting to write.
- Walk around, supporting and praising as they work.

Curriculum link: evaluating their writing with the teacher and other pupils; make simple additions, revisions and corrections

Evaluate and edit (CD)

Purpose: for children to evaluate their own and their partner's work against specific criteria and then discuss how they could improve their work

- Display **CD (file 10.3)** to show the evaluation points and read them aloud using MT/YT.
- As a model, select an example of work where the writing has met the criteria, and share this with the other children, explaining why it works well.
- Tell the children to take turns to read their partner's writing in pairs and discuss together how well each piece of writing has met the criteria.
- Ask children to discuss at least two changes they could make to improve their work.

proofreading to check for errors in spelling, grammar and punctuation

Proofread

Purpose: for children to proofread their work and make changes to improve the accuracy of their grammar, punctuation and spelling

- Now ask the children to proofread their work. If you have noticed that several children need to improve on a particular aspect of spelling, grammar or punctuation, use this as a focus for the Proofread activity. Write an example which includes common errors from the children's writing and use this as a model.
- The children should always be checking for standard use of punctuation and correct spelling of common exception words.
- The following points would be relevant as the particular focus for this Unit:
  - using tense correctly and consistently
  - checking spelling of ambitious vocabulary choices (i.e. those *borrowed* from the Pupils' Book or Anthology text).

Further activity

- Publish: allow the children to type up their stories.

READING AND WRITING NON-FICTION

The Non-fiction week, linked by the theme of chocolate, looks at developing children's awareness of information texts.

See p.166 for the daily timetable for the Non-fiction week.

Non-fiction

Reading

Children will:

- read and identify key points about chocolate and how it is made
- explore the features of information texts and how they make it easy for the reader to locate information
- consider the different ways information is presented to engage the audience, e.g. *pictures, diagrams, photos.*

Writing

Key writing purpose to be shared with the children:

To give the reader interesting information about chocolate, presented in an engaging way.

Writing evaluation to be shared with the children

Our chocolate exhibition:

- presents information in a variety of ways, e.g. *photos, quiz questions, fact files, pictures*
- includes an accordion booklet.

Grammar:

- uses capital letters for names of things or places.

See the Planning section of the Software ('Timetables' tab) for a printable version of the Writing purpose and evaluation.

DAY 11

Curriculum link: pupils should be guided to participate in discussion

Think and link

Purpose: for children to develop an interest in information texts via one of the Big Questions they have explored

- Display the Big Question from Day 8 on **CD (file 8.4)**:
  Should you always search for something you want?
- Ask the children to TTYP to recall some of what they discussed on Day 8 and take feedback.
- Remind the children that, in the story *Chocolate Planet*, Gala and Frag went in search of chocolate and found a monster.
- Explain that you have found a great poem that lists lots of monsters from myths, legends and other stories. Display **CD (file 11.1)** to show the poem 'A Monster Alphabet' by Gervase Phinn and read it aloud to the children.
- Re-read the poem and ask the children to listen carefully to the descriptions and think about which monster sounds the scariest.
- Now ask the children to TTYP to share their choices. Take feedback and use MT/YT to re-read some of the lines they pick out.

listening to, discussing and expressing views about a wide range of non-fiction

Alphabetical texts

Purpose: for children to revise their understanding of alphabetical order and to focus on information texts that use alphabetical order

- Remind the children that the poem they just read is special because it is written in alphabetical order.
- Ask them to TTYP to say where the moondog from *Chocolate Planet* would fit into the poem. Collect answers and check their understanding of the term *alphabetical order*.
- Now ask the children to TTYP to think of other things that are written in alphabetical order, e.g. *a class register, telephone directory, a dictionary, a thesaurus, an encyclopaedia*. Ask them to Popcorn (see Introduction p.17) their answers.
- Display **CD (file 11.2)** to show the front cover of the *Oxford First Dictionary*. Click 'TOL' to show a think bubble and use it to talk through the purpose and features of a dictionary. Click 'Dictionary entry' to show another think bubble and a close-up of the entry for *bark*. Clarify how the information is presented.
- Now navigate to the next slides and repeat the process.
- Say that if they wanted more information about any of the monsters listed in the poem, the children could look them up in an encyclopaedia or on the Internet.

being introduced to non-fiction that is structured in different ways

Presenting information

Purpose: for children to think about different kinds of information, how it can be presented and why different presentational features are used

- Remind the children that information is all around us. Say that texts are presented in different ways to make information easier for the reader to follow. Display **CD (file 11.3)** and use your own TOL to discuss the first extract. Explain that not all information texts are written in alphabetical order.
- Ask the children to TTYP to match the information text type to a heading in the table. Take feedback, clarifying where necessary, and click in the correct cell to show a tick. Repeat the process for *How is it presented?*
- Navigate through the rest of the slides, repeating the process for the other information text types.

- Ask the children to TTYP to think about why each of the texts is presented in a different way and how this makes the information easier for the reader to follow. Take feedback and draw out how the texts are used for different purposes and give different information.
- Now ask the children to turn to p.61 in their Pupils' Book and look at the Presenting information activity. Ask them to TTYP to read through the different information texts and match them to the headings. Choose two or three sets of partners to feed back their answers to the group.
- Now ask them to TTYP to discuss how the different texts are presented. Give prompts if necessary, e.g. *symbols, text with pictures, heading with lists*. Take feedback and clarify if necessary.
- When the children have decided how the texts are presented, ask them to TTYP to decide why each text is presented in this way. Encourage them to think about audience and purpose. Take feedback and clarify where necessary.

Curriculum link: answering and asking questions

Class log

Purpose: for children to share the process of keeping a class reading, writing and thinking log to record responses to texts and activities in a variety of forms

- Explain to the children that *Chocolate Planet* made you think about chocolate and that you would like to find out more information about it.
- Say that you want them to help you find out more information about chocolate and then work with their partners and the rest of the group to inform other children in school about it through mini-exhibitions and possibly a whole-school assembly. (The children will be creating various resources for their mini-exhibitions over the course of the week so you may wish to take this opportunity to give each set of partners a folder to keep this work in.)
- Now explain that you are going to add an *Information* section to the Class log. Write the heading *Chocolate* in the Class log. Ask the children to TTYP to think about what they already know about chocolate. Collect their responses and write them under the subheading *What we know...*
- Ask the children to TTYP to share ideas about what they would like to find out about chocolate. Collect their responses and model how to turn them into questions. Write their questions under the subheading *What we'd like to know…*
- Ask them to Popcorn answers to the question: '*Where might we find the answers to these questions?*' e.g. *websites, non-fiction books, encyclopaedias, leaflets.*

DAY 12

explain the meaning of new words, increase pupils' vocabulary

Information words (CD)

Purpose: for children to become familiar with vocabulary used in information texts

information index definition glossary heading exhibition

- Before the lesson, print a copy of the words and their definitions from **CD (file 12.2)**.
- Tell the children there are some words they will be hearing and using as they look at information texts that they may not have heard before.
- Display **CD (file 12.1)** to show the words and their definitions. Explain that these words will help us to identify, read, talk about and write information texts. Read each word and definition to the children. Ask the children to repeat them using MT/YT.
- Display the printed words and definitions from **CD (file 12.2)** on your Information texts wall for this Unit.

Curriculum link: answering and asking questions, think aloud as they collect ideas

Information 1

Purpose: for children to see a model of how to create their own questions after a close reading of a text

- Ask the children to turn to pp.22–24 in Anthology 2 Book 3 and look at the text 'Chocolate'. Tell them to follow the text as you read it aloud from your own copy.
- Say that you want to create some questions that others can find the answers to in the text.
- Display **CD (file 12.3)** to show a section of the text. Click 'TOL' and use the think bubble to model how to create a question that could be answered using this section of text. Type your question in the box provided.
- Now draw the children into the process using MT/YT to compose another question. Type your question in the text box.
- Navigate to the next slide and repeat the process, choosing two or three sets of partners to share their questions. Type their questions in the text box.

answering and asking questions; participate in discussion and consider the opinions of others

Write 1

Purpose: for children to develop their ability to create and write questions based on an information text

- Before the lesson, print the mock chocolate wrappers from **CD (file 12.4)**.
- Explain to the children that you want them to create a quiz about chocolate for other children to complete. Tell them that this will form part of their mini-exhibition on chocolate at the end of the week.
- Ask them to look again at 'Chocolate' on pp.22–24 of Anthology 2 Book 3 and TTYP to take turns to read one section at a time. If necessary, clarify the meaning of the word *edible* on p.24.
- Allocate a section of the text to each set of partners. (Some sets of partners will be working on the same section.) Choose the sections carefully to allow for some differentiation.
- Explain that you want them to TTYP to create at least two quiz questions using their section of the text.
- When they have finished, choose a set of partners to share one of their questions. Ask the rest of the class to TTYP to find the answer in the text. Develop their understanding of how to pose and answer questions in full sentences.
- Repeat the process with questions from other sets of partners.
- Ask each set of partners to divide their quiz questions between them and to write their share of the questions neatly on the mock chocolate bar wrappers from **CD (file 12.4)**.

compose individual sentences orally and then write them down

Personal log

You will need to bring in four different chocolate bar wrappers for this session.

Purpose: for children to keep a personal reading, writing and thinking log in order to record thoughts and ideas for their own writing

- Ask the children to find the heading 'Chocolate today' on p.24 of Anthology 2 Book 3.
- Explain that the bar chart shows how much chocolate is eaten in different countries. Remind them how a bar chart works and ask them to TTYP to find the answers to these questions: '*How many countries are listed in the chart? Which country eats the least chocolate? Which country eats the second largest amount of chocolate?*'
- After asking each question, tell the children to TTYP to discuss it before writing their answer down in their Personal log. Remind them to write both the questions and answers using full sentences.

- Now clear a space and place four different chocolate bar wrappers (or simply write the names of the bars on paper) on the floor.
- Explain that the children are going to make a human bar chart showing which chocolate bars are the most popular in the class. Ask them to decide which their favourite bar is, and form a line behind the relevant wrapper.
- Repeat with variations, e.g. which their least favourite chocolate bar is, which their second favourite chocolate bar is.
- Take photographs of the human bar charts for display in their mini-exhibitions and the Class log. Make sure you have a record of which questions match the different photographs. You will need to have enough photographs for each set of partners to have one to display in their mini-exhibition.
- When the children are back in their seats, ask them to TTYP to discuss why it was useful to show this information using a human bar chart. Take feedback, drawing out how some information is best presented visually.

DAY 13

Curriculum link: being introduced to non-fiction that is structured in different ways

Glossaries A

Purpose: for children to develop their vocabulary and understanding of glossaries

- Remind the children that they looked at the word *glossary* in Information words. Ask them to TTYP to recall what a glossary is. Take feedback and clarify if necessary.
- Explain that the text 'Chocolate' on pp.22–24 of Anthology 2 Book 3 contains lots of information but it doesn't have a glossary. Read the first section of the text chorally with the children and then ask them to TTYP to decide which words should be explained in a glossary.
- Take feedback and TOL about words they have chosen as you all decide whether they should form part of the glossary. Write any chosen words on a piece of card with a brief definition.
- Repeat the process for each section of the text.
- When you have a few words written down, allocate each word to a child. Tell them to come out to the front of the class and ask the rest of the class to help them to arrange them alphabetically.
- Display the words and their definitions on your Information texts wall under the heading *Glossary*.
- Ask the children if they can think of any other features of information texts that use alphabetical order. Take feedback and clarify if necessary, ensuring that children are familiar with an index and how it is used.

discussing and expressing views about a wide range of non-fiction

Information 2 CD

Purpose: for children to develop their understanding of information on packaging

- Tell the children you have found some chocolate bar wrappers. Display **CD (file 13.1)** to show an image of one of the wrappers. Explain that, as well as the name of the chocolate bar, the wrapper has lots of extra information on it.
- Click 'Information' to show labels about the different types of information shown on the wrapper.
- Use MT/YT to read the nutritional information. Guide them through what the information means, e.g. *GDA = Guideline Daily Amount*.
- Navigate to the next slide to show the wrapper from a different chocolate bar. Repeat the process. Encourage them to compare the fat and sugar content of the two bars.
- Ask the children to TTYP to discuss why it is important to have this information on a wrapper. Collect feedback and encourage them to link the information with making informed choices about what to buy.

- Tell the children that during the week you are going to paste items related to chocolate into the Class log. Ask them to bring in some things from home, e.g. chocolate bar wrappers, recipes involving chocolate, pictures of cocoa beans.

Write 2

Purpose: for children to be able to identify and record different kinds of information

- Before the lesson, print a copy of the Chocolate Fact File for each child or set of partners from **CD (file 13.2)** (there are two per sheet).
- Give each child or set of partners a copy of the Chocolate Fact File **CD (file 13.2)**. Now ask the children to turn to p.62 in their Pupils' Book and look at the Write 2 activity. Explain that they should use the pictures to find the information they need to complete their Chocolate Fact Files.
- When they have finished, go through the sections on the fact files, choosing two or three sets of partners to share their information.
- Remind the children that their Chocolate Fact Files can be used as part of their mini-exhibitions. Print images of the chocolate bars from **CD (file 13.3)** to display alongside the Chocolate Fact Files.

Curriculum link: discussing and expressing views about a wide range of non-fiction

Class log

Purpose: for children to share the process of keeping a class reading, writing and thinking log to record responses to texts and activities in a variety of forms

- Using a flipchart or a large piece of paper, create the beginning of a mind map on chocolate. Use the headings: *Records, Where is it from?,* and *Is it healthy?* for the branches and remember to use a different colour for each branch.
- Choose a branch and ask the children to TTYP to think about what could be recorded under that heading. Remind them to recall anything they already knew about chocolate and anything they can recall from the Anthology text and/or the chocolate wrappers.
- Collect answers and add to the branch using a minimum number of words. Ask the children to contribute ideas for symbols or pictures.
- Repeat for the next two branches.
- Explain that you are going to add another branch called *The Mayas*. Use MT/YT to say the name. Say that tomorrow they will find out more about the Mayas.
- Fold the mind map and put it inside the Class log.

DAY 14

Information 3

Purpose: for children to develop their understanding of how to make notes from an information text

- Remind the children that they have a branch on the class mind map for the Mayas. Explain that you are going to find information about them from different texts and make notes. The notes will be used to complete the mind map.
- Say that they are going look at a definition of *Maya* from an encyclopaedia. Display **CD (file 14.1)** to show the definition. Use MT/YT to read it aloud. Draw attention to the fact that the words *Maya* and *Native Americans* have been capitalised because they are the names of groups of people, and that *Mexico* and *Central America* have been capitalised because they are places.
- Blank the screen and ask the children to TTYP to summarise what they have just read. Choose two sets of partners to feed back. Make sure they have picked out the key points.
- On a board or flipchart, write the heading *The Mayas* and write one of their definitions/summaries underneath.

- Now navigate to the next slide to show the home page from a website about the Mayas. Ask the children to read it chorally with you. Click on the link to *Mayas and chocolate* and use MT/YT to read the information on the new slide.
- Explain that you want to record one important piece of information and add it to your notes. Click 'Highlights' to highlight information from the text. Use MT/YT to read it aloud.
- Model how to summarise and write it in note form on the board or flipchart.
- Click 'Highlights' again to highlight another part of the text. Ask the children to TTYP to discuss how they would put it into note form.
- Collect a few responses and clarify where necessary. Focus on the importance of picking out the key words and phrases to make the notes.
- Write an answer on the flipchart or board.

Curriculum link: encapsulating what they want to say, sentence by sentence

Write 3 PB

Purpose: for children to make notes from an information text

- Ask the children to turn to p.63 of their Pupils' Book and look at the Write 3 activity.
- Now tell them to TTYP and take turns to read the sections on the web page. Ask them to TTYP to share one thing they have learnt about the Mayas.
- Ask them to work together to summarise and make brief notes in their Personal log under the heading *The Mayas*, in the way you modelled. Remind them to say each point aloud to their partner before writing it down.
- Walk around as they work, giving clarification and support where necessary. Remember to praise them for good partner work and clear notes.
- Choose two or three sets of partners to share their notes. Clarify and paraphrase where necessary and then add their notes to the ones you have already made on the board or flipchart.
- Now turn to the mind map in the Class log and explain that you are going to add some of these notes to the Maya branch. Draw the children into your TOL as you create sub-branches and add symbols as well as the notes.

Personal log

Purpose: for children to keep a personal reading, writing and thinking log in order to record thoughts and ideas for their own writing

- Tell the children they are going to sell the idea for a brand new chocolate bar to a company that makes chocolate. Remind them that many different things can be added to chocolate to make interesting tastes and textures. Ask them to TTYP to think of some they are familiar with, e.g. *orange, mint, nuts, toffee, caramel.*
- Now remind them what kind of information their new product should include, e.g. *name, flavour, cost, nutritional information, weight, company name.*
- Ask them to TTYP to discuss the information they want to include on their new chocolate bar, then record a few of their ideas in their Personal log. Ask them to draw and label their new chocolate bar on paper and to keep them safe for display in their mini-exhibitions.

DAY 15

drawing on what they already know

Presentations 1 CD

Purpose: for children to develop their awareness of how information can be presented in different ways

- Tell the children that they are going to plan and prepare for their mini-exhibitions and presentations about chocolate.
- Ask them to TTYP to think of different places where they have been given information about things, e.g. *a wildlife park, a museum, a theme park.*

- Collect feedback and encourage them to think and talk about the different ways they saw information being presented in these places, e.g. *leaflets, labels, photographs, pictures, diagrams, charts, videos.*
- Open **CD (file 15.1)** and navigate through the slides. Talk through the different ways of presenting information using the examples shown in the slides. The children should be focusing on the methods of presentation, not reading the text on the examples. The final slide shows accordion booklets. Make sure you explain that these are pull-out booklets that are useful for displaying information.
- Ask the children to TTYP to recall two ideas for presenting information that they think they could use in their own exhibition. Take feedback and record their responses on a board or flipchart.
- Now ask them to Popcorn what they have to exhibit, e.g. *quiz questions, Chocolate Fact File, new chocolate bar wrappers with nutritional information and photographs of the human bar chart.* Tell them to write these down in their Personal log.
- Explain that these will be put together and labelled on the day of the mini-exhibition.

Curriculum link: discussing the sequence of events; planning or saying out loud what they are going to write about

Presentations 2

Before the lesson, you will need to gather for each set of partners: 1 A3 sheet of paper, 1 A4 sheet of thin, coloured card, 2 pairs of scissors, 4 x 8cm lengths of wool or ribbon, glue or sticky tape. You will also need to have made your own accordion booklet.

Purpose: for children to create an accordion booklet and write information in it

- Before the lesson, print a copy of the pictures on **CD (file 15.3)** for each child.
- Explain that you would like each of the children to make an accordion booklet to display information about chocolate to stand on their exhibition table.
- Display **CD (file 15.2)** and navigate through the slides to show step-by-step instructions for how to make an accordion booklet.
- Display the mind map from the Class log on the board or a flipchart. Explain that you are going to choose some information from the mind map to add to the first page of the booklet.
- Have ready a pre-folded booklet to model how to select and write information from the mind map into the booklet. Remember to model writing headings and simple labels as well. Remind the children that they can use pictures as well as words. Draw a simple picture or symbol on the page you have been writing on.
- Now give each set of partners the materials you prepared before the lesson.
- Show the first slide of **CD (file 15.2)** again. Talk through this and subsequent slides to instruct the children through each stage of making their own accordion booklets. (Each child should be working with their partner to create one accordion booklet).
- When they have completed their accordion booklets, ask them to TTYP to choose one piece of information from a branch of the mind map. Choose two or three sets of partners to share what they have chosen.
- Tell them to rehearse what they are going to write with their partner before writing it down. Remind them to use capital letters at the start of sentences, and for names of things or places. Tell them to leave spaces for pictures.
- Repeat the TTYP, sharing and modelling process for each page of the booklet.
- When all the writing has been completed, tell the children to cut out the printed pictures from **CD (file 15.3)** and paste them into appropriate spaces in their booklets. You may want them to print some relevant pictures from the Internet to use as well.
- You might need to allow an extra session for the children to complete their accordion booklets.

Curriculum link: proofreading to check for errors in spelling, grammar and punctuation

Proofread

Purpose: for children to proofread their work and make changes to improve the accuracy of their grammar, punctuation and spelling

- Now ask the children to proofread their work. If you have noticed that several children need to improve on a particular aspect of spelling, grammar or punctuation, use this as a focus for the Proofread activity. Write an example which includes common errors from the children's writing and use this as a model.
- The children should always be checking for standard use of punctuation and correct spelling of common exception words.
- The following points would be relevant as the particular focus for this Unit:
  - checking technical (subject specific) vocabulary has been spelled correctly, e.g. *Mayas, cocoa, chocolate*
  - checking capital letters have been used for proper nouns.

answering questions; read aloud what they have written with appropriate intonation to make the meaning clear

Exhibition

You will need to decide when and where the mini-exhibitions will take place.

Purpose: for children to display and present their chocolate exhibitions to others

- The exhibition should give the children the opportunity to work with their partners to display all of the work they have completed during the week and to present the information to others. The work they have to display should include: quiz questions, photographs of their human bar chart, Chocolate Fact Files, new chocolate bar designs and accordion booklets.
- You may want to have a table-top exhibition in the classroom or set up tables and display boards in the hall as part of a class assembly where children can present their information. You might also decide to have a display area and board in a corridor or the foyer.
- The children could create signs and labels for their exhibits. Small samples of milk, dark and white chocolate could be on paper plates on each table for visitors to sample. A simple tally of which type of chocolate visitors prefer could be kept and converted into a graph or bar chart.
- Walk around, asking the children questions about their exhibitions. Praise them if they explain the information clearly.
- You might like to have a comments book or board for children and adults to write down what they thought about the exhibition.
- Make sure you take photographs of the exhibition to paste into the Class log.

evaluating their writing with the teacher and other pupils

Evaluate PB

Purpose: for children to evaluate their work against specific criteria and discuss changes with their partner

- Ask the children to turn to p.64 in their Pupils' Book and look at the Evaluate activity. Tell them to TTYP to read through the question prompts.
- As a model, select an example of a piece of work that met the criteria, and explain to the children why it worked well.
- Tell the children to think back to their exhibition and TTYP to discuss how well they met the criteria and how it could have been improved further.
- Tell them to TTYP to talk about how they felt about the experience.
- Now ask them to write a few single words or a short sentence to describe the experience in their Personal log.

Curriculum coverage chart

England	*Literacy and Language* Year 2 is closely matched to the Programmes of study for the new *National Curriculum in England* from 2014 and the Year 2 grammar requirements listed in its Grammar appendix. See the overview chart on p.18 and the curriculum link boxes in the teaching notes for details. *Literacy and Language* is suitable for children working at National Curriculum level 2a and above and aims to take children to level 5 and beyond. See **www.oxfordprimary.co.uk** for curriculum updates.
Scotland	Primary 3 *Curriculum for Excellence* First level
Wales	*Literacy and Language* enables children to become accomplished in oracy across the curriculum reading across the curriculum writing across the curriculum. See **www.oxfordprimary.co.uk** for further details and a free downloadable correlation chart when the new *National Literacy and Numeracy Framework* is introduced.
Northern Ireland	Primary 3/Year 3 The following points from the *Language and Literacy* curriculum are covered in each unit of *Literacy and Language*: *Unit 1* Talking and listening: 1, 2, 3, 5, 6, 7, 8, 9, 10, 11, 12, 13, 14 Reading: 1, 3, 4, 5, 6, 7, 8, 9, 10, 11, 12, 16 Writing: 1, 2, 3, 4, 5, 6, 7, 8, 9, 11, 12 *Unit 2* Talking and listening: 1, 2, 3, 5, 6, 7, 8, 9, 10, 11, 12, 13, 14 Reading: 1, 2, 3, 4, 5, 6, 7, 8, 9, 10, 11, 12, 16 Writing: 1, 2, 3, 4, 5, 6, 7, 8, 9, 11, 12 *Unit 3* Talking and listening: 1, 2, 3, 5, 6, 7, 8, 9, 10, 11, 12, 13, 14 Reading: 1, 3, 4, 5, 6, 7, 8, 9, 10, 11, 12, 16 Writing: 1, 2, 3, 4, 5, 6, 7, 8, 9, 11, 12 *Unit 4* Talking and listening: 1, 2, 3, 5, 6, 7, 8, 9, 10, 11, 12, 13, 14 Reading: 1, 3, 4, 5, 6, 7, 8, 9, 10, 11, 12, 16 Writing: 1, 2, 3, 4, 5, 6, 7, 8, 9, 11, 12 *Unit 5* Talking and listening: 1, 2, 3, 5, 6, 7, 8, 9, 10, 11, 12, 13, 14 Reading: 1, 3, 4, 5, 6, 7, 8, 9, 10, 11, 12, 16 Writing: 1, 2, 3, 4, 5, 6, 7, 8, 9, 11, 12 *Unit 6* Talking and listening: 1, 2, 3, 5, 6, 7, 8, 9, 10, 11, 12, 13 ,14 Reading: 1, 3, 4, 5, 6, 7, 8, 9, 10, 11, 12, 16 Writing: 1, 2, 3, 4, 5, 6, 7, 8, 9, 11, 12